· · ·

AN OUTPOST OF COLONIALISM

· · ·

AN OUTPOST OF COLONIALISM

The Hispanic Community of Mérida, Yucatán, 1690–1730

ROBERT W. PATCH

STANFORD UNIVERSITY PRESS
Stanford, California

Stanford University Press
Stanford, California

© 2025 by Robert Warner Patch. All rights reserved.

No part of this book may be reproduced or transmitted in any form or by any means, electronic or mechanical, including photocopying and recording, or in any information storage or retrieval system, without the prior written permission of Stanford University Press.

Printed in the United States of America on acid-free, archival-quality paper.

Library of Congress Cataloging-in-Publication Data

Names: Patch, Robert, author.
Title: An outpost of colonialism : the Hispanic community of Mérida, Yucatán, 1690–1730 / Robert W. Patch.
Description: Stanford, California : Stanford University Press, [2025] | Includes bibliographical references and index.
Identifiers: LCCN 2024028002 | ISBN 9781503641907 (cloth) | ISBN 9781503642089 (ebook)
Subjects: LCSH: Spanish Americans (Latin America)—Mexico—Mérida—Social conditions—17th century. | Spanish Americans (Latin America)—Mexico—Mérida—Social conditions—18th century. | Mérida (Mexico)—Social conditions—17th century. | Mérida (Mexico)—Social conditions—18th century.
Classification: LCC F1391.M5 P36 2025 | DDC 972./650046802—dc23/eng/20240801
LC record available at https://lccn.loc.gov/2024028002

Cover design and photography treatment: Lindy Kasler
Cover photograph: Teoberto Maler, *Casa de Montejo, Mérida, Yucatán 1880s*, Wikimedia Commons / Public Domain
Typeset by Newgen in 10/14 Minion Pro

To my brothers and sister:
Jim, Tom, and Marianne

De todo lo que he dicho has de inferir, Sancho,
que es menester hacer la diferencia de amo a mozo,
de señor a criado y de caballero a escudero.

From all that I have said, Sancho, you may infer that
it is necessary to distinguish between master and apprentice,
between lord and servant, and between knight and squire.

Cervantes, *El Quijote*, I, 20.

CONTENTS

	Acknowledgments	xi
	Map of Yucatán	xiii
ONE	A New Year's Eve to Remember: A Prologue and Introduction	1
TWO	The City: The Founding and Establishment of Mérida	20
THREE	Death: Dying, Love, and Catholic Culture	33
FOUR	Life: Status, Relationships, and Children	57
FIVE	Migration: People in Motion	90
SIX	Immigrants and Society: Social Lives and Behavior	111
SEVEN	Social Status: Class and Political Power	137
EIGHT	Class and Wealth: Ranchers and the Urban Market	167
NINE	Rival Factions: Political Conflict in Mérida	185
	Conclusion: America, Yucatán, and Mérida	208
	Notes	221
	Bibliography	245
	Index	259

ACKNOWLEDGMENTS

I would like to thank all the many people who helped me throughout my life to become a scholar. Joseph L. Love at the University of Illinois got me started by telling me to become a historian. At Princeton University, my mentors Stanley J. Stein, Joseph R. Strayer, and James M. McPherson made me understand what it means to be a scholar. My fellow graduate student Teófilo Ruiz taught me that I didn't know as much as I thought and that what I was reading in books at the time was not enough to understand Latin America. Many people in Mérida taught me about Mexico and Latin Americans. Archivists in Mérida and Seville helped with guidance to the sources. Gil Joseph of Yale University offered unwavering support through good times and bad. Carlos Bojórquez Urzáiz of the Universidad Autónoma de Yucatán helped me get an academic position when I needed one, and I thank him for that. My students at the Universidad Autónoma de Yucatán, the University of Texas at San Antonio, and the University of California, Riverside were always an inspiration.

Research for this book was made possible in part by a Fulbright Foreign Area Fellowship, administered by the U.S.-Spanish Joint Committee for Cultural and Educational Cooperation, and by grants from the Academic Senate of the University of California, Riverside. Writing was helped by a fellowship from the National Endowment for the Humanities.

Two very competent anonymous readers commented on this manuscript for Stanford University Press. They made valuable comments that helped me focus the book, which is better because of their suggestions. Also useful were the bibliographical suggestions made by two anonymous readers of the journal *Entremons*. I thank all of these people for their time and effort.

For encouragement and good ideas, I would like to thank my colleagues in the History Department at the University of California, Riverside, especially Jim Brennan, Lucille Chia, Piotr Gorecki, and Tom Cogswell. I also thank Sergio Quezada of La Universidad Autónoma de Yucatán and my associates at CIESAS Peninsular in Mérida, especially Gabriela Solís Robleda, Pedro Bracamonte y Sosa, Patricia Fortuny Loret de Mola, and Paola Peniche Moreno.

Finally, I must thank my closest friends—Beatriz and my brothers and sister—who at times mentored me and helped me get through life.

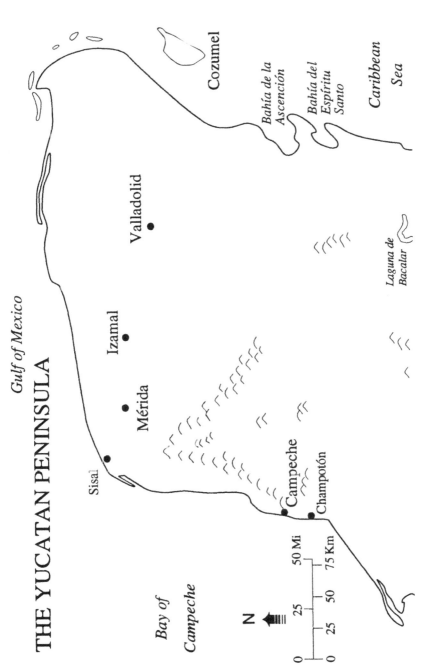

MAP: The Yucatán Peninsula. Source: Patch, Robert. *Maya and Spaniard in Yucatan, 1648–1812.*

AN OUTPOST OF COLONIALISM

ONE

...

A NEW YEAR'S EVE TO REMEMBER
A Prologue and Introduction

NEW YEAR'S EVE, 1714, was a busy night of political intrigue in Mérida, Yucatán. The following day the twelve city councilmen—the *regidores*—would meet to elect the officials who would hold political power for the next year. Municipal governments could stand up to royal officials, and some dissidents wanted the city government—the *cabildo*—of Mérida to stand up to and resist the policies of the royal governor. To do this they had to get their own people elected as *alcaldes* (justices of the peace, that is, magistrates who were executive officers as well as judges of first instance). The city, like all colonial cities but unlike modern ones, had two alcaldes, called the first and the second. They would be elected, however, not by the citizens at large but only by the regidores, who had purchased their seats on the city council and held them for as long as they wanted—or lived. The franchise, in short, was extremely restricted. This was naked elite rule, but it was the way things had always been done and no one questioned it.

The cabildo was split into two factions, and to get a majority the dissidents needed a swing vote.[1] Two of their number went to the house of Regidor Don Luis Magaña Dorantes to try to get him to support them the next day.[2] He was not at home, and so they talked with his daughter, and after explaining that they wanted to give her gifts in return for her father's vote, they left. What they did not know was that Magaña Dorantes was away from home because he was attending a secret meeting at the house of Regidor *Alférez Mayor* (titular leader of the city council—the man who carried the royal standard in all processions and stood at the head of the line)—*Maestre de Campo* (commander of a militia battalion) Don Juan del Castillo y Arrúe, the leader of the city council's opposing pro-governor faction. The dissidents did not know that their potential swing voter had already decided which side he was on, and he was not on theirs.

Later that night another city councilman, Don Nicolás Carrillo de Albornoz, showed up at the house of Magaña Dorantes, who in the meantime had returned home. They were soon joined by three other dissident city councilmen, who convinced their potential ally to accompany them to the house of Carrillo de Albornoz.

When they were later required to testify regarding their conspiratorial activity, the dissidents all said that it was pure coincidence. Individually they had left home that evening to stroll around looking at the Nativity scenes (*nacimientos*) displayed in the city, Christmas having been only a week before. One such Christmas scene just happened to be in front of the house of Magaña Dorantes. Since Mérida's Hispanic population was not large and lived near the city center, the regidores just happened to run into each other. One thing led to another, and soon they decided to hold a discussion indoors. It is unclear just who believed their story. Governor-Captain General Lord Don Alonso Meneses Bravo de Sarabia certainly did not.

Meanwhile, on that New Year's Eve, at the house of Carrillo de Albornoz, the leaders of the dissidents and several other regidores were waiting. First and foremost, there was Regidor Don Lucas de Villamil y Vargas, the son of a soldier from some other part of New Spain who had arrived in Yucatán in the middle of the seventeenth century. The father had married into a family descended from Yucatán's conquistadors. Villamil y Vargas's nephew, Regidor Don Pedro de Garrástegui y Villamil, the Count of Miraflores, was the other leader of the dissidents. The count was the only titled nobleman in Yucatán. His father, the first count, a Basque immigrant, had established the family's most important business: he bought the position as treasurer of the *Santa Cruzada* (Holy Crusade) and carried out the sale of indulgences on credit to the indigenous people in return for repayment in cotton cloth and wax. This was called a *repartimiento* (the allocation of something in return for repayment in kind). That, however, was also the principal business of the governor and his circle, who advanced cash or credit (mostly to pay taxes, called tribute) to the Maya in return for cotton, cotton cloth, and wax, which were Yucatán's important exports. The count and the governor therefore were competitors, and probably for that reason they were enemies.

The families of the two leaders of the opposition had been tied together since at least 1675, when Villamil y Vargas's sister Micaela had married Don Pedro de Garrástegui, the Basque who became the first Count of Miraflores and then a knight of the military order of Santiago (and endowed with the prestige attached to all members of that order). Villamil y Vargas had served as the godfather (*padrino*) of his nephew at the latter's baptism in 1685, and when he had married his second wife in 1697, the first count was the matrimonial godfather or sponsor (*padrino de boda*) of the marriage (and the groom's sister was the godmother). Finally, when the elder Garrástegui had to absent himself from his city council seat in 1688 in order to travel to Spain to purchase his title of nobility, he had appointed Villamil y Vargas to substitute for him as regidor. The first count had served as regidor for years, before being replaced by his son in 1709. Since Villamil y Vargas was childless despite two, and eventually three, marriages, it is possible that he had special affection for his nephew and godson. He had also been the matrimonial sponsor of one of the other city councilmen.

This was the group that met with the potential swing voter on New Year's Eve in the house of Carrillo de Albornoz. When Magaña Dorantes showed up, Villamil y Vargas approached him, and although they were known to be enemies, Villamil y Vargas embraced him, telling him, according to Magaña Dorantes's testimony, "that they should be friends, and that they should forget about past feelings." Everyone then begged Magaña Dorantes to vote for the Count of Miraflores and Villamil y Vargas. Then one of the city's alcaldes broke out a bottle of *mistela* (a sweet, fortified wine) and there were a lot of toasts ("*muchos brindis*").

Sometime after midnight, a group of these men accompanied Magaña Dorantes back home. There, they gave the latter's daughter 100 pesos and two pairs of stockings (presumably silk). They broke out another bottle of *mistela* and there was another round of toasts ("*se volvieron a repetir los brindis*"), this time with the daughter joining in. Before they left, they reminded him to vote the right way in the election that was only a few hours away.

The dissidents failed to achieve their goal, for someone had informed Governor Meneses of what was afoot. Luis Magaña Dorantes may have been the informant, but it could also have been Regidor Don Alonso de Aranda y Aguayo—the son of a royal government official who had been a city councilman and had passed his seat on to his son—for he later testified that the dissidents had tried to give him gifts too.

In any case, when the city councilmen arrived at the council chambers on January 1, 1715, they were presented with something unheard of in the history of Mérida: armed guards at the door. The governor was not a voting member of the city council, but as the chief royal official in the province he was allowed to attend city council meetings, and attend he did—with soldiers to intimidate his enemies. It worked.

Lucas de Villamil y Vargas and his nephew, the Count of Miraflores, were not elected. Instead, the regidores chose the governor's business partner as well as someone from a family that had been an ally of previous governors for years.

In the elections the governor got what he wanted. But he would have to answer for the use of soldiers to accomplish his goal.

This story is not important in the greater scheme of things about politics in colonial Spanish America. However, it is revealing and meaningful in other ways. Social classes exist first and foremost at the local level and serve as the base of a kingdom-wide, and eventually national and global, system of classes. In Spanish America, the focus of Hispanic life was urban, and thus it is in the cities that the social and political structures first intertwined.[3] Understanding these structures is impossible on a grand scale because there are too many cities and too many regional societies to study. It can only be done at the local level, that is, at the level of a Hispanic community in a single city. Only after a local society is studied can a region, nation, or empire of Hispanic communities be understood.

Focusing on a particular community at a particular time will allow for an analysis that is not based on abstractions of what social classes are, that is, groups that are assumed to exist. Frequently scholars have simply assumed that rich people and the upper class are one and the same. The lines dividing upper classes, middle classes, and people below them are not explained other than with references to occupation or wealth. Kinship is usually included as a factor tying some members of a class together, but affective and instrumental friendships, shared interests, and political alliances are other important aspects of the social network of class that are rarely mentioned. All of these must be included in any analysis that seeks to avoid shallowness and unsupported generalizations.

A community study permits the identification of the real people—individuals, affective and instrumental friends, associates, families, social networks, kith and kin—who were in those classes. By doing this, it then becomes possible to understand how that class was formed and how it reproduced itself. It makes it possible to identify the social networks that are an essential feature of social classes and at the same time to connect family history with the social structure. As one Spanish historian has recently argued, the history of social classes is the study of the connections of social networks and families.[4]

In all societies there is inevitably an overlap of political institutions with social class and economic power. Scholars of Latin America have provided a good understanding of colonial society and economic structures, but their connections with politics have not been well explored. At the local level, this means that the primary institution of political rule in cities—the city councils—must be incorporated into any explanation of class and power.

To be sure, local upper classes are rarely truly autonomous. That happens only when the state itself collapses or comes perilously close to doing so. Most of the time they must interact with a supra-regional state structure with varying degrees of power. As the events of New Year's Eve, 1714, make clear, in Spanish America cities were subordinated to a royal-colonial government that while not all-powerful could and did intervene locally and affect political outcomes. The regidores were able, within limits, to choose their local leaders but had no choice at all in the appointment or selection of the royal governor, who was almost always a Spanish-born person of high status.

Moreover, because Yucatán was exposed to foreign attack, from the middle of the sixteenth century on the governor was also a high-ranking military officer given the rank of captain general. The royal governor–captain general therefore had the charisma attached to men of the sword and the habit of command as well as the prestige of being the highest-ranking official representing the Spanish king's royal authority. He was one of the very few individuals in Yucatán who was called *Señor* (Lord). This was an outside force to be reckoned with, and the local community had to take it into account.

This book will focus on the Hispanic community in Mérida, Yucatán during the last decade of the seventeenth century and the first decades of the eighteenth century. The term "Hispanic" will be used to mean all the people who were classified as *españoles* regardless of where they were born. In this city they were Spanish-speaking, and many were bilingual in Spanish and Maya. Some of the immigrants probably spoke Castilian as well as some other Iberian language or Guanche (the language of the Canary Islanders). Still others spoke English, French, and either Genoese or some other Italian language. As will be seen, this Hispanic society included people from European countries other than Spain who were nonetheless classified as *españoles*.

This study is in the tradition of the regional or local studies of Spanish America, of which there are many.[5] Most scholarship, however, either covers a century or more or else concentrates on the later colonial period, that is, the era of imperial reform under the Bourbon monarchs.[6] This study will focus on forty years and will concentrate on the late seventeenth and early eighteenth centuries, that is, the late-Hapsburg and early Bourbon eras.

This book will concentrate exclusively on the Hispanic people rather than on everyone who lived in the town or city. This will distinguish it from many other works. Although the book will use many of the same sources as other studies, it will sometimes use them in different ways in order to illustrate human behavior. Mérida's history at times will be compared and contrasted with other places in Spanish America.

The chapters that follow also constitute a community study in the tradition of anthropology, although it will not apply anthropological theory. It is inspired in part by the classical pioneering work of Robert Redfield and J. A. Pitt-Rivers on Yucatán and Andalucía respectively.[7] Community studies are based on the supposition that what can be learned about people in one place and at one time can contribute to an understanding of the larger society that is made up of other such communities.

In modern times a significant number of scholars have devoted themselves to the history of colonial Yucatán, so this study will not have to enter uncharted historiographical territory. Spanish, American, Australian, German, and English historians have made important contributions to the subject.[8] However, scholars from Yucatán and other parts of Mexico have increasingly made their mark and have redirected the historiography.[9] This was made possible by institutional support within Mexico and the availability of good archival material. However, the new historiography of Yucatán could come to fruition only because of the talent of many first-class Mexican, especially Yucatecan, historians.

Most scholarship of the past fifty years has focused on the Yucatec Maya rather than on the Hispanic society. Important exceptions are the works of the Spanish scholar Manuela Cristina García Bernal and her students and the Yucatecan historian Marta Espejo-Ponce Hunt.[10] However, the Spanish historians did not have access to the sources available to scholars in Yucatán, and Hunt's work, unfortunately, was never published. Yucatecan and other Mexican scholars, on the other hand, have begun to direct more of their attention to Hispanic society, as is demonstrated by the recent works of Laura Machuca Gallegos on landowners and on the late-colonial and early-national city council of Mérida, as well as the study by Gabriela Solís Robleda of elites in the decades after the conquest and throughout the seventeenth century.[11] This book will continue in that direction.

It is important to note that the increased attention to Spaniards does not mean a return to the old historiography that studied Spanish elites as if they were the only people in history worth studying. Rather, it means bringing back into the analysis people who should continue to be studied. It entails taking into consideration the expansion of knowledge and insights resulting from the study of the indigenous and African American people. In the past historians paid attention to the differences between the encomenderos and all other Spaniards but said little or nothing about the Hispanic people who were not members of the elite. This study will include those non-elites in the discussion and will analyze social stratification, thereby deepening our understanding of Hispanic society as a whole.

Mérida was what might be termed a second-class Spanish city in America. It was not the site of a viceroyalty, an *audiencia* (high court), or a *consulado* (merchant guild), but it was one of a select group of cities that was the site of an episcopal see. It was important enough in the late colonial period to request the founding of a consulado, and although that request was denied, the Spanish crown did establish what was called a *diputación de comercio* (chamber of commerce) in the city.[12] Mérida's Hispanic population numbered around 5,000 people in 1700, which made it about the same size as Veracruz or Bilbao and half the size of the important city of Guadalajara. Its total population—Spaniards, Indians, Africans, and mixed-race people—in the 1790s was approximately 30,000. That made Mérida an important city in Mexico. Finally, its cabildo, while smaller than that of Mexico City, was as large as, or larger than, that of most cities in America. Mérida, therefore, was not of great importance, but it was clearly of significance.

The years from 1690 to 1730 are the focus of the book. Four decades for study are valuable because information from that time period is not taken from a single year that may have been extraordinary and therefore less representative. Hence the data in this study are more representative of the times. Moreover, four decades is a long enough time span to observe two generations of people and to examine a complete generational change. People in power in the 1690s are almost all dead by the 1720s. The analysis of two generations thus reveals the process of elite replacement, as the living take the place of the dead, and of the social reproduction of a Hispanic society.

It is important to emphasize that an analysis of a forty-year period or of two generations of people is not static. Significant changes in the economic or social structure may not occur during a few decades, but the people carrying out economic activity and forming a part of a society do change. Some people of lowly origins move up the social ladder. Others never even get onto that ladder. The families of people of high status sometimes move down the social scale, while others of high status but lacking in wealth find the means to consolidate their social position by acquiring a solid economic base. In other words, people move in and out, up and down, or stay in place.

An analysis of what happens will provide a better understanding of how and why this occurs. It will show to a certain extent how a society actually worked and how people behaved. Four decades therefore reveal not just an underlying continuity but also the dynamic process of change. There is value in studying a society not just over the *longue durée*—to use a famous phrase from French historiography—but also over what we might call the *courte durée*. What happens during a short period of time is not necessarily just *histoire éventuelle*—the history of events or "happenings." Rather, what "happens" can reveal the inner working of a society because those "events" have meaning to the people involved. In this case, a four-decade time period will reveal how political power, economic power, and social status—which together make up social class—are passed from one generation to the next.

The late seventeenth and early eighteenth centuries are the late-Hapsburg period of Spanish America. Most of the people who appear in this study were born before the Bourbon monarchs came to power and lived their lives before any major Bourbon Reforms went into effect. Scholars of Spanish America have not paid a great deal of attention to the latter portion of the seventeenth century in part because it was long believed to be a time of political and economic decadence, decline, and dynastic crisis and therefore lacking in significance. In the past several decades, however, historians have reinterpreted this era and have concluded that Spain in fact was recovering demographically and economically at that time, that the Spanish Empire showed significant "resilience" in the face of the threats from French and English expansionist policies, and that the commercial system linking

Spain with America continued to function effectively albeit imperfectly. Charles II and his ministers did not neglect business and made important decisions that had consequences. And Spanish America experienced some semi-autonomous regional development, but that was in tandem with the rest of the Empire.[13]

Of course, the Spanish state at the end of the Hapsburg era was not as strong as it formerly had been, and this created a power vacuum that people in America could occupy. In the case of Mexico, the recovery of silver production after 1670 gave merchants the means to gain greater control over international commerce, often by working with corrupt officials. This resulted in greater autonomous development than at any time since the early sixteenth century— and much more than they would have with the implementation of the Bourbon Reforms of the later eighteenth century.[14]

All of this means that Yucatán was not a backwater of a backwater. It was not tied to a corpse. Its history is not part of a decline affecting all parts of the Hispanic world. It was not isolated from the world, and local developments did not occur in isolation. Its history during this little-known period was a small part of the many small parts that constituted Spanish America. Yucatán and Mérida put the experiences of those other small parts into a broader perspective of the whole.

The last decades of the Hapsburg era are significant in the history of America and of Yucatán. By the late seventeenth century important structural features had emerged that had not existed in the first century of the colonial period. By the 1690s the region's small landed estates had been accumulating debts for over a century, and in many cases a tipping point had been reached. That was when the value of the debts approached or matched the value of the estates themselves. As a result, new people with money had the opportunity to become landowners and achieve social mobility.

At the same time, Spanish immigration was continuing, and therefore Hispanic society was still characterized to an extent by the presence of people born and raised elsewhere. Nevertheless, because of continuity with the past, when all Hispanic people were immigrants or the children of recent immigrants, there was no easy distinction between "creoles" (American-born people) and "*peninsulares*" (those from the Iberian Peninsula). In Yucatán at the time people did not often make that distinction in documented ways. People born in Mérida were used to having people from Spain and elsewhere around.

Conflict between the two groups could easily have developed. This is because people from Europe (Spain, Italy, England, France, Belgium, and Ireland) formed a significant part of Mérida's Hispanic society. Moreover, that society was augmented by migrants or immigrants from other parts of the Spanish Empire, especially from the Canary Islands. People born elsewhere formed a distinct part of Hispanic society in Mérida, and they behaved in ways to maintain their distinctive nature. They were not all the same, however. Some assimilated quickly. Other groups tried to stick together as immigrant colonies-within-a-colony.

If such small groups of distinctive people had monopolized power and positions in government and the Church, then one can easily imagine that conflict would have developed. But in Mérida these colonies-within-a-colony cooperated rather than competed with the American-born. They shared power. Political conflict during this time, as in Guadalajara, did not pit Europeans against Americans.[15] The major disagreement of the time was the result of something else. For example, the dispute described at the beginning of this chapter was not between the foreign-born and the Yucatán-born. Both groups were to be found on both sides of the conflict. In fact, when the collective interests of the Hispanic community were threatened, political leaders born in Yucatán and those born elsewhere worked together quite effectively. Class interests prevailed over regional identities. If there was any hostility between the two groups, it is likely to have occurred within the religious establishment, as manifested to an extent in the struggle between the secular clergy (usually American-born) and the Franciscans (frequently Spanish-born) for control over Indian parishes and hence income—a topic in need of further research.

This study will demonstrate that American identity was not defined simply by place of birth but by interaction with a group of people who tried to maintain their Spanish identity *even when born in America*. This was made possible by immigration, a topic that scholars thus far know little about. Important exceptions include the works by Thomas Calvo on seventeenth-century Guadalajara, David Brading on late-colonial Mexico, and Mariana Alicia Pérez on late-colonial Buenos Aires.[16] Emigration from Spain is better known, thanks to the work of several scholars.[17] However, while available knowledge allows us to know a great deal about where Spaniards were leaving from, it tells us little or nothing about where they ended up after crossing the Atlantic. Only after Independence did governments in America start to pay attention to immigration and gather information about it.[18] This book will address this issue by looking at one place where migrants to a great extent settled down.

Moreover, the decades under study in the middle colonial period were a time before the imperial reforms of the last two-thirds of the eighteenth century. Those developments led naturally to the great transformations leading up to the Independence era and after. The middle colonial period gives us a last glimpse of a traditional colonial society still based to a certain extent on the resources extracted from the indigenous economy. Much of this was paid as tribute through a system known as *encomiendas*. These were grants given to individuals entitling them to annuities, called tribute, paid by the Maya in cotton cloth, cotton thread, and wax as well as money, maize, and turkeys. These goods were handed over to *encomenderos* (the people granted encomiendas by the crown), who for the most part were descendants of conquistadors.

The survival of the encomienda until nearly the end of the colonial regime demonstrates how different Yucatán was compared to most other parts of the Spanish Empire. Most commonly, the royal government gradually took control of tribute revenue and ceased to appoint new people as encomenderos. In a few places, however, the old system lingered on for decades well into the eighteenth century. This happened in modern-day Colombia, Chile, and Paraguay. However, in the latter places the indigenous population was small in number, especially compared to that of Yucatán, and lacked a surplus-producing economy allowing for the payment of tribute. As a result, the encomenderos of Colombia and Chile exploited the native people through forced labor to work in gold mining, while in Paraguay the labor was used on a small scale in agriculture or domestic service.[19] In Yucatán, on the other hand, there was no gold or silver, but the Maya economy produced a significant surplus, thereby allowing the native people to survive as well as to pay the tribute that was the lifeblood of the Hispanic community well into the eighteenth century.

The Maya thus had to subsidize the existence of the descendants of the people who had conquered them. Yet settler colonialism in Yucatán did not destroy the indigenous society and economy. The Spanish crown permitted the encomienda system to survive in order to prevent Hispanic people from abandoning a province that had virtually no resources other than the Maya themselves. At the same time, the above-mentioned repartimientos, whether carried out by the governor and his agents, by the treasurer of the *Santa Cruzada*, or by others, were also based on goods extracted from the indigenous people and their economy.

Encomiendas and repartimientos thus resulted in the accumulation of cotton cloth, cotton thread, and wax. These were Yucatán's most important exports, which were sent to the mining towns of northern Mexico and the textile industry of Puebla, while the wax was shipped all over Mexico to be made into candles. The Maya of Yucatán, therefore, helped clothe the miners of Guanajuato, Zacatecas, and Parral and provide light for churches, houses, and mines throughout Mexico. These exports paid for the imports—such as the *mistela* mentioned earlier in this chapter—that were the basis the wealth of the province's merchants.

A factor of great importance in the history of Yucatán's Hispanic community during the colonial period is the province's relative poverty. All visitors at the time commented on this. It was manifested in various ways, including in the institutions that ran the Church. During the entire colonial period the Cathedral Chapter of Mérida could only afford eight salaried prebendaries, while in other parts of Mexico the number was as high as twenty-seven.[20] This was because diocesan income, as opposed to parish income, was based overwhelmingly on tithes paid by Spaniards on the production carried out on their landed estates. There was so little production in Yucatán that tithe revenues could not support a full-scale cathedral chapter.

The poverty of the province is shown in the low value of its landed estates. The average selling price of 46 estancias sold between 1718 and 1738 was only 1,471 pesos, while the median price was a meager 1,175. Decades later, after the emergence of the agricultural and stock-raising estates called haciendas, values had increased, but even then 54 haciendas sold between 1756 and 1803 had an average selling price of only 2,324 pesos, while the median was 1,962.[21] Meanwhile, in central and northern Mexico in the second half of the eighteenth century, in a sample of 113 haciendas belonging to the elite landowners, 77 percent were worth over 50,000 pesos and 34 percent were worth more than 100,000 pesos.[22] The difference is extreme.

Yucatán's relative poverty was not the result of isolation from the world economy, as has sometimes been alleged. Indeed, as we have just seen, the province in fact was an export platform tied into the wider world economy and the province's merchants imported valuable textiles, iron products, wine, olive oil, books, paper, and other European-made products, as well as cacao from Tabasco, Honduras, and Venezuela.

Yucatán's Hispanic people were poor because they had no way to get rich. The first colonists tried to establish sugar plantations and indigo enterprises, but these required forced labor, and the royal government quickly suppressed these by prohibiting Spaniards from forcing the Maya to work in these enterprises. Sugarcane and indigo thus failed as a source of income for members of the Hispanic community. There were limits, in short, to exploitation—at least in the sixteenth century. Only near the end of the colonial period, when Bourbon kings ran the empire, did the royal government authorize the use of forced labor to coerce the Maya to work in sugarcane fields.[23]

Before then, at least in the area around Mérida, the only forms of productive property that Hispanic people owned were cattle ranches (*estancias*). These produced some leather and tallow, for local consumption as well as for export, and beef for urban markets. However, the profits from these activities were meager compared to those of the great haciendas of other parts of Spanish America. Moreover, the cloth production carried out by the Maya meant that non-Indians found it unprofitable to set up privately owned textile mills (*obrajes*) such as existed in other regions in Spanish America.

Spaniards therefore had to rely on encomiendas and the repartimiento as their most important sources of income. These yielded some personal wealth, but not on a scale compared to what rich people in other parts of Spanish America were accumulating. Moreover, income from these sources was not based on production carried out on property owned by the Hispanic people. On the contrary, these were parasitic activities based on the exploitation of the indigenous people through colonialism. The means of production remained mostly in Maya hands. As a result, no one in Yucatán was rich.

The very nature of colonialism, which allowed the conquerors and their descendants to live off the Indians without engaging in significant entrepreneurial activities on their own property, had a profound impact not just on the Maya but also on the Hispanic people. Since no one could get rich, Hispanic society was not characterized by extremes of wealth and poverty. This should come as no surprise. Decades ago the economist Simon Kuznets showed that substantial economic growth in history has almost always produced economic and social inequality.[24] Conversely, little economic development would have the opposite effect. To be sure, Mérida's Hispanic people were not members of an egalitarian community. Some people had a lot more wealth than others. But the differences between the two were not as great in Mérida as in many other places in Spanish America. Social stratification was not based primarily or overwhelmingly on property ownership, which is the usual situation in almost all societies. As a result, it was difficult for the people in the upper class to distinguish themselves from the middle class below them.

It is frequently believed that in colonial American societies like Yucatán, where the indigenous population greatly outnumbered the Hispanic people, those classified as Spaniards or *españoles* were wealthy. This was not the case. In Mérida, as elsewhere, Hispanic society, although surrounded by a largely indigenous society, was stratified.[25] Yucatán's relative poverty, of course, meant that the class structure of Hispanic society in Mérida was different from Hispanic communities elsewhere that were larger and wealthier. In Yucatán, for example, there was no landowning aristocracy that combined wealth, status, and power. Class structures differed from place to place, and generalizations for all of Mexico or for all of Spanish America, while useful, will be misleading when applied to specific cases.[26]

This study will hopefully contribute to an understanding of how social classes operated within Hispanic society in the middle-colonial period. Did the upper class act like a ruling class by monopolizing political power, or did a middle class participate in politics and share power? Did the upper class monopolize economic opportunity, or did a middle class share in that opportunity? This book will answer those questions. Many other questions of course cannot be answered, but the ones that can are important.

In Yucatán and Mérida, the lack of opportunity to get rich meant that social mobility upward did not require much wealth. Immigrants and other newcomers therefore could move in and, if they acquired some wealth, move up. This resulted in demographic growth and contributed to the continual reinforcement and replenishing of Spanish culture, thereby helping the Hispanic community to survive as an outpost of colonialism, "a Spanish island in a sea of Indians," a phrase used by an anonymous author of a manuscript written in the second half of the nineteenth century about the Caste War of Yucatán.[27]

That character has survived to the present. Mérida currently has several universities, modern hospitals, classical ballet classes and performances, a symphony orchestra that plays mostly European classical music, a country club with golf and black-tie debutante balls, yoga and Pilates classes, a large number of upper- and middle-class people who have traveled to Europe (as well as to Disneyland, Disney World, and Las Vegas), and a literate public that reads the great works of European literature in addition to what is written in Latin America. At one time French and Italian films were just as popular as those from Hollywood.

The sources used for this study give a good indication of the book's contents. The Archivo General de Indias in Seville provides a small quantity of vital information. That is the only archive that contains a virtually complete set of the records resulting from what was called a *residencia*, the trial of someone for conduct in office. When a governor–captain general left office, he had to stay around for the trial, and people were invited or required to testify regarding the performance of his duties. Although one might suspect that these trials were mere formalities, in practice they provide the scholar with valuable information about the nature of politics and of the colonial system.

That is not all, however. At a residencia, all people who had held elective or permanent positions in municipal government were also put on trial, and thus residencias reveal a great deal about the exercise of political power at the local level. They provide information on the alleged and real abuses of city governments. Moreover, in order for people to be held accountable, they had to be identified; thus residencias, in the absence of city council records (which exist for Mérida only after 1747), provide information that is unavailable anywhere else. They give us the names and offices held of everyone who served in city government. The Archivo de Indias therefore provides us with the names of the men—but not the women—who exercised political power.

Who were these people? Names are a good place to start what might be called a group biography, but without more information they are just names. The Spanish scholar Ana Isabel Martínez Ortega managed to use the sources in Seville to create nineteen family trees and identify the councilmen who were encomenderos and *estancieros* (cattle ranchers), but she did not have complete information about family ties and property ownership. The first place to look for that information is in Mérida itself, in the Archivo General del Arzobispado, that is, the General Archive of the Archdiocese. This contains the records of baptisms, matrimonies, and last rites of the people who were born, who married, or who died in Mérida. The task of the scholar is made easier by the organization of the records according to ethnicity or "race": there were separate registries for *"españoles"* (Spaniards) and *"indios"* (Indians), as well as for the residents of the parish inhabited by mixed-race people called *"castas."*

These records allow the historian to focus on the Hispanic people and find out about death rates and the impact of epidemics. They can help identify the disease causing some epidemics and contribute to the study of other demographic factors such as trends in births, marriages, remarriages, and the process of migration and immigration. In addition, in this book they will be used to estimate child mortality and poverty in the Hispanic community. They also reveal the great importance of illegitimacy and the widespread practice of abandonment of newborn infants. They allow the scholar to identify who were members of the hidalgo class (lower nobility) and who were not, thus providing insight into social stratification within Hispanic society.

Ecclesiastical sources therefore do not merely provide cold demographic figures. They tell us a great deal about social life and human behavior. They show connections between people. Marriage records tell us not just who married whom but also who their in-laws and matrimonial sponsors—*padrinos de boda*—were. We see who attended as witnesses. In other words, we see not just marriages but weddings. We sometimes see who attended weddings—and who did not. Political alliances and friendships were established or reinforced and are revealed. The social networks of class are identifiable. And women, who of course did not hold political office, are shown to be wives, sisters, and mothers of important people and thus to have power that can only be imagined. Anyone who thinks that men in Hispanic society pay no attention to what their mothers, wives, and sisters say does not know much about Hispanic society. Indeed, John Tutino has argued that women who were not from rich families probably had more control over their lives than those in the extremely wealthy elite of central Mexico.[28] In Yucatán, women were never from truly rich families.

Having identified the ruling elite and other members of Hispanic society as human beings belonging to a community, we then need to know about their economic activities and property ownership. These are revealed to a great extent in the unfortunately incomplete notarial records. These exist intermittently since only 1689 and are continuous only after the middle of the eighteenth century. Yet the quantity of information provided by the surviving records is substantial, and the quality of that information makes them indispensable. Notaries in societies like Italy, France, Spain, Portugal, and Latin America did more than just notarize or sign off on documents. They made detailed inventories or descriptions of what was being bought and sold—including not just landed estates and real estate but also human beings—of financial or commercial agreements, of wills, of apprenticeships, and of the posting of bail. The dowries provided to women and recorded in the documents tell us what kinds of luxury clothing and jewelry were desirable and provide us with information about Mérida's connections with the world economy.

An entire historiographical tradition utilizing notarial records began to emerge in the 1960s with the work of James Lockhart, whose first book was based on the documents left by notaries. He even dedicated the book to the sixteenth-century notary whose documents he used.[29] Lockhart also carried out a group study on the conquerors of Peru that included the commoners rather than just the leaders.[30] He therefore returned to the study of Spaniards but did so in a new way by analyzing them sociologically as a society rather than as the only people worth studying. As Lockhart and his many students have shown, notarial records provide a deeper understanding of Spanish society in Spanish America.[31] One of Lockhart's students, Marta Espejo-Ponce Hunt, used those sources to write an excellent although unfortunately unpublished study of Mérida in the seventeenth century.

After Hunt's work, much remained and remains to be done. Matthew Restall used a variety of documents, including notarial records, to provide a much better understanding of African and African American people in Yucatán. Restall and Philip Thompson also used Maya-language notarial sources to provide a great deal of insight into Maya society.[32] Indeed, the work of these two scholars led to a revolution in the understanding of the Maya in the colonial period.

The notarial documents of the time period under study can even provide us with some knowledge of feelings like love, fear, guilt, and thankfulness of Hispanic people. Wills as well as documents founding chantries (*capellanías*) occasionally mention those feelings and allow us to go beyond the written words and into the minds and culture of real people. They do not figuratively bring the dead to life, but they do give us some insight into how they acted and what they thought and felt.

Finally, the Archivo General de la Nación (National Archive) in Mexico City provides the scholar with many sources for the study of Yucatán. It provided us with a document providing detailed information about one particular obligation of the city government of Mérida: to provide a meat supply—the *abasto de carne*—for the Hispanic population and other carnivores of the city. Normally, this was done in a perfunctory manner. A single individual promised to organize the cattle ranchers to market their meat throughout the year (except for Fridays, Lent, and religious holidays) and sell it at a price agreed upon in advance.

But frequently no one was willing to take the risk of guaranteeing a low price. When that happened, the city council itself took on that task, and it apparently did so frequently in the early eighteenth century. In the 1720s it provided a detailed list of the individuals and institutions allocated market days. The list, therefore, is a registry of Yucatán's cattle ranchers, who changed from year to year because of death and the entry of their replacements. And since the regidores were frequently ranchers themselves, they allocated market shares to themselves and, of course, to their family members—including their mothers, wives, and in-laws. Here we will clearly see the overlap between political and economic power held by the upper class.

These documentary sources are not the only ones available, and someday other scholars will use them and arrive at different conclusions. This study, therefore, cannot be considered definitive or to have the final word. It will, however, contribute to the discussion of how the various classes of colonial society created a community with a basis that has survived to a great extent to this day in the social structure, which manifests a correlation of race, class, and culture. Part of that history is the survival and expansion of Hispanic society in a place where initially the Maya population greatly outnumbered Spaniards. This is what distinguishes much of Spanish America from Portuguese, British, French, and Dutch America, where there was always an indigenous presence but never an indigenous majority in the European-occupied areas.[33] In Yucatán, the Maya presence and impact on Euro-American people was much greater than in the colonies far to the north or south. And the indigenous people even sneak into the sources supposed to be exclusively for Spaniards. The book of "Spanish" marriages sometimes records matrimonies of Maya people. Their children then could do the same and their descendants might eventually have been counted or accepted as Spanish, not Maya. Indigenous genes thus passed into Hispanic society.

The information available reveals that Maya society made inroads into Hispanic society. Spaniards were not unchanged by their surroundings. At the same time, documentary sources show how Hispanic society succeeded in maintaining to a certain extent its Spanish nature. Mérida was an island in a sea of Mayas, and the island was sometimes partially inundated by that sea. Nevertheless, that society kept enough of its own traditional culture to be recognizable to all European immigrants as partially, although not exclusively, Spanish.

A study based on these sources and analyzing a community by necessity has to provide evidence in the form of names. How else can it be demonstrated that immigrant communities existed other than by identifying the leaders and other persons who attended the social events of those communities? How else can it be shown that at a particular moment in time five city councilmen were the sons of Spanish immigrants and many others were immigrants from Spain, the Canary Islands, or Portugal? Fortunately, many of these people show up in this study over and over again and in different contexts, thus challenging the reader to remember some of them by name. It cannot be said, therefore, that this book treats people as an amorphous or anonymous mass revealed only in statistics. On the contrary, it shows that these people were real, had first and last names, did or did not have relatives, in-laws, and godparents, lived long or short lives, maintained or lost status, and acquired or failed to acquire wealth.

Why did the Spaniards stay in Mérida rather than leave, as happened in some other parts of America with no mineral resources to exploit? Such was the fate of many small cities in colonial Central America and Colombia, where Spanish civilization effectively collapsed in the seventeenth century when colonists no longer had resources or indigenous people to exploit.[34] In Yucatán, on the other hand, the colonists had the Maya as their source of wealth. As a result, Hispanic people have been vilified in post-Revolutionary Mexico as racist parasites who denigrated and obliterated indigenous culture. The same is often said of their descendants. However, the community's survival as a cultural entity contributed to the eventual outcome that includes in the present a Spanish-speaking society that is proportionately larger than ever before and is growing larger still. These people therefore contributed, like the indigenous and the African people, to the formation of Spanish America and modern Mexico and Latin America, even as many members of that Hispanic society benefited in one way or another from the colonial system in Yucatán based on the exploitation of the Maya and African Americans.

TWO

. . .

THE CITY
The Founding and Establishment of Mérida

MEXICO, GUATEMALA, AND THE central Andes region were to a certain extent urbanized long before the European invasion. Many important cities had emerged, and a large part of the indigenous people already lived in either large villages or full-scale cities. Spaniards preserved urbanization and even extended it further, for they came from a society in which the terms city and civilization were intertwined. They believed that civilized people lived in communities with other people, which is why few Spaniards, except in northern Mexico and in some thinly populated regions of South America, lived permanently on rural estates. Most landowners had a house in the city and visited a rural property only sporadically. Cities therefore were the focal point of Hispanic life in Mexico and in Yucatán, as well as in most of Spanish America.[1]

They were also the focal point of Hispanic political life. All Spanish cities in the Old World and then the New had the right to a city government that represented the inhabitants. That right included many legal privileges and a certain degree of self-government. As a community, a city had the right to communicate directly with the king without the approval of any intermediate authority, and thus the inhabitants felt they had a direct tie to the monarch. The strong Mediterranean tradition of city-states exercising and sharing power with the king resulted in a strong sense of local sovereignty and the belief on the part of the citizens that they were sharing sovereignty with the king and with no one else. After Independence there was no longer a king, and therefore they claimed full sovereignty, thus leading to political disorder and making it difficult to create unified nations.

This is why the first thing that Cortés did when he landed at Veracruz was to found a city. By doing so he could bypass the political authority of his rival, the governor of Cuba, and appeal directly to the king to be recognized as an entity independent of that governor. Immediately the conquistadors set up a city government as an instrument of their political pretensions, and the leaders assumed all the positions.[2] Cities, therefore, were the essential element that connected the new Spanish society in America with the king in Spain. The Hispanic communities in America made up what was called the Commonwealth of Spaniards—the *República de Españoles*—which was separate from the indigenous people and possessed its own set of laws distinct from those of the native people, who belonged to the *República de Indios*.[3] In addition, as political units with a limited form of representative government, cities imparted a strong sense of identity to their inhabitants. Hispanic people referred to their city and surrounding area as their *patria* (homeland), and the permanent inhabitants of cities were called citizens (*vecinos*) rather than just residents. Only later did the word *patria* take on a broader national meaning.

Cities were centers of imports, exports, consumption, and production. Food products that Spaniards and Indians produced flowed into local markets, but little of this could be exported because of the high cost of transportation for bulky, low-value goods like corn. Foreign-made goods coming to the cities were of high value for the same reason. Books and paper were imported for the most part, but because of low literacy rates they were not in great demand. Mexico did not produce much wine or olive oil in the colonial period, so those goods were brought in from Spain. They were in great demand, the former in part because it was essential for Mass. Religious art—especially portraits of saints—was also imported and was listed in wills as a valuable possession. By far the most significant import, however, was material for clothing: silk, silk cloth, golden filigree thread, and linen.[4] These were not just for utilitarian function, however. They were markers of status. Only Hispanic people could afford to buy them, and clothing became an essential way for people to display their wealth. Just as important, it became a way of stating cultural and ethnic identity. Dressing in silk and linen clothing cut in the European style was a way of proclaiming "I am not an Indian. I am a Spaniard."

Mérida and the other Spanish cities in Yucatán were the products of a long history of Hispanic and indigenous urban traditions. The Spanish conquest of Yucatán ended a generation after that of central Mexico, and it was only in 1542 that the conquistadors of Yucatán felt themselves secure enough to found a city in the interior of the Peninsula. Mérida thereby became an outpost of colonialism.

Meanwhile the *villa* (small city or town) of Campeche had already been established on the west coast in 1540. However, the conquerors could not project power far into the interior from such a remote location. To be sure, Campeche, located on a safe shore, was necessary to maintain lines of communications with any Spanish settlements in the interior. But only full-fledged cities well beyond the coast could dominate and control the conquered, tribute-paying Maya of Yucatán. Therefore, after founding Mérida, the Spanish invaders founded farther to the east the *villa* of Valladolid in 1543. The latter had to be relocated to its present site in 1545. In that same year the conquistadors also proclaimed the founding of Salamanca de Bacalar, on the east coast. However, that town was located on a dangerous lee shore in a region that very quickly lost most of its indigenous population because of disease and the violence of Spanish conquest, and so it never prospered.[5]

Mérida was the most important of these four cities and from the beginning was the capital of the province. It remained the capital until the State of Campeche separated from Yucatán in 1858, and its control was restricted even more when the territory, now the State, of Quintana Roo was separated from Yucatán in 1902. In the meantime, for the entire colonial period, Mérida was the capital of a large region with a large indigenous population. It was also the seat of an ecclesiastical capital, for the diocese of Mérida, Yucatán, founded in 1518, had its first resident bishop beginning in 1561.

All cities have hinterlands that they rely on for provisions and exportable goods, but the urban centers in Yucatán, like many others in Spanish America, were the products of conquest and colonialism. These factors shaped not just the founding but the very development of the cities. The income of the new, Hispanic ruling class as well as much of the food that provisioned the cities were based on a colonial institution: the encomienda. This allowed encomenderos—those awarded encomiendas—to extract resources from the indigenous people. It was a result, therefore, of the Spanish domination of the Maya through colonialism.[6]

In return for this grant of an income, the encomendero had to help defray the costs of Christianizing the Indians, although in fact they contributed very little to that. Their most important obligation was to serve as members of a colonial militia that could be called up to put down rebellions or defend the province from enemy or pirate attacks. All other adult males in the city were also expected to perform service as soldiers when needed, which meant that Mérida, like medieval Castilian towns, was to a certain extent a society organized for war.[7] The requirement to serve in the militias was a serious matter, for on many occasions the units were mobilized and sometimes even sent into combat against pirates. This military function affected the development of the social structure, for as will be shown, military service could speed up social mobility. It should also be noted that it was the governor who made appointments to positions as militia officers, and as a result he could use this power to his political advantage.

Encomiendas in Yucatán were hereditary for only two generations, after which time it was allocated to a different person for two more generations. The royal governor was the person who chose who got an encomienda when it became available, and this gave him considerable leverage in dealing with members of the elite who wanted to be granted an encomienda. This continued allocation and reallocation of encomiendas did not end until 1785. The Spanish government in that year decided that it was no longer necessary to keep the elite from collapsing, and it was abolished.

When the conquest was over, between 140 and 150 Spaniards received encomiendas. Half of them, about 70 in all, settled in Mérida. The second largest concentration of encomenderos was in the small eastern city of Valladolid, where some 39 to 40 of them resided. Campeche, the small port on the west coast, was the home of 30 or so. Finally, about 10 encomenderos tried to live on the east coast in Salamanca de Bacalar—a settlement that was a city in name only—but these people eventually gave up and moved away. Encomendero society, therefore, was concentrated in three relatively small urban centers, which collectively projected their power over the countryside and therefore over the great majority of the conquered Maya tribute-paying population. The city and the two *villas* were islands in a sea of Mayas.

The conquistadors founded the city of Mérida on the site of an already-existing Maya city called Ti-Ho. In fact, the colonists chose to name their city after Mérida, in Extremadura, a Roman city, precisely because the existing buildings reminded them of a city filled with Roman ruins. There were good reasons to establish a city on top of, so to speak, an indigenous urban center. First, there was a large Maya population settled in the area. These were people who could deliver their tribute without the difficulty of transporting goods over a great distance. The city council explained the situation well in 1579. It wrote to the crown that "Mérida is established in a region of four Indian provinces ... and each province has many villages of native Indians with lords and governors who come to this city ... and bring to it the necessary sustenance that the earth produces, with which we, the Spanish and foreign residents who live in it, sustain ourselves."[8]

Second, the royal government permitted the colonists to extract labor services from the nearby indigenous people. Their labor resulted in the construction of the city's numerous buildings, and in addition the Maya were required to perform household service for the Spanish colonists. Mérida was well located to receive large quantities of Maya labor from the people living around them Finally, the preexisting cities had stone-built structures that could be torn apart and used for material for the new Spanish buildings. Thus an urban civilization continued to exist because it was in the interest of the Spaniards to maintain it.

The Spanish conquerors of Yucatán never found much in the way of natural resources or precious metals and therefore they had to live off the conquered Maya population. Spanish society in Yucatán survived through a parasitic relationship with the native people. The Maya paid their tribute at first in kind, in the form of maize, beans, squash, turkeys, dried fish (from villages near the coast), beeswax, cotton, and woven cotton cloth. There was a great deal of economic continuity because the conquerors, finding that the Maya already had a monetary system, found it necessary to keep the Maya system in place. The ancient Maya had used cacao beans as coins, and so did their descendants in the colonial period. Since cacao was not produced locally, it had to be imported from places like Tabasco and Honduras and eventually even Venezuela and Ecuador. Of course, the Spaniards would have liked to replace the native currency with Spanish silver coins, but these entered the provincial economy by exporting something in return. In the urban market, therefore, people exchanged goods for the old cacao beans more often than for the new Spanish *reales* (8 reales = 1 peso). Taxes on transactions in Mérida's markets continued to be collected partly in cacao beans until at least the middle of the nineteenth century, that is, decades after Mexican independence. In the realm of money, therefore, the Maya successfully resisted the Spaniards for a very long time.[9]

The city of Mérida began to take on its modern look immediately upon its founding. After a formal ceremony on January 6, 1542, or perhaps even before, the Spanish colonists laid out the urban core.[10] They did this in a way that was repeated throughout the Americas. At the center was a square plaza, and around a grid of roughly square city blocks the rest of the city took shape. A priority was the church, which was always on the block to the east of the plaza. The entrance was on the side facing the plaza, and the church faced east. The faithful faced the altar to their east, that is, the direction of Jerusalem. The first construction was provisional, for shortly after construction had begun, and once the permanence of the city was established, the colonists began to build a more imposing structure that would become the cathedral of the diocese of Yucatán. It was a huge and expensive project requiring a considerable outlay of funds and utilization of indigenous labor. The Cathedral of San Ildefonso, which cost 330,000 pesos, was completed in 1598, making it the second oldest cathedral in America; only the one in Santo Domingo is older.

To the north of the central plaza workers constructed the first government buildings, one of which eventually became the office and residence of the governor. Next to it was a city council building and a granary, although that building was eventually abandoned and a new one constructed on the block on the western side of the plaza.

As was the custom, the block to the south of the central plaza was used for the construction of the residences of the leading conquistadors. Most important was the house that the chief conquistador, Francisco de Montejo, constructed for himself. Built in the Renaissance style, the Casa de Montejo became a gem of colonial architecture.[11] It is still imposing today, although its transformation to largely commercial use in the twentieth century tends to distract from the beauty of its unity. Other important leaders also built houses in and around the central plaza.

At the same time, a special barrio (neighborhood) was created to the southeast of the urban core in order to house the indigenous people from Mexico City who had served as military allies and servants of the conquistadors. Similar barrios were also founded in Campeche and Valladolid, as well as in the large village of Izamal, located midway between Mérida and Valladolid. In Mérida this settlement was called San Cristóbal (Saint Christopher).[12] It still has a special devotion to the Virgin of Guadalupe, a cult originally of Mexico City origin. The first church for these "Mexicans" (as they were called) was undoubtedly rudimentary, but in the eighteenth century an ornate Baroque-style church was built in the barrio.

Because of natural reproduction and immigration, the Hispanic population of the city grew over time. Mérida had at least 300 vecinos (permanent residents who were heads of households) in 1588, which would have amounted to a total population somewhere around 1,500. In 1636 the city was estimated to have 400 heads of families, and despite a yellow fever epidemic of 1648 the total in 1700 probably reached close to 900, which is to say a total Hispanic population of between 4,000 and 5,000.[13] In 1722 Mérida was reported to have 1,320 Spanish heads of family, that is, over 5,000 people (assuming four or more persons per family).[14] Rapid population growth continued in the eighteenth century.

A growing city needed more building activity, and this was begun in the second half of the sixteenth century.[15] Across the street to the north of the cathedral a hospital took shape. Eventually this was run by the order of San Juan de Dios (Saint John of God), which built hospitals all over the urban Hispanic world in the Americas. Since Yucatán did not have trained doctors until later in history, it is likely that the hospital was more like an apothecary that treated the sick rather than a hospital in the modern sense of the term.

In the early seventeenth century the bishop authorized the construction of more buildings for religious purposes. A seminary founded by the Society of Jesus (Jesuits) was built somewhat to the north of the cathedral and opened in 1624. This institution educated male members of the elite, some of whom became priests. Since there was also the need for an institution for women, the Church constructed a convent for nuns one block west of the modern City Hall. This was for the Nuns of the Immaculate Conception, and it was certainly not a place to discard unwanted females. Entry required the payment of a significant dowry, just as in the case of marriage, and thus an elite family saved nothing financially by putting a daughter in the convent. The convent's administrators loaned the money gathered from dowries at interest, to members of the elite with the collateral required for a loan, and the interest payments received covered the convent's expenses.[16] It was, therefore, a bank. By the eighteenth century the nunnery was the single most important source of loan capital in Yucatán.[17] A respected gentleman of the community was entrusted with carrying out the convent's business of lending money. The nuns took vows of chastity, but they did not live in poverty. They were allowed to bring female servants and slaves with them, and they lived in separate living quarters like families. They did not eat communally but did enjoy a significant social life within their community.

The Franciscans, the only missionary order in Yucatán, had an imposing presence in Mérida. They built a large convent to the southeast of the plaza called, appropriately, San Francisco. This, however, was much more than a convent, for it was surrounded by a defensive wall and was manned by a small body of soldiers. It was called the citadel (*ciudadela*). Presumably this would serve as a refuge should the Maya rise up in large numbers in an attempt to kill the Spanish invaders. It was never needed for that purpose, and in the nineteenth century it was torn down to expand the space available for the city market.

By the second half of the seventeenth century the continued arrival of African slaves and the growth of the Afro-Maya population led to the founding of a church to serve that population. This was *El Dulce Nombre de Jesús* (the Sweet Name of Jesus), the parishioners of which were at first the offspring of male slaves from Africa and indigenous women working in the houses of the Spanish. Thereafter the records of the sacraments administered to these people, who were eventually called *castas*, were kept in separate books. Thus, the Church established administrative segregation.

As Mérida grew in size and, to a lesser extent, in importance, it expanded from the inner core outward in all directions. Because of the need to attend Mass within walking distance of residences, new churches were constructed every few decades in all directions. The private residences of the wealthy, of course, occupied most space, and because of the hot climate and the Spanish culture houses were built of stone and tended to be large in terms of terrain occupied. Typically a high stone wall with openings for a door, a gate, and windows faced the street. In the center of the lot was an open-air patio sometimes containing a well but always containing trees, shrubs, flowers, and/or a fountain. The lots were square, with the front wall occupying the street side. In the back, on the other side of the patio was another wall that separated the lot from the house on the opposite side of the block. The front and back walls were connected to each other by walls on the two sides, which separated the house from the other houses on the block. The front gate of the largest houses led to a stable and a place to park a carriage. (The smell of horses, urine, and excrement must have penetrated every square inch of the city.) This is one more reason why the lots were so large: they had to be. The living quarters tended to be located in rooms along the front or side walls. The back of the house was usually the kitchen area. Ceilings were high to allow for the circulation of air, which entered through grated windows. People of lesser means, of course, had more modest dwellings that were usually thatched, like those of the Maya.

Since Spanish cities usually grew in size over time, the nearby Maya villages became the sites of a new colonization by colonists. When the original city center grew overcrowded and real estate values rose, Hispanic people started to buy property in those villages, and when they were joined by other, similar people, the villages were converted into new, smaller versions of the original city.[18] The spillover in effect was a process similar to what is now known as gentrification. However, these satellite cities or towns never had their own city government. The whole urban center and a good deal of the surrounding hinterland were under the jurisdiction of the center city government.

In practice this meant churches built by and for the Maya soon had nonindigenous parishioners. To the north a Maya village was the site of the Church of Santa Ana. The village and the church were incorporated into the city. The same happened to Santiago, about four blocks west of the plaza. In an indigenous neighborhood five blocks to the east, the Church of Nuestra Señora del Tránsito (Our Lady of the Assumption), which looked like a church in Madrid called La Mejorada, was finished in 1640 and became one of the city's largest religious constructions. The neighborhood became known as La Mejorada. The urban space of Mérida was saturated with religious buildings.

In the late seventeenth and eighteenth century urban life revolved around family, marketing, religion, and politics. In the 1750s Mérida had between seventy-two and seventy-eight stores that paid municipal taxes and undoubtedly many, many peddlers who, like today, avoided taxes.[19] Many of these commercial establishments were founded by immigrants, and in fact Mérida had a large number of residents who had been born elsewhere. Most important, of course, were people directly from Andalucía, the Basque country, and Cantabria (but not Aragon or Catalonia). All of the people who came to occupy important political positions as governors or accountants of the Royal Treasury were from Castile and the Basque Country. A good number of immigrants came from the Canary Islands, and in fact *isleños*, as they were called, were especially represented among the small merchants. People from truly foreign countries, like England, Ireland, Belgium, France, and Italy, were also to be found in the city. There was even a family named Garibaldi. Still others came from other parts of the Spanish empire in America like Caracas, Havana, and Mexico City.[20]

Why would people come to Mérida, Yucatán? Certainly it was in part the result of the ease of getting there. The fleet leaving annually from Seville, and later from Cádiz, put in to Veracruz, which was well-connected by sea to Campeche. After 1718 the Canary Islands and Campeche were allowed direct contact with each other, which meant there was no longer any reason for *isleños* to go to Veracruz.

Apparently people found out that a reasonably prosperous life might be had in the provincial capital. No one came to get rich, of course, because Yucatán lacked precious metals, and indeed no one got rich. But the exports of cotton textiles and wax to Veracruz tied the province to the mining economy of northern Mexico and thus brought in a flow of silver coins and commercial goods.[21] Immigrants could integrate quickly into the society and culture and become relatively important in a relatively unimportant place. In any case, the presence of so many people from elsewhere shows that Yucatán was well connected to the regional and world economy.

Also present in the province and in Mérida was a large number of people of African origins. Many of them were slaves brought directly from West Africa. Every upper-class family owned a slave or two who worked as domestic servants. Some slaves worked as skilled laborers. The presence of Maya as well as African women in the city allowed for intermarriage on a much larger scale than was the case for slaves working on rural estates. Yet only in the Campeche region, where sugarcane was cultivated, was slavery commonly used for agricultural production, albeit on a small scale. In Mérida, as in most cities in Spanish America, there was a historical trend toward the emergence of a free African American population. This was in part because the children born to a free mother were always born free, and also because of a tendency on the part of slave owners in the city to make provisions in their will for the emancipation of many or all of their slaves. This free Black or racially mixed population served as an important recruiting base for the provincial militia.[22]

Finally, Mérida of course had a large number of Mayas, although the community of "Mexicans" in San Cristóbal was also significant at first. The Hispanic families regularly received labor services from the native people for household work, including childcare, and this contact especially between indigenous women and Hispanic men led to the gradual growth of the *mestizo* (part Indian, part white) population in the city. Moreover, as the urban center expanded and absorbed nearby villages, the indigenous people came into more and more contact with the Hispanic people. The market, located midway between the central plaza and the barrio of San Cristóbal, was not just a place but also a daily event, where people of all backgrounds interacted. Most of the commercial establishments were located here, and the shop owners, frequently immigrants, would have had to learn some of the Maya language to get along. All the American-born members of the elite learned some Maya from their indigenous nannies. In the early eighteenth century the bishop of

Mérida even complained that the Hispanic community spoke Maya too often, at the expense of Spanish, and also that elite women wore immodest but comfortable Maya clothing in the privacy of their own homes. The bishop ordered these practices to stop.[23] We can be sure that his mandates were ignored.

Unfortunately, since the Spanish government would not authorize a printing press in Mérida until the early nineteenth century, at the very end of the colonial regime, we are lacking in newspapers for accounts of social life and news in the city in the colonial period. However, surviving cabildo records give us at least a glimpse into some activities. A major function of the government was to organize the systematic provisioning of the city by closely regulating the entry of cattle into the market. It was also responsible for the purchase in advance of maize and wheat flour (imported from abroad) for the granary and bakeries. Subsistence, which is to say survival, was the primary function of government, and this was frequently put to the test in the eighteenth century because of frequent poor harvests resulting from drought, hurricane, or locust plague. The cabildo often resorted to the rationing of both maize and bread, and tried to punish hoarders and speculators.[24]

Politics was a major activity and was a concern for the elites of the city. To a great extent politics revolved around conflicts with the royal governors. The latter were almost always Castilian-born military officers who, like officials everywhere in the Spanish colonial empire, engaged in illegal commercial activities, frequently with the indigenous population, to augment their meager salaries. The issue was: should the elite try to resist an especially extortionate governor, or should the Hispanic leaders cooperate with him in order to moderate the governors' activities? Those who cooperated stood to gain, because it was the governor who allocated encomiendas when they became available as the result of the death of an encomendero, and the governor tended to reward his "friends."[25]

These conflicts were played out in the city council, the institutional representative of the Hispanic population of the city.[26] Mérida had twelve permanent city councilmen, or *regidores*. These positions were purchased from the crown and were permanent; that is, a regidor stayed on the cabildo as long as he liked. Usually he served until he died or resigned. Every January 1 the regidores met to elect the city officials for the incoming year. They chose two alcaldes, who were charged with actual leadership and served as judges of first instance. Another of the most important elected officials was the procurator, who served as the city attorney. Finally, usually a person who had never served in office before was elected to run the granary and arrange for the purchase of maize from villages within the province and wheat flour that was imported. It was a thankless job, but good service would allow someone to move up to a higher position in the future.

The city council had many responsibilities and few resources. The lack of documentation makes it difficult to generalize about city finances, but a surviving budget from 1756 will give us a good idea of what the cabildo of Mérida spent its money on in the middle of the eighteenth century.[27] This in turn will tell us a great deal about the culture of the time. Expenses totaled 488 pesos 4 reales. By far the single most important outlay was for the doctor's salary of 200 pesos. Mérida did not have a resident doctor during much of the sixteenth and seventeenth century because of the unattractiveness of the place and the inability to pay a significant salary. Apparently 200 pesos—41 percent of the city budget—was enough in the eighteenth century to have a permanent doctor on hand.

After that, religious festivals occupied an important place in city expenses: 92 pesos 6½ reales were paid to the Indians who came in from the nearby villages to work on the palm thatching needed for the Feast of Corpus Christi, which was the biggest religious festival of the year in colonial times. Similarly, 30 pesos were paid to the Guardian of the Convent of San Francisco for the Feast of Santa Inés (Saint Agnes, a companion of Saint Francis of Assisi), 25 pesos went for the Feast of St. John, 12 pesos for axes to work on the constructions for the Epiphany and the Immaculate Conception, 7 pesos 3 reales for the work of a sculptor who made statues for the Corpus Christi procession, and 2 pesos 2 reales for the clothing put on those statues. The total for religious celebrations thus came to 169 pesos 3½ reales, or 35 percent of the budget.

Outlays also went for maintenance and repair projects, salaries, and payment of past debts. Thirty pesos went to the repairs of the stone arches over the street leading to the barrio of Santa Ana, while 2 pesos 2 reales were paid to "the Indians" who cleaned out "the cave that serves as a drainage canal" for the city. These two expenses accounted for almost 7 percent of the budget. Salaries, amounting to 5 percent, did not account for much: 22 pesos 1 real to the school master—there was only one in the city—and 2 pesos to the doorman who worked at City Hall. It is important to note that the regidores themselves received no payment for their civic service.

Deficit financing was necessary for city expenses. About 10 percent went to pay the previous year's deficit of 44 pesos 3½ reales. The previous year's procurator received that sum as reimbursement for expenses. Since total municipal income, derived from commercial taxes, fees from the slaughterhouse, and rent paid on municipal property, came to only 399 pesos 6 reales, there was a new deficit of 88 pesos 6 reales. The procurator of 1756 paid that himself and could expect reimbursement the following year.

We see, therefore, a city culture that cared a great deal about having a professional doctor and enjoying religious celebrations. Since buildings had been constructed at an earlier time, only maintenance was necessary. Street illumination, not to mention cleaning, was considered unnecessary. We know nothing of garbage collection. It is likely that pigs, dogs, and buzzards took care of that.

Mérida was one of many Spanish settlements in America in which European and Euro-American people tried to benefit from their close relationship with and proximity to indigenous people without being overwhelmed by the latter's culture. They tried to maintain their separate Spanish identity but were not completely successful. They ended up creating a new one, a Spanish American one.

THREE

* * *

DEATH
Dying, Love, and Catholic Culture

I. Colonialism and Classifications

After the Spanish occupation of a large part of America, the Spaniards imposed a European-like system of estates. These were called the *República de Indios* (Commonwealth of Indians) for the native people and the *República de Españoles* (Commonwealth of Spaniards). The members of each estate had special rights, privileges, and obligations, and the Indians and the Spaniards were supposed to be kept separate. That is not what happened. The two groups mixed with each other, and the one with the power tried to exploit the weaker group. Moreover, the African slaves brought to America reproduced and mixed with the other two, thereby creating a group of people called *castas*, who did not fit into either estate.

The attempt to put everybody into neat categories meant that the Catholic Church kept separate records for *indios* (Indians), *españoles* (Spaniards), and *castas* (mixed-race people). Of course, a neat classification of human beings does not always work.[1] Unlike most other parts of Spanish America, however, this was made somewhat easier in Yucatán by the continued use after the Spanish conquest of indigenous surnames: those who were *indios* with only a small number of exceptions used Maya surnames and people with Maya surnames were understood to be *indios*.[2] This allows us to separate the indigenous people from the records kept for people called *españoles*, who always used European surnames.

The people classified as *españoles*, however, frequently must have been of mixed race. This is because the *Libros de españoles* included a significant

33

number of people of uncertain parentage. For example, as will be seen in the next chapter, between 1710 and 1729 almost exactly one-third of all infants baptized were recorded as either illegitimate children or *expósitos* (foundlings), that is, someone left on someone's doorstep.[3] On rare occasions both parents of illegitimate children were recorded, and almost always the mother of an illegitimate child was identified. In the latter cases, therefore, one of the parents was known. Seldom, however, was there any identification of the mother or father of foundlings.

The same uncertainty evident at the time of baptism also made its appearance at the time of marriage. Of those receiving the matrimonial sacrament between 1716 and 1721, fully 21 percent were either illegitimate, foundlings, or adopted. Their parents were therefore not recorded, although one suspects that many people knew very well whose children they were. For reasons of decorum and discretion, no one came forward to identify them. Mérida's society knew how to keep its secrets.

In any case, the inclusion in the books for Spaniards of marriages and baptisms of people who were not entirely of European origin means that these people's children would most likely have been registered in the book of "Spaniards," and if they had children their genes would have passed into the Hispanic population. Many members of Hispanic society therefore were in fact of mixed race. One suspects that all of the current members of the elite who had ancestors in colonial Mérida have some indigenous and/or African ancestry. And that is not all. Living in such close proximity to the Maya people, everyone in Hispanic society would have had extensive interaction with people of a different culture and could not have escaped the cultural influence that must have resulted.

And these are important points. Despite ancestry, a society founded by people from Spain gradually became a society that was different from those in towns or small cities in Spain, especially after the expulsion of the Moriscos (Muslims) after 1607. Many people in Mérida although classified as *españoles* were of mixed-race ancestry and belonged to a new, American, Hispanic society. Many children of uncertain parentage were Hispanized. Consequently the individuals in the books of *españoles* were accepted as Hispanic people (unless priests noted otherwise), and we can accept as Hispanic, although not Spanish, with a high degree of certainty those who appear with Hispanic surnames in the books for *españoles*. The experience of Mérida, therefore, was not like that of all Spanish cities in America. In Guadalajara and San Antonio (Texas), for example, the immigration of people from other parts of Mexico and the almost total absence of new immigrants from Spain eventually led, with some exceptions, to the breakdown of the socio-racial classification system.[4] In Yucatán, and in many other places in Mesoamerica, the tradition survived.

Mérida was "an island in a sea of Indians," but that sea influenced that island in a variety of ways. Its shoreline was continually shifting because of erosion and inundation. Consequently, despite the people's determined efforts to remain Spanish, their environment was different from that experienced by people in Spain. America was not Spain. The social context was different. Mérida's Hispanic society was gradually becoming an American society with deep Spanish roots yet changing because of cultural and biological interaction with indigenous people.

II. Sacraments and Disease

Yucatán was not a healthy place for human beings. The environment was very good, however, for tropical diseases and bacteria. The long periods of heat and high humidity caused the rapid putrefaction of food and the proliferation of dangerous microscopic life forms in the food and water. Since germ theory had not yet emerged, people were unaware of the causes of many of the diseases that killed people. Medical knowledge was unable to make a diagnosis, and in any case the priests who recorded the administration of Extreme Unction—the last rites of the Church—only rarely commented on the cause of death of the people receiving the final sacrament. However, when medical knowledge improved and record-keeping was secularized in the nineteenth century, it is understandable why doctors frequently diagnosed dysentery and gastroenteritis as causes of death. Presumably such diseases had always been common in Yucatán.

Then, in the seventeenth century the disease environment got a lot worse. Somehow the larvae of the *Aëdes aegypti* mosquito survived the passage across the Atlantic from Africa, and eventually this new insect found good conditions throughout tropical and semi-tropical America for massive reproduction. This was important because this mosquito was the vector of yellow fever. The first epidemic of this new tropical disease hit the French Caribbean colony of Guadeloupe in 1635. The second was the catastrophe that afflicted Yucatán in 1648.

A first epidemic is usually the deadliest, because some diseases provide survivors with immunities that lessen later impacts. This happened in the case of yellow fever in Yucatán. According to the sacramental records for Spaniards in Mérida, priests had to administer the last rites of the church an extraordinary number of times in 1648. This is demonstrated in Figure 3.1. After that, epidemics returned but never again reached the level of 1648.[5]

As already noted, the priests did not attempt to diagnose the causes of death. But they did at times provide us with some clues. It should be remembered that church records are not registries of births, marriages, and deaths but of the administration of the sacraments of Baptism, Matrimony, and Extreme Unction. The so-called *Libro de Entierros* of the *españoles* in Mérida therefore is not a book of burials but rather a record of the administration of Extreme Unction. Entries reveal, however, that most people received three sacraments to prepare their souls for the afterlife: Confession, Holy Communion, and Extreme Unction. Confession was supposed to remove the stain of sin from the soul, thereby preparing the individual for sanctifying grace provided by Holy Communion. This second sacrament, received in a sinless state, insured entry into heaven. Finally, Extreme Unction, the sacrament usually received only once, just prior to death, provided even more sanctifying grace for the soul.

Not all of the dying, however, received all three sacraments. Young children—those who had not yet reached "the age of reason"—were excluded from Confession and Communion because they were thought to be too young to sin, and their Original Sin had been removed by Baptism. The very young were in fact perceived as a distinct category of human beings and, consequently, the names of dead children were not even recorded. Sanctified by the grace provided by Extreme Unction, small children would go straight to heaven without having to suffer through Purgatory. Some priests therefore registered the last rites of a child as for "a little angel" (*un angelito*)—someone already in heaven by the time the entry was made. Adults who were either unconscious or delirious also received only one sacrament since they could not confess or swallow the host. They could, however, receive Extreme Unction in a last, desperate effort to save their immortal souls.

During some years a large number of adults did not receive all three sacraments, and the priests sometimes tell us why: because of "*vómitos*" (vomit) or even more specifically "*vómitos de sangre*" (vomiting blood).[6] That is the term used until the late nineteenth century for what is now called yellow fever. Yellow fever produces internal hemorrhaging that fills the stomach with blood, which is soon regurgitated as the dark vomit that people found so horrifying.

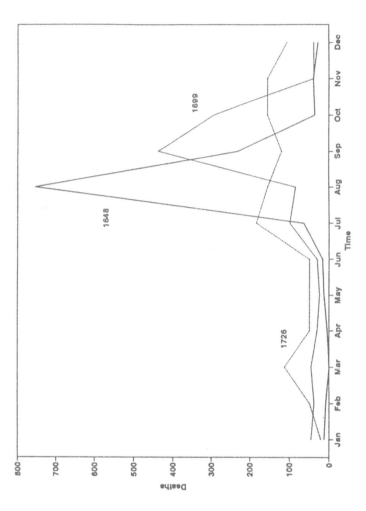

FIGURE 3.1: Month-by-Month Death Index of Spaniards in Mérida: 1648, 1699, 1726. Source: Robert Patch, "Sacraments and Disease in Mérida, Yucatán, Mexico, 1648–1727," *The Historian* 58, no. 4 (1996): 731–43.

The symptoms of yellow fever changed the administration of the sacraments. The priests decided that the people with *vómitos* would receive Confession and Extreme Unction but not Holy Communion. Why? In the priests' words, "because of the vomiting." The consecrated host was believed to be the Body of Christ, so holy that only consecrated priests were permitted to touch it. The regurgitation of the Body of Christ must have been horrifying to the faithful, and a consecrated host, once vomited, would have to be handled and disposed of by a priest. Understandably, clergymen chose not to take the risk of such an occurrence. The dying would have to make do without Holy Communion.

The priests therefore provided clues that permit the diagnosis of at least one disease. Someone with *vómitos* had yellow fever, and if many people died of that disease, then an epidemic was in progress. The records of last rites in Mérida between 1697 and 1729 reveal that a yellow fever epidemic occurred in 1699. On the other hand, high levels of mortality also occurred in 1709 and 1726 but there is no evidence that yellow fever was the principal factor involved.

The seasonality of death helps distinguish between yellow fever and other diseases. Since *vómitos* were the result of the transmission of a virus by a vector, the *Aëdes aegypti* mosquito, yellow fever tended to cause most fatalities during the hot, wet summer months of August and September. Then, it tended to taper off. It coincided with the rainy season in Yucatán, which provided mosquito larvae with the water necessary for mass reproduction. The onset of slightly cooler weather in October and November, combined with the decline of precipitation, slowed the reproduction of the vectors and dried up surface water, thereby killing the mosquitoes or driving them into a prolonged larval stage. Thus yellow fever all but disappeared every winter.[7]

This seasonality is demonstrated in Figure 3.1, which includes information from 1648, the year of the first yellow fever epidemic in Yucatán. It also includes data from 1699 and 1726. The records of 1648 demonstrate extremely high mortality, reflecting the newness of the disease and the concomitant lack of immunity. In the nineteenth century, observers in Yucatán noted that yellow fever tended to be most lethal to "foreigners," that is, people not native to the Peninsula.[8] This suggests that the local population had developed some immunities to the disease. In 1648 deaths in large numbers did not begin until late July and peaked in August. In 1699 fatalities were much less skewed toward the months in which the epidemic was raging. After that, yellow fever reappeared every summer for the next three years, but the number of deaths was not abnormally high.

If 1699 was a year of yellow fever, what can be said of 1709 and 1726? There is no mention of *vómitos* in those years, so some other pathogen was at work. The epidemic of 1726, which coincided with a famine, started not in July or August but rather in March. The mortality seems to have abated somewhat for several months, but in July deaths increased significantly, making that the month of greatest mortality. The number of deaths again declined slightly in August and tapered off considerably in September, only to increase again in October and November. In December mortality declined once more, only to rise dramatically again the following month. Clearly the epidemic and/or famine was carrying over into the next year. The dead in January 1727 outnumbered those of every month of 1726 except July. The epidemic is therefore most unlikely to have been yellow fever.

Although the high mortality of July 1727 might suggest the presence of a tropical disease, in fact the seasonality of disease in Mérida demonstrates that high death rates in the hot, wet summers of Yucatán were the norm. In the thirty-one years between 1698 and 1728, more people died in August than in any other month. In eighteen of those years, the months of highest mortality were either July, August, or September, whether yellow fever was present or not. In modern times those months are especially marked by gastrointestinal diseases, and in colonial times the lack of antibiotics would certainly have meant high death rates in Mérida's hot summers.

Identifying the disease that killed so many people in 1726–27 is not possible. Circumstantial evidence, however, allows for a good guess. It will be recalled that the epidemic, although starting in 1726, carried over into 1727. That was a year in which central Mexico suffered a severe outbreak of either measles (*sarampión*) or German measles (*rubeola*).[9] The seasonality of those diseases is different from that of yellow fever, for death rates tend to be higher in the colder months of the year. That is consistent with the death rate in Mérida, and the large number of deaths in July 1726 probably reflects the normal high mortality rate in the summer.

The highest mortality rates of all in this period, however, occurred in the four years between 1708 and 1711. Indeed, more people died in 1709 than in 1699 (yellow fever) or in 1726 (probably measles). Once again, precise diagnosis is not possible, but the records of the last rites provide some suggestions. The large number of deaths in 1708 was probably not caused by yellow fever because there was no change in the administration of the sacraments. Most people received Confession, Holy Communion, and Extreme Unction. Moreover, the months of highest mortality were April and May, when yellow fever was unusual because the rainy season had not started. Death rates then declined in June but rose again in July and August, although somewhat below the norm for that time of year. Moreover, throughout the whole summer there was no change in the administration of the sacraments and there was no mention of *vómitos*.

The illness of 1708 carried over into the next year, peaking in April of 1709. The number of deaths diminished considerably from May to July, only to rise again in August and September to higher levels than for the same months in the previous year. The Church records also show a change in the administration of the sacraments: many people received Confession and Extreme Unction but not Holy Communion—the tell-tale sign of yellow fever. However, the number of deaths from what was probably yellow fever did not approach the epidemic level. But because there may have been two diseases at work in the same year, 1709 had the highest mortality in the thirty-one years under discussion. It was also the only year in which the number of deaths was larger than the number of births.

The next year, 1710, was unlike either of the two previous years. There was no late winter or spring epidemic, and consequently the pattern of death for the first part of the year was normal. But mortality rose to high levels in August and September. Once again, the administration of the sacraments was changed, indicating the likely presence of yellow fever. The last of the four years in question, 1711, was also unlike any of the previous three years. Mortality during the first half of the year was normal. Then death rates in August and September rose to very high levels, but this time with no accompanying change in the administration of the sacraments. It was probably not yellow fever that was killing so many people.

All of this suggests, first, that in 1708 an epidemic of unknown origin took place and carried over into 1709. Then, yellow fever broke out in the late summer. By 1710 the first unidentifiable epidemic was over, but yellow fever returned again in the summer of that year. Finally, in 1711 very high death rates were reached during the season of the year when yellow fever usually reigned supreme, but the absence of any change in the administration of sacraments suggests that this was not yellow fever. The earlier epidemic may have returned or still another illness may have caused the large number of deaths. Finally, it is also possible that there was no epidemic at all, and that the large number of deaths in August and September was simply a function of Mérida's hot, humid summer months.

The epidemics and high death rates in fact marked the end of an era. After 1727 the population of Mérida and of Yucatán began a period of demographic growth interrupted in the 1770s by still another famine, which was followed by recovery. There were more outbreaks of yellow fever, of course, but they never reached the level of mortality as in 1648 or 1699. Other epidemics took place, but none had the same impact that yellow fever once had. The growing population needed resources, and the result was the expansion of production on haciendas, the growth of urban markets, and the struggle between Hispanic people and the Maya over land. The early eighteenth century, therefore, was a transition period between the early and late colonial eras. It was also a time when the American-born Hispanic population greatly outnumbered those born in Spain and had to struggle to maintain its Spanish cultural roots in order to avoid being overwhelmed by "the sea of Indians" that surrounded them.

III. Dying

If diseases did not kill people, other things could. Childbirth itself was of course dangerous, and sometimes priests recorded that fact. On March 9, 1726, María de la Cruz Villarreal, the wife of Pedro Campos, "died suddenly and without the holy sacraments because of childbirth."[10] Infant mortality, of course, was high for a variety of reasons. The death records offer some idea of the likelihood of early death. The priests wrote down the names of most of the people who died, but did not usually do so in the case of infants and young children. Perhaps this was because the latter were not considered to be full-fledged persons; "personhood" may have come later.

In any case, some people were given a name at baptism but not always at death, and those without names were either infants or the very young. The data regarding deaths, baptisms, and last rites are included in Table 3.1. They show that in the thirty-two years between 1698 and 1729 priests recorded the deaths of 2,990 people, and of these 788—that is, 26.4 percent—were buried without their names being mentioned. Of course, some of these people were possibly not children and their names went unrecorded because of the inattention of priests or lack of information. Still, the figures do suggest that over one-fifth, and possibly as many as one-fourth, of the Hispanic population did

TABLE 3.1: Baptisms, Marriages, and Last Rites, 1697–1726

YEAR	BAPTISMS	MARRIAGES	LAST RITES
1697		32	
1698		33	67
1699		51	159
1700	158	48	83
1701	167	53	81
1702	111	35	88
1703	164	31	91
1704	162	40	77
1705	180	42	105
1706	189	61	84
1707	198	66	87
1708	186	44	132
1709	177	47	188
1710	195	51	138
1711	193	31	163
1712	185	38	84
1713	228	48	62
1714	182	27	86
1715	186	30	113
1716	221	40	127
1717	220	61	98
1718	209	63	110
1719	179	56	87
1720	203	37	53
1721	256	60	22
1722	226	38	52
1723	175	58	34
1724	250	55	61
1725	228	49	73
1726	240	26	171
1727	142	38	101
1728	174	53	59
1729	282	52	54

Source: Archivo General del Arzobispado, Españoles, Bautismos, Libros 4–8; Matrimonios, Libros 4–7; Entierros, Libros 2–3.

not even reach adolescence let alone adulthood. That is not unexpected, for in the United Kingdom in 1725 life expectancy as a whole was only about thirty-one years. However, at the same time in the English colonies of what is now the United States, where population density was much lower than in Yucatán or in England and where a large part of the population lived outside of the areas with endemic yellow fever or malaria, life expectancy was fifty. That, of course, was highly unusual in the world at that time.

The precarious nature of life for the young is further demonstrated by the frequent need to administer baptism as soon as possible after birth. This was done so that infants could get into heaven even if they did not get into adolescence or adulthood. For example, in the records of the ten-year period from 1720 to 1729 there was a total of 2,176 baptisms, and of these there were 219—10.1 percent—registered as "urgent." In short, the number of infants baptized in dire danger of dying was one in ten.

That danger was faced by the high and mighty as well as by the poor. La Señora Doña María Violante de Salcedo Enríquez y Navarra, the wife of Governor Juan José de Vertiz y Ortañón—and the only lady other than the Countess of Miraflores who could use the lordly title of *Señora*—gave birth to a baby boy who was baptized on February 2, 1718. He was buried three months later, on May 29. He was given a name at baptism but no name at death. Don Mateo de Cárdenas, an immigrant from Andalucía who had married in Mérida in 1693, died in July 1707, leaving behind a pregnant wife; but his newborn child died only a few months later and was buried, without a name, in the cathedral. Regidor Don Felipe de Ayora, the assistant commander of Mérida's citadel, and his wife, Doña Andrea Beltrán, lost one unnamed infant daughter on September 25, 1711, and then another one less than three months later, on November 11.

Older children, adolescents, and young adults also died, but their names were recorded. Don Manuel Carrillo, a bachelor, the son of Captain Don Juan Manuel Carrillo and Doña María Cervera, died in 1712, but he did not make a will "because he is child of a family." That meant he was living with his parents and was considered a dependent.

Many people died so rapidly and unexpectedly that they could not receive all the sacraments. In 1698 Alférez (ensign) Don Juan Domínguez, the husband of Doña Rosa Carbajal, came down with an *achaque* (which usually meant an infectious disease) that "deprived him of his senses" and as a result did not receive communion or confession and did not even have the time to make a will. The same death was experienced by many others. Doña Isabel

Delgado died in 1701 without the sacraments because she was away at Estancia Sacalá (probably near Izamal), and there was no time to get a priest.

People died in many ways and circumstances. In 1698 Blas Pinelo, the husband of María Villegas, was "brought from the sea drowned" and was given a pauper's grave. This means that the body had to be transported from the coast to the city, a distance of over 35 kilometers. That was a journey of more than a day, and whoever transported the body went to a lot of trouble for a dead person whose burial would be paid for out of charity.

Pedro del Bullon, a Frenchman, died in 1708 in the house of Governor Martín de Urzúa, thereby suggesting that he and the governor had business dealings together. On July 30 and July 31, 1700, two dead infants were found in the barrio of Santa Ana. Their parents could not be found or identified. The priests could have chosen to bury them in the local Indian parish but instead had the two deceased infants interred in the cathedral crypt and recorded in the books for Spaniards. The priests may have known something that they did not put into the records.

Alférez Mayor of Valladolid Don Miguel Ruiz de Ayusa and former alcalde of Valladolid Captain Don Fernando Urquizu y Tovar were in Mérida and knew that death was near. They had time to confess and receive communion before they were hanged on May 28, 1705. In the struggle for the profits from the repartimiento in their home region, they had encouraged supporters to murder their political enemies, two former alcaldes, and because of the importance of the crime they had received the death sentence. Moreover, because Governor Martín de Urzúa y Arizmendi had failed to exercise his authority in time to prevent the crime, he was suspended from office, and so the execution took place during the tenure of Governor Álvaro Rivaguda.

It did not go as planned. Gallows were built in the patio of Mérida's jail, which shows that capital punishment was rare. Some leading citizens and priests gathered to witness the event. "Death is a dignitary who, when he comes announced, is to be received with formal manifestations of respect," as Ambrose Bierce wrote in a fictional account of a similar event.[11] Urquizu Tovar died quickly, but Ruiz de Ayusa had an excruciating wait during his final moments on earth. In the first attempt to hang him the rope broke and he fell to the ground. So, the authorities tried again, but with the same result. Ruiz de Ayusa begged for mercy, but the governor responded that he would show the same mercy that the murderers had shown their victims. They tried again. Third time was a charm. Sometimes truth is stranger than fiction.

Since capital punishment was much less common in the Spanish colonies than in the English, executions stand out as rare. The only other case occurring in the entire province of Yucatán in the early eighteenth century was the execution of Gregorio Lugo, a native of Havana, and Basilio Laguna in 1726. They died together for an unspecified crime.

It is unknown if Western medicine helped cure disease in Mérida in the eighteenth century. Nevertheless, from early on the city leaders had faith in the value of medicine and therefore tried to recruit a professional doctor to settle and practice in the city. For lack of one, sometimes an herbalist or someone with similar aptitude was available. In 1691 a priest named Domingo Hidalgo was said to be *"platicante [sic.] en Medezina"* (practitioner of medicine), and he may have helped people somewhat.[12] However, a trained doctor does show up in the records in the late seventeenth century. This was Don Manuel Jiménez Amador, who was identified as a doctor when he died in early 1700.[13] His family apparently had come with him on the trip from Spain, for when his daughter Manuela married in 1699 it was recorded that she was a native of Seville. It is likely that Don Manuel was either from Seville or had studied medicine at the University of Seville and found a wife there.

After the passing of Doctor Jiménez Amador, there is evidence of a "Professor of Medicine" named Bachiller Manuel de Rivera Sumbado in the city in 1709.[14] In 1722 there was a doctor and a surgeon in Mérida: Don Juan Gregorio Calvo, a doctor, and Don Melchor Herrera, "master surgeon and apothecary of this city." They signed a certified document to the effect that they had treated and attempted to cure the Indian servants of many Spanish citizens of Mérida.[15] Calvo was still working as a doctor as late as 1729, when it was said that he owed money to the estate of the late regidor of Mérida Don Juan del Campo.[16]

Of course, medicine in the seventeenth and eighteenth centuries was not always helpful and was sometimes downright dangerous for the patient. Nevertheless, it is also likely that the treatment of a doctor was a benefit to some people if for no other reason than a placebo effect, and the usual medical practice at the time of administering brandy to the sick might also have made people feel better. At a later time, as we have seen, the city government paid the salary of the doctor, and it is likely that Doctor Jiménez Amador, Doctor Rivera Sumbado, Doctor Calvo, and Master Surgeon Herrera were also paid by the city government.

Death was a frequent occurrence and therefore people sometimes tried to get ready. Ignacio Manzana prepared for his death in a unique way. He got a rope and hanged himself in the back yard of a house in the barrio of San Cristóbal in November 1716. People who committed suicide were not allowed to be buried in sacred ground, but the diocesan vicar (executive officer of the diocese) investigated and declared that Manzana was mentally deranged. Therefore he was buried, like practically everyone else, in the crypt of the cathedral. It was a pauper's grave, and he left a wife behind.[17]

Don José Domínguez de la Cámara had no time to prepare for his death. While in the house of Don Domingo Cayetano de Cárdenas, he was fencing—apparently people fenced in colonial Mérida—with Don Juan Bolio y Solís when the latter accidentally inflicted a mortal wound on his partner. This was a double tragedy, for the event caused Bolio y Solís to fall into *"melancolía y demencia"* (depression and mental illness). He began to go into indigenous villages and abuse the people. In a rage he even hit a Maya woman. Eventually Mérida's authorities acted, put him into protective custody, and refused to endorse his request for an encomienda.[18]

Death caught many people financially unprepared—that is, poor. Sometimes the priests recorded the deaths of people who could not afford to pay for the last rites, and this gives us an idea of poverty among the Hispanic population. During the epidemic of 1726, 48 of 171 burials—28.1 percent—were free (*gratis* or *de caridad*), which suggests that a significant portion of Hispanic people was in fact poor. A similar percentage of indigent people was found in the death records of Guadalajara in 1691.[19] Also in that year there was an increase in the number of foundlings left on doorsteps, which, as will be shown in the next chapter, suggests that parents sometimes had to abandon their children because they could not afford to support them.

And what about the wealthy? Church documents say nothing about how much money was collected or spent on funerals, and in fact there is almost nothing known about what people of means did upon the death of a family member. There is one indication: in his will in 1691, Captain Francisco Domínguez Palacios stated that upon the death of his wife, Doña María Díaz Santiago, he had spent 400 pesos on the funeral.[20] That was a small fortune, and it is unlikely that many people could afford such an expense. It does illustrate, however, the possibilities of what wealthy citizens like Domínguez Palacios—an Andalusian immigrant from Ayamonte engaged in lots of business operations with the Maya carried out by him, his creditors, and his debtors—were capable of.

Sometimes the pretensions of the elite could not hide economic difficulties. Doña Antonia de Arrúe, the mother of Don Juan del Castillo y Arrúe, was the daughter of Captain José de Arrúe, a native of Navarre, and of Doña Lorenza de Loaiza, a descendant of conquistadors of Yucatán. When she made her will in the village of Maní in 1691, she stated that upon marrying Juan del Castillo y Toledo, a native of Andalucía, in 1669 she had received a dowry. However, that document, she said, "was made in confidence for certain motives." It eventually becomes clear that she was subtly saying that the dowry was somewhat fictitious. The agreement, recorded in a notarial document that has not survived, stated that the dowry was to be provided in part by Captain Don Juan de Sosa y Magallanes and his wife, Doña Antonia de Sosa. For unexplained reasons, the latter couple had raised Doña Antonia de Arrúe, but when she was on her deathbed she claimed that because of *"cortedad"* (hard times) her adoptive parents had failed to deliver the money to complete her dowry. She had only received 1,000 pesos, which was supplemented by 600 pesos provided by Castellan Don Juan Jiménez de Rivera. Therefore, in her will she declared that her husband was not responsible for the portions of the dowry that had never existed; after all, the people who had promised to provide it failed to do so because of their bad financial situation. She herself claimed to be on hard times, for her husband had spent most of the family's money on an *entrada*—an Indian-catching expedition—that he had led into the wilds of the south. Even though she was the daughter of a Spanish-born alcalde of Mérida and of an encomendero family, she chose to be buried not in the cathedral of Mérida but in the church in Maní. And she was illiterate: she did not know how to sign her name.[21]

IV. Getting Ready to Die: Love and Money

Most people of means prepared for death by making their wills. Many residents of Mérida did not do so because they had no property, money, or possessions. Indeed, the priests keeping the death records frequently noted that many *españoles* died intestate because they had no reason to make a will.

For people with property, of course, death was something to prepare for, and before leaving this earth they had to account for dowries received—or not received. When Nicolás Trujeque prepared for death in 1689, he said that his first wife, Catalina de Salazar y Figueroa, had brought no dowry with her to the marriage. On the other hand, his second wife, Luisa de Tolosa, brought with her "a silver spoon, two pack horses, and a small patch of *milpa* [corn field]." Trujeque had some success at business and was able to provide a dowry of 200 pesos for each of his two daughters. His possessions included his furniture, a house, and some clothes, including a hat from Castile and another one from Puebla.[22]

Leonardo Peñeda Suárez, an immigrant from Tenerife, received no dowry when he married in the Canary Islands prior to emigrating. That was, as he put it, *"porque nos casamos pobremente"* (because we were married poorly). He left his wife and children behind when he departed from the Islands. He ended up with a store in Mérida and was owed money by various people. His estate was valued at 2,922 pesos 5 reales, so he had done well in America.[23]

Even people in the elite of encomenderos were sometimes near penury and could not provide dowries. When the encomendera Doña Gerónima Castellanos made her will in 1720, she stated that when she married her first husband, Don Pedro Guillermo de los Guillermos (a British immigrant whose name was undoubtedly Williams), she received no dowry at all, for she had married *"pobrement."* However, she provided herself with 500 pesos when she married her second husband, Matías Ontiveros, and she and her late husband had been able to provide a house worth 1,000 pesos as the dowry of their daughter. Unfortunately, the house had deteriorated in value, and her second husband had contributed 600 pesos to repair it. Furthermore, although she was the encomendera of the village of Citilcum, her possession of the title had yet to be confirmed because the paperwork had gone down with the Spain-bound fleet (probably in the hurricane of 1715).[24]

Epidemics certainly encouraged many to prepare for death. In 1729, when Yucatán was still suffering the effects of what was probably a measles epidemic, Captain Don Martin Antonio de Noguera and his wife, Doña Isabel María de Ávila y Carranza, made their will because they were afraid of the "illness" (*achaque*) that was killing people at the time. They had no children together (although she had an illegitimate child as a result of a relationship with Governor Antonio de Figueroa y Silva), and so they named each other as executors.[25]

Doña Manuela de Osorio y Cervantes, widow of Captain Francisco Ortiz del Barrio, vecina of Mérida, encomendera, also prepared for death by making her will in 1718. She was very well-off by local standards, for she was the granddaughter of the first Count of Miraflores. Her grandmother and guardian, la Señora Doña Micaela de Villamil y Vargas, the Countess of Miraflores (and the sister of Don Lucas de Villamil y Vargas), had provided her with 12,000 pesos in cash as a dowry, and since her late husband, an immigrant from Spain, had worked as a repartimiento agent for the governor, she had inherited some *"casas tiendas"* (stores) in the city of Campeche. Her property also included some jewelry and clothing given to her by her father, who like her husband was an immigrant from Spain.

In her will, Doña Manuela provided for the women who had served her. She gave 100 pesos to Pasquala Chac, the daughter of Juana Chac, her wet nurse (*chichigua*).[26] She also freed her slave Inés (no surname provided), "because she served me since my tender years." Inés's son Gregorio, also a slave, was to be given to her grandmother the countess to serve for ten years, at which time he too would be freed. Moreover, Doña Manuela stipulated that Gregorio could not be sold to anyone else or be moved outside of Yucatán, thereby ensuring that he would remain close to his mother. Since she had no children herself she used all of her wealth to establish a *capellanía* (chantry—see section V) for the souls of her parents and of her late husband, "for his Christian zeal and the much love and affection" (*"amor y cariño"*) between them. She appointed her grandparents, the count and countess, and her uncle to be her executors.[27]

Doña Manuela was not the only one to mention love in a will. José Fernández Palomino, a man from England who had a Spanish name, provided 25 pesos to Doña Francisca de Lara "for having assisted me with much love and good will."[28] When encomendero Don José Rodríguez Vigario made his will in 1722, he passed his encomienda on to his wife, Doña Inés de Sosa. He also recognized some debts, and therefore he asked his wife, for the love that they shared together (*"por el mucho amor . . . que hemos tenido"*), to pay off his obligations.[29] Although many or most marriages among the higher status people were arranged by parents and relatives, this did not preclude the development of love between husband and wife.

Love could also be found among men. After the death of Major Don Matías Beltrán de Mayorga, the latter's father-in-law, Regidor Captain Don Diego de Aranda y Aguayo, founded a *capellanía* for his daughter's late husband. Aranda y Aguayo referred to Beltrán de Mayorga as his son, and established the chantry, he said, "because of the great love [*mucho amor*] . . . I had for the Sargento Mayor."[30]

Many features of life among Hispanic people in the mid-colonial period is provided by the will of Captain Don Pedro Carvajal, an immigrant from Triana (across the Guadalquivir River from Seville), who prepared for death in 1692.³¹ In Veracruz he had married Doña María Montalvo, who came into the marriage with the sizable dowry of 8,000 pesos. The family was in Veracruz during the famous attack by pirates in 1683, and Carvajal's wife was killed. All of the cash of the dowry departed with the pirates, so the widower was left *"sumamente pobre"* (overwhelmingly poor). He owned a slave named Lucía, whom he left in Veracruz—for unexplained reasons—and then he settled in Mérida with his four children and two slaves, Pedro and Juana.

We do not know what Carvajal's slaves thought of their master, but we do know that the master thought very highly of Pedro. During the pirate attack in Veracruz, Pedro had rescued the children and carried them to safety. Carvajal promised then to free Pedro in the future. The slave also had for a while managed Carvajal's rancho in Veracruz and then managed a general store for his master in Mérida. Pedro was clearly faithful and had served his master well, and therefore Carvajal kept his promise by freeing Pedro in his will. He also freed his female slave named Juana as well as her daughter, born in the house in Mérida. Carvajal admitted that he was the father of the child, thereby testifying to a sexual relationship. Such arrangements may have resulted in affection, but slave women had no choice in the matter of having sex with their masters. The relationship was clearly among unequals, and coercion—that is, rape—was probably used in almost all cases of sexual relations between masters and slaves.

Carvajal's brother, Don Fernando, was in Mérida at the time of the will (and would marry the daughter of a regidor in 1705), so he must have accompanied his brother to America, preceded him, or joined him later on. Don Pedro owed his brother 700 pesos and was owed quantities of money by someone in Puebla. He also owned some bales of cotton thread in the possession of Alférez Miguel Azevedo, and he tried to have that property collected. In the will Don Pedro named his brother and his son-in-law, Juan Domínguez, as executors of the estate. The latter two in turn eventually arranged for the sale of the house in Veracruz, which sold for 1,980 pesos. However, liens on the house totaled 1,500 pesos, which left only 480 pesos to the estate.³² Finally, Don Pedro Carvajal declared as his heirs his legitimate children. Despite his poverty, he was able to provide a 500-peso dowry for his daughter Rosa and to donate 300 pesos to establish a chantry for his wife's soul. However, he did not provide for his illegitimate daughter by his slave and also willed nothing to his faithful slave Pedro. Perhaps there was nothing more to give.

V. Preparing for Purgatory

Since preparation for death also meant preparation for the afterlife, many people of property tried to find a way to get themselves out of Purgatory and into Heaven faster. At least that was the hope. If sinners did not go directly to Hell, then prayer could help get them out of Purgatory and into Heaven. The best way to ensure that the living prayed for the souls of the dead was to establish a *capellanía* (chantry). This was a fund set up by someone with money or property to pay for Masses for the souls of the dead. The fund would pay a priest to say a certain number of Masses per year, an arrangement that was supposed to be perpetual. The chantry would have a designated patron who would appoint a priest to perform the Masses. However, the founder would normally start the process by appointing the priest, who was called the *capellán* (chaplain).[33]

A good example is provided by the will of Doña Mariana de Sosa y Nortes in 1689. She left her house, which she had received as her dowry, to her daughter, and also willed 50 pesos to Juana Lizama, her loyal servant, so that she could buy the plot of land on which she had her house.

Doña Mariana must have been very religious, for she was a "*cofrada de todas las cofradías*" (member of all of the cofradías) of Mérida. Cofradías were religious "brotherhoods," but since she was a member of all of them, they must have been open to women as well as men. They were an important part of Catholic culture in the world, and leadership roles in them added prestige to those who held them. Among the activities of cofradías was group prayer for the souls of the departed members, and perhaps for that reason they were supported financially by people like Doña Mariana de Sosa y Nortes. In her will she established a chantry to provide funds for Masses to be prayed not only for her own soul but also for the souls of the members, past and present, of all the cofradías. She appointed her nephew, Father Juan Gaspar Bojórquez, to be the interim chaplain, who would be succeeded by another nephew, Hermenegildo González, should he become a priest. If he chose not to, or died, then the position as chaplain would pass to one of her two other nephews. Her son-in-law, Juan González Mangas—the father of the three young nephews—was appointed as patron of the chantry.[34]

Chantries therefore in reality provided not just Masses for the dead but also incomes for priests, especially family members, in the present. They encouraged young men to become priests if for no other reason than to get a steady income, and should they choose to be wastrels instead they might end up in conflict with their families.³⁵ Capellanías therefore resulted in an enlarged priesthood filled with people who were not engaged in the pastoral duty of curing the souls of the living.³⁶

Chantries were also important in economic history because they had to be funded. The founding of a capellanía required not just sins in need of forgiveness but also capital. Sin will be discussed below, but what we can be sure about is the importance of chantries in what Kathryn Burns has called "the spiritual economy."³⁷ Sometimes the founder would simply donate a quantity of money to the fund, and the capital would then be loaned to someone at 5 percent interest to produce an annual income to pay the priest. However, cash was always scarce in colonial Yucatán, and therefore the vast majority of capellanías were set up by putting liens on property. That meant a debt that was recognized on a landed estate or on a house or houses, and the owner of the estancia or of the houses had to pay the chantry fund annually 5 percent of the value of that debt. In effect, therefore, a capellanía was a 5 percent tax on part or all—depending on the size of the debt—of profits earned by landed estates, rental properties, or any kind of income. Thus, a 1,000-peso chantry established as a lien on an estancia or house required the owner to pay 50 pesos per year to pay for Masses for the dead. And that payment was supposed to be paid forever.

Chantries had great economic significance because the debts were permanently attached to properties no matter who owned them. When a landed estate or house with a lien attached to a chantry changed hands, the new owner had to recognize the debt and continue to make the payments. The new owner therefore not only had to pay for the sins of previous owners but was also burdened with debts that could not be canceled. Moreover, the new owner might also set up a chantry, which the next owner had to recognize and pay for as well. As a result, landed estates, stores, and urban rental properties tended to build up debts to the point that the value of the property sometimes equaled the value of the debts. Capital accumulation, therefore, rather than being invested in agriculture, stock-raising, or industry, went into the service sector and led to the proliferation of priests.

Nevertheless, as always, there was a difference between theory and reality. All who purchased estates and houses with chantries attached recognized the debt because they had to do so in order to gain legal possession of a property. However, once in possession some new owners ignored the debts and refused to pay the money owed to a chaplain. In other cases, the properties lost so much value over time that the owners could not pay anything for the required

Masses. Bishop Juan Gómez de Parada took notice of this, and in his rules announced at the Diocesan Synod of 1722 that he convened, the bishop pointed out that failure to pay for chantries was contrary to both civil and canon law. He ordered people to pay up.[38] One suspects, however, that this had little effect.

The very existence of *capellanías* could contribute to the further proliferation of priests in the diocese. In 1751 the bishop imposed a 3 percent tax on all chantry income to pay for the new seminary of Our Lady of the Rosary and Saint Ildefonso being established in Mérida. This forced contribution fell on forty-seven priests in Mérida, thirty-five in Campeche, and seven in Valladolid, all of whom were receiving funds as chaplains of chantries. The seminary, of course, then trained more priests, some of whom would presumably get income from *capellanías*.[39]

Catholic culture thus had a significant impact on the economy, for estates became encumbered with debts of people who feared Purgatory. We will never know if chantries helped someone get into Heaven faster, but whatever the case they were not necessarily unproductive in an economic sense. Many priests who served as chaplains of the chantries invested their income to establish or purchase landed estates engaged in productive activities. Moreover, when people put up cash to establish a *capellanía*, the money immediately became available to lend to reputable borrowers. For example, in 1692 Father Francisco Gómez, the curate of Peto, borrowed 400 pesos from the estate of the late Doña Melchora Pacheco, who had specified that the money was for a chantry. Gómez promised to pay the requisite 5 percent annual interest. To guarantee the loan he recognized a debt of 400 pesos on his Estancia Bitunthul, which had cattle, horses, and burros in sufficient quantity to serve as collateral. The curate's estate already had a 1,000-peso lien on the property, so the chantry would simply add to the debt. In this way, Doña Melchora Pacheco's capital designated for a capellanía found an investment to fund it, while the priest got money to invest in his productive property.[40]

Similarly, when in 1692 Alcalde Captain Pedro de Rivero repaid a debt of 400 pesos owed to a chantry (and then promptly asked for a new loan from the Jesuits), 300 pesos were immediately borrowed at 5 percent interest by Captain Antonio Ruiz de la Vega. The latter was an immigrant merchant with commercial interests and landed estates, and thus the money from the chantry probably ended up stimulating commercial and/or stock-raising activity. The remaining 100 pesos of the *capellanía* fund was borrowed on the same day by a priest, Licenciado Father Salvador Gorosica, who promised to pay the requisite 5 percent interest on the loan.[41] In 1720 a priest named Miguel de

Cervantes [sic.] owned a store in Mérida that had a 200-peso chantry attached, thus showing the overlap of commerce and spirituality.[42] In other words, a *capellanía* was like a bank, and the profits from loans went not to a banker but to a priest who prayed for the dead and who may or may not have put the capital to economically productive use.

The significance of chantries is revealed by the example of the *capellanías* set up in the Campeche region between 1680 and 1730. Although some of the documents were destroyed during pirate raids, there is extant evidence for forty-one chantries set up during that fifty-year period. These had a total value of 55,857 pesos, although only 7,008 pesos were paid in cash. The rest was in the form of liens on property with the promise to pay for Masses. Thirty of the forty-one were based on houses alone, thereby demonstrating the importance of urban real estate as the source of chantry income in the Campeche region. Two were based on estancias alone and two on a cash payment alone. Four were based on a combination of cash and houses and one on cash and an estancia. Finally, two were based on a combination of cash, estancias, and houses.

A similar registry does not exist for region around Mérida, but if it did, it would certainly show a different pattern. Campeche was a seaport and was the residence, if not the permanent home, of many sailors and merchants. The commercial nature of the city is demonstrated by the existence of a large number of rental houses, used either for business or as temporary residences. Mérida, in contrast, had a hinterland comprising more Indians and a much larger number of estancias and other landed estates, and on a per capita basis probably had fewer rental houses and more residential property than the western seaport. The extant documentation does not permit a precise analysis, but most of the chantries that show up in the surviving notarial records were based on liens on landed estates, not on rental houses. But whatever the case, it is clear that *capellanías* were an important part of the social and economic structure of Mérida and its surrounding area. It is likely that the loss of income resulting from the need to pay for chantries led to social mobility downward for some families, for without wealth people sooner or later fell out of the upper class. The spiritual economy had an impact well beyond the spiritual.

People established chantries, which in fact were expensive, because they feared for their souls. Sometimes this fear could have been based on guilt and resulted in efforts to make restitution. For example, when Juan Romero de

Salazar, a resident of Valladolid, faced death and made his will in Mérida in 1690, he noted first that when he married his wife brought with her a dowry of 130 pesos and his capital amounted to 200 pesos. He got involved in the cotton business, which flourished around Valladolid, and therefore his property included numerous bales of cotton. He also owned a small bit of land with 100 beehives as well as three shotguns, a horse, and silver dishes and utensils. He was not wealthy, but he provided for several chantries, one for his soul and the for the souls of his parents. Another one, endowed with 100 pesos, was for Masses to be prayed "for the souls . . . of the Indians with whom I had business dealings, as a means of remuneration." He also canceled the debts that the Indians owed him.[43]

Nicolás Ortes was wealthier, and the capellanía that he founded on his estancia in 1700 for the Indians of the villages of Telchac and Sinanché was for 1,000 pesos.[44] Captain Don Juan Santiago González was also wealthy. When he made his will in 1722 he established a lien of 1,000 pesos on his Estancia Humul and also paid 1,000 more in cash for ten Masses per year "for his soul, for his wife's soul, and for the souls of his parents and of the Indians with whom he had business in this Province."[45] Don Diego del Campo did not have much in the way of assets, but when he made his will in 1727 he allocated what he had—200 pesos—to establish a chantry for three Masses per year "for the souls of the Indians I had business with."[46] In this way profits made at the expense of the Maya sometimes were used as a form of spiritual reparations felt to be necessary in preparation for death.

In many cases, of course, guilt may or may not have been involved. When José Fernández Palomino, the man from England with a Spanish name, made his will in 1690, he declared himself to be a Catholic and desired to be buried in the cathedral of Mérida. He was apparently a retail merchant who kept a *libro de tienda* (his store's account book) and also served as a pawnbroker. He acquired some tobacco in a trade with a merchant in Campeche, demonstrating that there was demand for tobacco in Mérida. He was owed small quantities of money and owed even smaller quantities. He had 300 pesos in cash and wanted 250 pesos used "*del descargo de mi consciencia*" (to unburden my soul). Perhaps this had something to do with Viviana Hau, a Maya woman, for he left 50 pesos to her two daughters. His figures did not add up, however, for he left an additional 25 pesos to Doña Francisca de Lara, "*por averme asistido con mucho amor y voluntad*" (for having assisted me with much love and good will). Perhaps she was the one who bothered his conscience.[47]

Paradoxically, some people prepared for death by getting married. There were many reasons for doing so, but one of these was the desire to legitimize long-standing—and, in the eyes of the Church, sinful—relationships before it was too late. The priests recording matrimonial information did not always pay attention to this, but some of them did. In the years between 1697 and 1710 the priests recorded the names of several couples who were said to be living in a *unión libre* (free union) or who had been *casados muchos años* (living together for many years). They may or may not have had death on their minds, but seventeen other people who married in those years were specifically said to be dying. Most of them were non-elites, but even members of the elite occasionally got married because of imminent death. For example, when Doña Josefa de los Santos Heredia was dying in 1709, she quickly married a man named Pablo Ricalde. Despite the rush, the ceremony included both matrimonial sponsors and witnesses.[48] That was unusual for a quick marriage.

In cases like this, the Church chose to marry the couples without publishing the usual marriage banns (*amonestaciones*). There was no time to lose, for couples living in free unions were couples living in sin. Confession, matrimony, and the last rites sometimes went together as a package.

Practically all Hispanic people in Mérida, even the poor, upon dying were wrapped in a shawl or in the habit of a Franciscan and buried in the crypt of the cathedral. Given the high humidity and heat of Yucatán, their bodies must have decomposed rapidly. That may have made the church an unhealthy environment. The stench of death might have been perceptible, thereby reminding the faithful of their own mortality.

FOUR

. . .

LIFE

Status, Relationships, and Children

I. Documents and Colonialism

In the Spanish colonial system, there was always a difference between theory and practice, and ecclesiastical record-keeping that divided people into estates was no exception to that rule. While most Hispanic people in Mérida were undoubtedly registered—if they were registered at all—in the books for *españoles*, some people's origins were only partly known or were unknown because they were illegitimate children or *expósitos* (foundlings). Others, moreover, who were identified as either mestizos or *indios* chose to have their marriages registered in the books for *españoles*.

As Marc Bloch once said, documents are like witnesses: they must be cross-examined, and this is just as true for ecclesiastical records as for anything else.

Sometimes the limited usefulness of the sources is revealed in the sources themselves. In Mérida in 1718, Bishop Juan Gómez de Parada scolded the priests in charge of the matrimonial records, noting that some entries were drawn up by some people but signed by others, names were left blank, etc. The modern reader can see that priests would sign blank documents with the expectation that the information would be filled in later. Sometimes someone later on did not know or could not remember who had gotten married. The bishop ordered the priests to obey the rules laid down by the Council of Trent and the Council of Mexico City. Yet only nine years before Bishop Pedro de los Ríos Reyes had signed off on the books—possibly without even looking at them.[1]

What is certain, nevertheless, is that not all of those whose names appear in the books for Spaniards were, strictly speaking, Spanish or "white," to use a current word. In fact, the term "white" did not begin to be used until the late colonial period, and after Mexican Independence uncertainty over terminology continued to exist. "Spanish" was no longer appropriate, but what should the non-Indians be called? In Yucatán some people chose at first to refer to the people formerly called *españoles* as *gente de color* (people of color). However, in this case the color in question was what is now referred to as white.[2] Therefore in the mid-colonial period the sources used the term *españoles* to refer to all people who were not Indians and who could not be classified as racially mixed. Consequently, European immigrants from England, Ireland, France, Italy, and the Low Countries were forced into the category of "Spaniards." That is because race, in the modern sense of the term, was a concept intimately related to social factors such as class and culture. Colonial society had a flexible concept of identity, and people could in fact change their "race" according to their social characteristics.

The presence of non-Spaniards is clearly manifested in the records of marriages in the twenty-five years between 1697 and 1722. In all, 108 people of the 2,252 who married—4.8 percent of the total—were registered as Indians, mestizos, or persons *de color pardo* ("of dark color"), the phrase used to refer to those of part African ancestry. In other words, almost one out of every twenty was genetically part or even all Maya or African. The presence of non-Spaniards in the books supposedly for Spaniards also shows up in the birth records. In the ten years from 1720 to 1729 there were 2,176 baptisms registered in the *Libros de Españoles*, but in 140 cases—6.4 percent—one of the parents was registered as a mestizo or an "Indian." Almost always, the non-Spaniard was female, usually an indigenous woman with an illegitimate child.[3]

On occasion color was used to try to determine someone's identity when parentage was completely unknown. For example, a female foundling left at the door of Micaela de Vargas and baptized on July 9, 1718 was said to be "*de color pardo.*" She was registered in the book of Spaniards anyway. Also registered in that book was a female foundling left at the door of Fabiana Chi (Maya surname) in the mostly indigenous barrio of Santiago and baptized on June 16, 1726; she was registered as a "*mestisa conosida por el color*" (known to be a mestiza because of color).

Priests were of course not alone in using color to distinguish between or categorize people. Notaries did the same, for mixed-race people frequently needed to get matters notarized. One such person was Captain Mateo Aldana, identified in 1720 as a *pardo libre* (free person of dark color); he was an officer in one of Yucatán's mixed-race militia companies and was described as "*de color pardo*" (of dark color).[3]

These observations made in marriage and baptismal records as well as in notarial documents demonstrate that the colonial regime's efforts to make everyone fit neatly into the three social or cultural categories of *indios*, *españoles*, and *castas* were unsuccessful. Moreover, when parentage was uncertain, the priests had to search for a reason to classify people into one of the three categories. This meant that something other than culture had to be used, and as a result all over the colonial world people turned to color as a possible marker of identity and/or ancestry.[4] Color, then, understood to be the result of ancestry, became a guide for classification when there was no other information. The colonial records are testimony to the significance of color—a biological characteristic—on the way to the development of full-fledged racism.

By far the largest group among the non-Hispanic people who were registered in the books for Spanish marriages were the sixty-five Maya women who married non-Indian men. There was not one case of a Maya man marrying a Hispanic woman. Of course, in the absence of letters, diaries, or other sources there is no explanation of why there was such a sharp difference in the experience of men and women. It is likely, however, that Hispanic men insisted on being classified among the *españoles* and therefore their wives accompanied them in the records. It may be for the same reason that the illegitimate children of Maya women were also sometimes registered in the books for *españoles*: the unidentified Hispanic fathers of such children may have insisted on it.

There were of course obvious reasons for Maya women, but not men, marrying non-Maya people. Hispanic households, whether legally or extra-legally, found indigenous women, as well as African slaves, to serve as domestic servants. Unlike men, they were more likely to be live-in domestics, and thus indigenous females more often lived among the Hispanic people. Such circumstances led to sexual abuse by the males in the house. At the same time, however, as the records demonstrate, Hispanic men who were not of the hidalgo class (lower nobility) living in Mérida sometimes found wives among the Maya women living in close proximity. It could be that the arrival, albeit in small numbers, of immigrants who were overwhelmingly male resulted in a shortage of marriageable Hispanic women. All of this may explain why Maya women sometimes married Hispanic men.

Hispanic women, however, never married Maya men—at least not in the cathedral curacy (*Sagrario*) of Spaniards in Mérida. It is certain that it was socially undesirable or almost unacceptable for a Hispanic woman of any status or class to marry an "Indian." Sexual relations between the two undoubtedly took place, and in fact a significant number of Hispanic women gave birth to illegitimate children who could have been of mixed race. But since the identity of the father was usually not recorded, there is no evidence to support any conclusion.

Identity is always a confused concept. In Spain, people in small cities and towns could remain Spanish despite minor experiences of social mobility. In America, however, class and status were made more complicated by biological factors—racial mixing—that produced people who did not easily fit into preconceived categories. Moreover, Hispanic people in Mérida interacted on a daily basis with people of a profoundly different culture. As a result, categories and identities were frequently unclear. Lack of consistency and confusion reigned. This was small-town America, not small-town Spain.

II. Class and Status

Status is important in all societies, and it is usually connected in some way with social class. The sources give some clues about status determination in Hispanic society in Mérida. The priests in charge of the books for Spaniards made important distinctions between the people getting married or buried or having their children baptized. The record keepers adhered to the socio-cultural attitudes of the time and place, and they were not always liberal in their interpretation and assignment of social status. They noted who was, and therefore who was not, a *doña* (lady) or *don* (gentleman), that is, a person of *hidalgo* status.[5] Hidalgos were supposedly members of the lower nobility. In Europe, of course, that was a hereditary status intrinsically related to the possession of honor. All such people in America tried to assert and protect their special status The very few people of higher nobility were recorded as lords and ladies, that is, *señores* and *señoras*. Meanwhile, most members of the Hispanic community were left out of the hidalgo class, as the members of the higher class asserted their social superiority.

To be sure, these records are inconsistent and sometimes contradictory and therefore the sources cannot be accepted as precise. The priests got careless at times. Nevertheless, there are indications that the status distinctions made in the records reflected generally accepted social differences among people.[6] They closely correlate between wealth and class, as in the case of the forty-eight Hispanic people who died in 1726 and who could not afford to pay for the last rites. Not one of the poor men or boys was identified as a *don*, and only two of the females—Doña Juana Montero, a *doncella* (maiden), and Doña María Magaña, a widow—were of sufficient social status to merit being called a *doña*.[7] In short, forty-six of the forty-eight poor people were of lower social status.

Moreover, people at the time clearly thought these distinctions to be of importance. For example, in 1710 a baby girl born to the Canary Islanders Cristóbal de Herrera and his wife, Juana de Córdoba, was baptized, but the priest did not specify that the parents were a lady and a gentleman, thereby implying that they were not. So, later in the century a priest, undoubtedly responding to a request of the daughter or a descendant of the daughter of Herrera and Córdoba, went into the records and added the *don* and *doña* before their names—using a different color of ink.[8]

A similar situation resulted when the priest failed to identify José de Segovia as a gentleman when his son was baptized in 1712. The baby's descendants discovered this and at a later time convinced the provisor-vicar general of the diocese to go back into the records and change them. Thus it was written in the book: "By order of the Lord Provisor Vicar General and Governor of the Bishopric and in accordance with the procedures . . . the Don [capitalization and underlining in the original] was added" to everyone's name, and they were declared to be "españoles." The procedures mentioned included testimony by respected members of the community that all the people involved were accepted as "Spaniards of pure blood, free from any taint of the bad race of mulattoes or of base people." One man testified regarding the father of the child that "he knew him as a foreigner and that in the City he was taken for a person from the Basque Country."[9]

In a colonial Spanish American society, the difference between a European-like person and someone else was of great importance. In late colonial Buenos Aires, parents of hidalgo status could legally deny their children the right to marry if the prospective spouse was a non-hidalgo.[10] Similarly, Mariana Alicia Pérez found that in late eighteenth-century Buenos Aires the marriage records reveal, as do those in Mérida, that the people making the records paid attention to these details. "Without a doubt, access to the privilege of being called 'Don' expressed the place that each person had in society and the recognition of all members of society" of that place. And although the criteria used to assign status were not clearly explained, "it is very clear that the utilization of the [appellative] 'Don' during the eighteenth century was a sign of prestige."[11] In other words, even at a later time in history compared to that of early eighteenth-century Mérida, and in a place without the major presence of an indigenous society, the terms *don* and *doña* had significance. The same was true in the case of colonial Chile and undoubtedly in many other cities as well.[12]

The priests in Mérida may have made mistakes and errors of omission, but they (almost?) never assigned *don* or *doña* status to anyone thought to be undeserving. As a result, an important social distinction is preserved in the records. Of the 2,180 Hispanic people—that is, those who were not Maya or identified as mixed-race—who married in Mérida in the twenty-five years between 1697 and 1721, 26.5 percent were recorded as either a *don* or a *doña*. They were members of a class defined by status whose qualifications to belong to that group were largely hereditary or had been achieved by serving as officers in the militia. Three quarters of the Hispanic people therefore were not recognized as ladies or gentlemen and belonged to a lower status group.

It is important to note that the percentage of people in Mérida classified as hidalgos was much larger than in Spain itself, where, with the exception of the Basque Country, the percentage was only between 5 and 10 percent.[13] Once again, we see that America was not Spain. Moreover, a group as large as one quarter of the total is likely to be too large to be an upper class. There undoubtedly was social stratification within the hidalgo class, as discussed in a later chapter.

Of course, the documents do not explain the criteria used for the assigning of status. Nevertheless, we can be sure that ancestry played a major role. A century and a half after the conquest there was a large number of people descendant from the original conquistadors and from high-status Spanish immigrants like military officers and treasury officials. Intermarriage between the two groups and high levels of fecundity resulted in a large class of people who felt themselves to be worthy of new grants of encomiendas. Indeed, whenever an encomienda became vacant, a large number of people applied for it.[14]

Some idea of the proliferation of offspring of conquistadors is provided by the cases of two of the most prominent conquerors. Juan de la Cámara had eleven children and at least fifteen grandchildren. Diego de Magaña had at least twenty-five grandchildren or great-grandchildren.[15] With examples like these it is easy to see how by 1700 there were hundreds of people who qualified to be an encomendero by being the descendant of one. Moreover, encomiendas changed hands after two generations, thereby creating expanded opportunities for other people to become encomenderos.

This ended up creating a class people without a great deal of wealth but with relatively high status because of ancestry. In modern times they would be said to be from "good families." This meant that there were always people ready to move up once they had again acquired the wealth necessary to rejoin the upper class. They may be considered as a middle class, and as will be shown later in this study, the difference between the middle and upper classes can to a certain extent be measured because of the overlap of political power, wealth, and status. If these lesser hidalgos had been less numerous or practically nonexistent, the upper class would undoubtedly have closed ranks and maintained strict endogamy to keep people who were not from "good families"—some of whom would have some Maya or African ancestry—from moving in. That would have led to a caste-like social structure with little or no social mobility upward. This is what is frequently assumed to have been the case in much of colonial Spanish America. Yet it was not the way it was in colonial Mérida.

This was probably the result in part of the lack of extreme economic inequality within the Hispanic community of Mérida. The economic structure of Yucatán provided no means for people to get extremely rich compared to people in other parts of America. Only one family ever came up with the money to purchase a title of nobility, and that family—Pedro de Garrástegui and his descendants—owed its wealth to control of the sale of bulls of indulgence on credit to the indigenous people. This was simply parasitic activity; the income of the counts did not result from any productive activity carried out on the family's own property. Indeed, as will be shown, the family members of the original count were not even significant landowners in the early eighteenth century.

Encomiendas provided income for those lucky enough to hold them, but even then very few encomenderos were rich unless they had additional sources of money. In the early eighteenth century, the 115 surviving encomiendas in the province yielded an average annual income of only 348 pesos. That would barely have provided for a comfortable existence for a large family with hangers-on. Of course, a handful of people received up to 600 pesos, but that was a pittance compared to the wealth of the really rich in other places. By the late eighteenth century the median income yielded by the surviving seventy-three encomiendas in Yucatán was a mere 323 pesos.[16] All of this helps explain why merchants, who derived their wealth from the import-export business, were so important in Mérida's society and politics. They did not have many wealthy competitors.

The differences between the rich and the others within the Hispanic community, therefore, were not as great as those found elsewhere. The lack of extreme inequality meant that people in the upper class were not radically different from those in the middle class. Moreover, it would not have taken a great deal of newly acquired wealth to move someone into that upper class. As landownership began to yield more wealth as the eighteenth century progressed, estancias and then haciendas might have provided just enough to make the move up. While that was happening, however, class structure would have been changing because of the gradual emergence of a wealthy class of landowners who increasingly saw themselves as a landowning aristocracy. That is what lay in the future.

If a quarter of Mérida's Hispanic population of 5,000 qualified as hidalgos, as the marriage records suggest, then the total number of hidalgos would have been well over 1,000. Most of them were probably descendants of conquistadores or encomenderos, and the status of hidalgo was routinely passed on to children. This is too large a proportion of the total population to be considered the upper class. Many of these people were not wealthy, and some of them did not exercise political power. As we have said, they were a middle class, people from "good families" but who were not in the upper class or ruling elite. They were distinct from the non-hidalgo people below them—three-quarters of the Spanish population—and their descent from high-status people in the past was certainly not forgotten and was just as certainly used to display high status. Moreover, they were able to move into the upper class if the opportunity presented itself.

At the same time, this means, as will be seen in a later chapter, that those who held encomiendas did not rule Mérida. Rather, the ruling elite was made up not only of many current encomenderos but also of people descended from *past* encomenderos, who in turn were joined by high-status immigrants from Spain and other immigrants who achieved hidalgo status after arriving in Yucatán. All these people would of course pass their status on to their descendants, some of whom would become encomenderos in the future. These people certainly knew each other or knew of each other. They knew who had elite status by birth and who did not.

In marriage records, status seems to have differed significantly depending on gender. Among males, only 19.2 percent merited the *don* category, while 34.2 percent of females were recorded as *doñas*. A small part of this is the result of sixty-five Hispanic males, none of whom was classified as a *don*, marrying Maya women, and the latter are not counted among the Hispanic women. And of course it should be remembered that the data are not precise and that these percentages provide at best the minimum rates of acceptance of high status. That is because, as noted, priests never—or almost never—assigned the *don* or *doña* status to the undeserving. Of course, errors of omission certainly took place, as is suggested by examples in the records of people not identified as ladies or gentlemen even though their parents were identified as high-status individuals.

However, it is likely that the statistical difference between males and females cannot be attributed solely to clerical errors or omissions. It may be the result of priests making status distinctions for reasons unclear to us. But why would females pass the status test more easily? The immigration of lower-status Europeans cannot be the cause of that difference. Indeed, as will be seen, male immigrants, who greatly outnumbered females, in fact were more likely to be recognized as hidalgos than Hispanic males born in Yucatán when it came to getting married. The presence of immigrants in the sample therefore raised, not lowered, the proportion of gentlemen.

Some high-status young men certainly left Mérida to study law at the university in Mexico City, and if they chose not to return they would not marry in Mérida and be recorded in the marriage documents. That exodus of elite men, however, was probably offset by the number of elite women who became nuns or who never married, and therefore also failed to show up in the marriage records. It is possible that migration within Yucatán contributed to the higher status of women in Mérida, for more elite men may have left the capital city than elite women. Other factors, like dress, overall appearance, and behavior, including religious piety, may also have played a part in women getting accepted as *doñas*. Finally, it is probable that women frequently had higher status simply as a result of the respect that men were supposed to have for women because of their special role in preserving and perpetuating the culture. In other words, there may have been status rewards for being put on a pedestal. But in the end, we can only speculate.

The status difference between men and women reflected a social reality: women were social capital. They were human assets of great value to a family.

High-status parents did not always have sons, and some had sons who did not contribute to the maintenance of status or the perpetuation of power and wealth. The behavior of male children was hard to control precisely because they were male. Parents got the sons who were born, not necessarily sons with good character traits. Daughters, on the other hand, could be expected or even forced to behave in a way that preserved status, thereby making it possible for them to marry someone of power and prestige. In Hispanic society, sons-in-law as well as daughters were social capital who could contribute to the family's social and economic position. In other words, while parents could not choose their sons, they could choose their sons-in-law. But to get good ones, parents had to guard their daughters to keep them desirable as marriage partners for prospective sons-in-law. This undoubtedly helped preserve high status for women.

It is widely assumed that throughout colonial Hispanic America parents controlled or arranged the marriages of their children. There is not much evidence regarding marriage choice, however, but what does exist most often shows up in documentation when sons or daughters resisted their parents and tried to marry whom they wanted.[17] Nevertheless, as a later chapter will show, there is some indirect evidence that in Mérida Spanish immigrants did indeed arrange, or try to arrange, the marriages of their daughters and probably of their sons too. The children of non-immigrants may have had more freedom of choice, however, since it was not until 1778 that a royal decree requiring parental consent to marry was implemented. Many scholars unfortunately have inadvertently assumed that the strong parental control of the late colonial period had been in existence for centuries. As Kimberly Gauderman has pointed out, however, this was not true. Earlier in history young people were freer to marry the spouse of their choice, which is why in the late colonial period the Spanish crown decided to give parents much more control over their children.[18]

In any case, in the marriage records in Mérida women appear as ladies in greater numbers than men appear as gentlemen. There were numerous instances in the marriage records in which all of the women but none of the men were recognized as being of high status. For example, in 1698 Jacinto de Loaysa, the son of Juan Martínez de Loaysa and Doña María Flota, married Doña Ana Robles, the daughter of Diego de Robles and Doña María Martina Negrón y Cisneros. The bride was from the large village of Ticul, not Mérida, and yet she still kept her high status when she married in the capital.[19] Indeed, between 1697 and 1725 of all Hispanic females identified as originally from villages who got married in Mérida, fully 20 percent were categorized as *doñas*. They had clearly maintained their Hispanic identity in their hometown and residing there had not lowered their status in the capital. Meanwhile, not one Hispanic male from a village was classified as a *don*.

High status seems at time to have stuck to women like glue, which would be expected of hereditary condition. As we have seen, two women who died in 1726 and were too poor to pay for the last rites were nonetheless classified as members of the hidalgo class. Behavior that we might think would lower a *doña*'s status does not seem to have done so. For example, in 1711 Doña Ana Alpuche gave birth to an illegitimate son yet was still registered as a lady, as was Doña María de Alpuche—possibly a relative of Doña Ana—after her illegitimate son was baptized in 1722. In 1728 Doña María Francisca León, identified as an unmarried woman, gave birth to an illegitimate daughter and yet was not demoted in status. Doña Antonia de León—probably a close relative—served as godmother.[20]

Having an illegitimate child not only did not cause a woman to lose her status as a *doña*. It also did not prevent important people from having a major role in the baptism. In 1710 Doña María de Salazar had an illegitimate daughter, yet Colonel Don Juan de Solís y Casanova, a person of high status, served as the godfather. Other times a woman's status eventually went up after having an illegitimate child. In 1727 Felipa de la Cruz Malaver gave birth to a "natural son" but in 1742, when the boy was legitimized, Don Agustín de Argaiz was recognized as the father, and the mother was re-categorized as a *doña*. Thus in some cases a man who was classified as an hidalgo could end up raising the status of the mother of his children even if the couple were not married.

Nevertheless, it is worth noting that there is no record in the *Libros de matrimonios de españoles* of any of these ladies who had illegitimate children marrying in the curacy of Mérida. It is possible that they married in a village or outside the city, but it is also possible that their extramarital sexual activity harmed their chances of finding a husband within the Hispanic community in the city. This seems to have been the case in other parts of Spanish America as well.[21] Some unwed mothers, of course, might have continued to maintain a relationship with someone outside of marriage.

There is no evidence of hidalgo women losing their status, suggesting that hidalgo status was indeed hereditary. It is possible that women who had illegitimate children could keep their status as ladies because of the status of the fathers of the children. If that were the case, then the identity of the father would have been known although not recorded—in other words, covered up. Certainly priests sometimes violated their vows of celibacy, as was the case of Father Don Pedro del Espíritu Santo Pacheco. The bishop brought charges against this priest for having baptized two boys claiming that the father was unknown, when in fact Pacheco himself was the father.[22] Doña Manuela de Salazar had an illegitimate child named Bernardo Flores, whose father, Father Don José Flores de Aldana, was a priest. Years later Bernardo later tried to follow in his father's footsteps by becoming a priest, but to do so he needed special dispensation from the bishop. That was authorized by the vicar general in 1752, but that permission was rescinded by the bishop in 1756.[23] There were consequences for being the illegitimate child of a priest.

III. Birth, Remarriage, and Extramarital Sex

Expected responses to demographic crisis are first an increase in marriages and then an increase in births requiring baptism. This happened among the Hispanic people of Mérida in the case of the epidemic and famine of 1726. As the data in Table 3.1 show, in the year before the sharp increase in deaths, there were 228 baptisms, and the number went up in the following year, as children conceived before the epidemic were born. Then, the number of baptisms fell to only 142 in 1727. Undoubtedly some pregnant women and many people of child-bearing age died and did not reproduce. In the following year, the number of baptisms rose to 174, and then went up sharply in 1729 to 282. Similarly, the number of marriages declined from 49 in 1725 to 26 in the year of epidemic and famine. Then it rose to 38 in the following year and went up to 53 in 1728. Society recovered from a demographic decline through sex, marriage, or both.

Life goes on, even for those who had lost a spouse. As in all societies at the time, the low life expectancy resulting from high death rates meant that many people were widowed at a fairly early age. At the same time, as was also true in practically all societies at the time, males and females held somewhat complementary positions in a household or family and therefore there was a desire on the part of many widowed men and women to remarry. This tendency was evident in Mérida. Between 1697 and 1721, there were 111 widows and 182 widowers, a total of 293, who remarried. That was 13 percent of the 2,250 people who received the sacrament of matrimony. This means that one out of every eight persons who got married was either a widow or a widower. There were 90 cases of widows marrying widowers. Of those remarrying, 62.1 percent—five out of eight—were men and 37.9 percent were women.

Males therefore had more chances, or likelihood, of remarrying than females. Of course, men who were wealthy and powerful have always had the best opportunities when it came to marriage and remarriage. Don Juan del Castillo y Arrúe, the leader of the pro-governor party in the city council in the early eighteenth century, married Doña Tomasa Cano in 1692, and after being widowed he remarried in 1711. His second wife, Doña María de Solís y Lara, had married her first husband in 1708, but the husband died shortly thereafter. Don Juan had children with both wives.

Castillo y Arrúe's political opponent, Don Lucas de Villamil y Vargas, had even more wives but no children. In 1688 he married his first spouse, Doña Beatriz de Aranda y Mijangos, the daughter of an important Spanish immigrant. He was then widowed and remarried in 1697. His second wife, Doña Manuela de Cepeda y Lira, was also the daughter of a Spanish immigrant who was a knight of the prestigious Order of Calatrava. She died in 1710, and Don Lucas married for a third time in 1717. His last wife was Doña Josefa de Sánchez de Aguilar Cepeda y Lira, his second wife's niece. She therefore was the granddaughter on her mother's side of a Spanish immigrant but on her father's side was a descendant of one of Yucatán's original conquistadors. Don Lucas always married well. After his death in 1724, the third wife inherited her late husband's estancias and remarried in 1726. Her second husband was the Spanish-born lieutenant governor.

Villamil y Vargas's political ally, his nephew Don Pedro de Garrástegui y Villamil, the second Count of Miraflores, also married more than once. His father, the first count, was a Spanish-born immigrant whose marriage to the sister of Lucas de Villamil y Vargas ended only with his death thirty-seven years later. In 1707 the first count's son Pedro, who would become the second count, married Doña Josefa de la Cerda, a member of the encomendero elite. The first wife died in 1727, and two years later the widower, who by then was the count in his own right, married Doña Felipa del Puerto. Both of her parents had been born in Mérida.

Widowers always had an advantage over widows when it came to remarriage if for no other reason than there were always more of the latter than the former.

Although there are no census data to prove it, there were certainly more Hispanic widows in Mérida than widowers. That was also common throughout the world. If the census for Mérida were available for any of these years, it would undoubtedly show that many households were headed by women. It is highly likely that women significantly outnumbered men in the city, as was true elsewhere.[24]

Since many of the women undoubtedly had more years to live, this reality had an impact on family life. Younger people undoubtedly sometimes took in a widowed parent or parents or simply continued to live in the house they grew up in. A Hispanic household, then, would frequently, or even most commonly, have been multi-generational and sometimes headed by women. As we shall see, many families probably included adopted children. The high death rates resulting from tropical disease and contaminated water would undoubtedly have reinforced this tendency. At the same time, young widows and widowers who remarried still had the opportunity to have children and thereby contribute to recovery from demographic decline.

The great majority of those who married in Mérida between 1697 and 1730 were of course people getting married for the first time. The age of first marriage is an indicator of perceived opportunity to support a family and therefore is a rough substitute for what in modern times is called consumer confidence. Unfortunately, it is impossible to determine the average or median age of first marriage because priests never recorded anyone's age. Moreover, many of the people who received the sacrament of matrimony had been born somewhere other than Mérida, and their birthdates are unknown. As the next chapter will show, the marriage records of Spaniards in Yucatán's capital included people from the province's other cities (Campeche and Valladolid), villages far and near, other Spanish colonies, the Canary Islands, and Spain or some other European country. Since priests did not ask the ages of the couples getting married, birthdates for many brides and grooms cannot be determined.

A very small sample of people from the elite might be useful if not as a valid measurement than at least as a suggestion of possibilities. A published genealogy—which of course includes only people judged by the genealogist to be important enough to include in his book—reveals that twenty-two of the men who appeared in the records between 1690 and 1730 had an average age of first marriage of 22.7 years, while for twenty-five women that average age was 19.4 years.[25] The extremely small size of this sample makes it difficult to compare with other places in Spanish America. Thus, while it is possible that the age of first marriage in Mérida was somewhat above or below that found elsewhere, there is not enough evidence to confirm either conclusion.[26]

Not all marriages are happy, of course, and there is some evidence of failed relationships. Doña Francisca de Espinosa identified herself as *"separada por Divorcio"* (separated by divorce) from her husband, Juan Echavarría. When she drew up a power of attorney with her mother in 1692, neither of the two women were able to sign their names.[27] However, the husband's permission to give power of attorney was not needed because of the separation. In this case divorce meant separation according to canon law and did not give either person the right to remarry.[28] In 1698 Francisca Cornelo died and was said to be *"suelta de matrimonio"* at the time. That meant that she was unattached to marriage, that is, not living with her husband. She was poor, and so she did not make a will.[29] In 1720 Doña María de Garibaldi was described as *"malcasada"* with Don Ignacio Barboso when she died.[30] This possibly means that she was not carrying out her marital duties, so the marriage was probably not a good one.

Some people were in a hurry to enter the holy state of matrimony. Others probably had to get married because of family, societal, or ecclesiastical pressure to do so. Sexual relations sometimes started before marriage and the people involved were rushed into matrimony. Normally the Church published banns of matrimony to give people the opportunity to inform on would-be bigamists or to investigate if those who wanted to marry were too closely related to each other. However, this procedure was sometimes dispensed with, and in the twenty years between 1697 and 1716 (during which time the priests seem to have kept good records) a total of eighty-seven marriages took place without the publication of the banns of matrimony. In eighteen cases these were marriages between someone who was dying and someone who was not. There were sixty-nine instances of other rushed cases, thirty of which (43 percent) were among hidalgos.

Many of the marriages without banns involved widows and widowers. There were fourteen such cases among hidalgos, and three of these were widows marrying widowers. In such cases it is likely that the Church was more lenient regarding the banns because one or even both of the partners had already gone through the process for their first marriage, and in a small society like that of Mérida it was easy to decide quickly that some people were known to be unmarried. For example, in 1708 Captain Gaspar de Salazar y Córdova, the widower of Doña Catalina de Ancona, was allowed to marry Doña María Avellana without the publication of banns.[31] Similarly, in 1709 Captain Don Nicolás Carrillo de Albornoz, the widower of Doña Petrona Chacón, married Doña Josefa Velasco, the widow of Don Alonso Valverde, without the formality of banns.[32] Apparently the Church found no reason to impede those who wanted to remarry.

The priests kept records but except in the case of imminent death they never gave an explanation for such quick marriages. They did, however, occasionally use cryptic phrases that can only make us wonder—and speculate. Sometimes they said that the banns of matrimony had been dispensed with for what were called "*justas causas*" (just causes). For example, when Don Pedro de Ancona Hiniestrosa, the son of a regidor and the grandson of the lieutenant governor, married Doña Jacinta Castellanos, from a high-status family, in 1699, there were no banns. But the Church did issue a special license "*por justas causas que para ello huvo*" (because there were just causes for this).[33] Similarly, Nicolás del Canto and Josefa de Armenta, who were not identified as hidalgos, were married without banns in 1702 "*por justas causas.*"[34]

The phrase "*por convenir así*" (because it is convenient) was also used to explain the absence of banns. When Alférez Francisco González married Angela Ulibarri in 1701, the marriage took place "without going through the usual procedures because it was convenient to do it this way." And when Alonso Fernández and Catalina Sansores married in 1703, there were no banns "*por convenir así*" and the priest did not even bother to record the names of the parents of the couple.[35]

Of course, a large number of people having extramarital sex did not bother to marry. As we have already seen, one-third of all infants baptized between 1710 and 1729 were illegitimate or were foundlings left on someone's doorstep. In a few cases both parents of illegitimate children were recorded. Don Luis Magaña Dorantes, encomendero, descendant of at least one conquistador, had a son out of wedlock with María de Segovia.[36] He later married Doña Susana Iguala and became a regidor in Mérida's city council. Basque immigrant Don Juan de Urquizu eventually married Doña Andrea Beltrán de Mayorga and served on the city council, but before that he had an illegitimate daughter with Doña Magdalena de Armenta.[37] It was much more common for the mother to be identified but not the father. In these two cases, both of the illegitimate children took the surnames of their fathers.

Of course, by no means were all urgent marriages the result of premarital sex. Yet that had to be taking place, and in fact it was permitted if the couple had exchanged promises to marry.[38] On the other hand, sexual relations without such promises certainly took place. In fact, we know that they did, and that they could involve people from the best of families. Among the very best of families was that of Don Pedro de Garrástegui, the Spanish-born Basque who became the Count of Miraflores. The documented part of the story began on September 23, 1706, when a foundling was baptized and given the name Juan Francisco. The baby had been found on the doorstep of the Spanish-born Basque Captain Don Juan de Vergara and his wife, Doña Eugenia de la Cerda. This couple served as the foundling's godparents.[39] Thus ended the first phase of what has been called a "private pregnancy."[40]

Then, less than four months later, Don Pedro de Garrástegui y Villamil, the son of the Count of Miraflores and the future second count, married Doña Josefa de la Cerda, the younger sister of Doña Eugenia de la Cerda. Thirteen years later Juan Francisco, who had been left on the doorstep of Captain Vergara and Doña Eugenia de la Cerda, was legitimized by the bishop. He was in fact the son of Don Pedro de Garrástegui y Villamil and Doña Josefa de la Cerda. He had been left at the doorstep of his mother's sister. Why did it take the parents thirteen years to legitimize their son? There is no way of knowing. Unfortunately for Don Pedro de Garrástegui y Villamil, he and his wife had no more children, and their son Juan Francisco died in 1727. Therefore the second Count of Miraflores had no heirs and the title passed to his eldest sister, Doña María de Garrástegui, and her husband, Captain Don Pedro Calderón, a Spanish-born immigrant from Extremadura.

One of the most important members of the political elite, Captain Don Juan de Mendoza, was also almost certainly involved in an extramarital affair that was taking place without any promise to marry. He first entered the state of holy matrimony in 1691, but his wife died shortly thereafter, and then in 1700 he married Doña Francisca de Vargas, who had not been previously married. This took place in a ceremony so quickly arranged that there was no time for the publication of the banns of matrimony. This was said to be *"por justas causas"* (for just causes). There also were no marital sponsors for the couple.[41] Between 1705 and 1723 he served in five elective offices (four times as alcalde and once as market inspector), and he was a permanent regidor of the city between 1706 and 1726.

Another case of elite extramarital sex became famous locally and the story was passed on as oral history. It began in 1724, when a new governor, Captain General Don Antonio de Figueroa y Silva, Lazo de la Vega, Ladrón del Niño de Guevara, took up his post in Yucatán.[42] Soon he met Doña Isabel de Ávila y Carranza, a widow who was the daughter of Don Francisco de Ávila, the former lieutenant governor. According to local legend, the governor was attracted by her "virtues" as well as by her "beauty," and although neither of those attributes can be verified, it is known that Doña Isabel ended up getting pregnant and giving birth to a son. The baby was left as a foundling at the door of her niece, Doña Francisca de Ávila, and the latter's husband, Don Juan Quijano, who was the son of prominent Spanish-born immigrants. The child, baptized in early January 1729, was named Juan Esteban and took on the name Quijano.

The genealogist Valdés Acosta, writing two centuries later, noted, without providing a source, that "there is reference" to a secret marriage of the governor and his lover. Presumably this would have been done in an effort to get around the law that prohibited high-ranking government officials from marrying local women. In fact, special permission to marry local women could be obtained by making a request from the king, but that meant sending the request to the Audiencia of Mexico, which passed all such matters on to Spain, where a decision was made. Then that decision had to be communicated back to the Audiencia and then passed on to the local official. Such a process took years, and in this case the couple expecting a child could not wait that long.

In any case, the alleged marriage was almost certainly just a convenient myth, for in April 1729, just months after dropping off her baby at the house of her niece, Doña Isabel married Don Martín de Noguera, a widower and important rancher. Governor Figueroa, however, was still alive and did not die until 1733, while Doña Isabel and her husband went on to appear in society weddings as matrimonial sponsors and witnesses. Had the governor and the mother of his child been married earlier, it is hard to imagine that the Church would have permitted bigamy. It is likely that a false and romantic historical memory was created to hide what was simply extramarital sex.

It is notable that in both of these documented cases the unmarried pregnant women turned to their female relatives for help. One suspects that many such women did the same, and therefore it is likely that many of the large number of foundlings in the baptismal records had been left at the doors of relatives, female or otherwise.

IV. Children Illegitimate or Abandoned

Foundlings and illegitimate children were a significant part of Hispanic society in Mérida. Information about the status of children baptized during the last ten years of the time period under analysis (1720–1729) is included in Table 4.1, which shows that in those years a total of 2,176 children were baptized. Of

TABLE 4.1: Status of Baptized Children, 1720–1729

YEAR	NUMBER OF BAPTISMS	LEGITIMATE	ILLEGITIMATE	FOUNDLING
1720	203	109	57	37
1721	256	146	76	34
1722	226	147	57	22
1723	175	112	36	27
1724	250	162	64	24
1725	228	149	60	19
1726	240	158	43	39
1727	142	95	31	16
1728	174	119	43	12
1729	282	167	83	32

Source: AGA, Españoles, Libros 7 y 8 de Bautismos.

these, 62.7 percent were legitimate, 25.3 percent were illegitimate, and 12 percent were foundlings. The *espósitos* and illegitimate together therefore made up 37.3 percent.

Mérida was by no means a unique Spanish American city with respect to illegitimacy and abandonment of infants. The incidence was much higher than in Europe, and other cities in the Spanish empire in America also had very high rates of illegitimacy and abandonment.[43] Almost everywhere, it seems, America was not Spain.

It is of course impossible to know why so many children were being abandoned and left on someone else's doorstep. Poverty clearly was a cause, as is proved by a unique case of clarification of the parentage that provides insight into what was sometimes happening behind the scenes. In 1730 a baby boy was left on the doorstep of Don Sebastián de Herrera and his wife Doña María Muñoz, who served as his godparents and "adopted him and raised him" as a foundling. More than fifty years later, however, it was revealed that in fact the boy had been the legitimate son of Don Francisco Zapata and Doña Jacinta López de las Nieves, but "because of their extreme poverty, the multitude of children [that they already had] and their inability to raise him" they had left the child with Herrera and Muñoz. The parentage was clarified later because it was said that status as a foundling "can cause grave harm" in the future.[44] Poor parents, in short, had secretly given up their child for adoption. It is probable that others did the same. In cases like this, the children therefore were not illegitimate at all. They were just abandoned.

Demographic crisis sometimes caused impoverishment and therefore also led to child abandonment. There was a notable increase in the number of *expósitos* baptized in Mérida during 1726, a year of epidemic and famine, while at the same time there was a decrease in the number of illegitimate children who were baptized. This suggests that disease and death were causing the parents of these infants to abandon them rather than try to provide for them. The same probably was true during other years of epidemics, such as 1699 and 1707–1711.

Clearly family honor had to be involved in the decision to leave an infant on someone's doorstep. It would have been scandalous for an unmarried Hispanic woman to raise an illegitimate child herself, and so to preserve a family's good name it would have been convenient to drop the baby off at someone else's house. After that, it is unknown if the mother or father had any personal relationship with the child who was growing up with people other than the parents.

The large number of foundlings in the baptismal records means that something had to be done with so many abandoned infants. The convent of nuns apparently took in very few of these, and there was no orphanage in Mérida or apparently anywhere else in New Spain at that time. Special houses for foundlings—sometimes called *casas de cuna* (cradle houses)—were in existence in Lima and Bogotá before 1700, another one was established in Havana in 1710, and more homes for foundlings were set up in Buenos Aires, Mexico City, and Santiago de Chile sometime in the late eighteenth century.[45] This reflected the widespread nature of the problem. As far as is known, nothing similar was founded in Mérida during the colonial period.

It is by no means certain that abandoned children would have been better off in houses for foundlings. In the cities with such *casas de cuna* mortality rates among the children were shocking by modern standards. Usually half of the children were dead within a year and three quarters never lived to reach five years of age.[46]

Poor or even nonexistent nutrition was undoubtedly a major cause of such a catastrophic mortality rate. A newborn infant needs food immediately, and although the foundling houses were supposed to have a wetnurse on permanent standby, one suspects that this was not always the case. After a few days the child was supposed to be passed on to a paid nursemaid, some of whom may have simply taken the money and ignored the child. Moreover, going from one wetnurse to another increased the chances of infection, which was probably another major cause of death. In these circumstances, it is possible that a foundling in Mérida was better off being left at someone's doorstep. This is suggested by the pattern of abandoning children, which, as we shall see, was not random in nature. Still, very few *expósitos* show up as adults in the marriage records, which suggests that most moved away, did not marry, or died young.

Presumably some unwanted children were secretly left to die, as was the case, as we have seen, of the two dead infants found in the barrio of Santa Ana in 1700. Others would have been secretly disposed of, but a very large number was taken to the church to be baptized and had people willing to be their godparents. Someone, in other words, was taking at least some responsibility for abandoned children.

Some lucky illegitimate children did receive support from members of the community, although this was usually done anonymously. For example, sometime before 1738 an unidentified benefactor ("*persona bienhechora*") provided 200 pesos for the dowry of María Antonia de Villacís, the daughter of Juana de Villacís.[47] Doña Anna de Salazar, the daughter of Doña Catarina de Salazar, received 1,665 pesos 2 reales anonymously for her dowry. Of this, 200 pesos was in cash, the rest consisting mostly of clothing and jewelry.[48] Her benefactor must have been wealthy and generous. She and her mother were recognized by the notary as members of the hidalgo class, while the Villacís women were not.

As we have seen, a few foundlings survived into late adolescence or adulthood and got married. Therefore, some must have been taken in and raised by families. Given the large number of infants left on the doorstep, it is likely that many, and possibly even most, Hispanic households had foundlings living with the family. Some probably became domestic servants. Others could very well have become members of the family, and indeed may very well have actually been biologically members of the family because they were the illegitimate offspring of someone in the household. And, of course, many abandoned children must have died.

There is rarely any proof that the foundlings were in fact related to the people at whose houses the babies were left. However, there are documented cases that demonstrate that some infants became members of the household and were in effect adopted. For example, Alférez (later Captain) Francisco Pérez, a merchant and later an important cattle rancher, raised a girl who took his surname, and she married in 1705. He also took in a boy who used the surname Pérez when he married in 1731.[49] An infant boy left on the doorstep of Captain Don Lucas de Villamil y Vargas in 1719 married eighteen years later and was named José de Villamil. He was said to have been raised by Villamil's last wife, Doña Josefa Sánchez de Aguilar.[50]

There are of course cases of formally recognized adoptions, although the limited documentation includes only a few references to them. In 1690 José Fernández Palomino, the man from England who had a Spanish name, stated in his will that he had adopted an "Indian" named Antonio de Palomino. The latter was to inherit 30 pesos and three pounds of silk.[51]

When adoptions do show up in wills, however, the context sometimes suggests that the adopted children could well have been foundlings. In a testament drawn up in 1728, Doña Seferina de Garrástegui y Villamil (the daughter of the first Count of Miraflores) declared that she and her husband had adopted a child, while in the following year Doña Juana de Vargas (the widow of Regidor Don Juan de Mendoza) stated that she and her late husband had adopted two children, and Doña Catarina Dorantes Magaña and her late husband had adopted one.[52] Some years before all of these people had found children abandoned on their doorsteps.[53] Were the adopted children those same foundlings? We will never know, although it is obviously possible.

Many times there are suspicions of biological connections between foundlings and the families that took them in. For example, a woman "of unknown parents" who had been raised by Captain Don Francisco Raymundo González married in 1729, and at the time of her marriage she bore the surname González. Although her husband was illegitimate, the marriage was attended by very important people, namely, Alcalde Don José Bermejo and his wife, Doña Josefa del Castillo, who served as matrimonial sponsors. The latter lady was the daughter of Don Juan del Castillo y Arrúe, who served as a matrimonial witness.[54] It is hard to imagine that neither the bride nor groom was unrelated biologically to someone of such power and prestige.

It is unlikely that all foundlings were taken in by the families at whose doorsteps the children were left. It is possible that an unofficial adoption service existed to help find people willing to adopt, although we will never know how it worked. We do know something, however, because sometimes priests recorded the names of the people at whose doorstep children were abandoned, or "*botados*" (thrown out), in the phrase used at the time. Between 1711 and 1729 a total of 309 children whose baptisms were recorded in the books for *españoles* were left on the doorsteps of houses of 252 identified Hispanic individuals or married couples in Mérida. The number of houses in Mérida at the time is unknown, but if the population was approximately 5,000 then 252 houses must have represented a large part of the total. If even a small number of the foundlings were raised in the households where they were abandoned, then a large number of families must have had abandoned children being raised there.

Moreover, if 309 children were left on the doorsteps of 252 houses, then many of these residences were the site at which more than one child was abandoned. The imbalance between the number of *expósitos* and the number of houses at which they were left means that some people had to decide what to do with more than one foundling. Indeed, twenty-eight people found two *expósitos* on their doorsteps. Seven people found themselves with three. No one beat the record of Lorenzo de Argaiz, however, at whose house no fewer than eight infants were abandoned between 1712 and 1727.

It is likely that many mothers and/or fathers decided where it was best to leave a child. Only six foundlings were left at the houses of people with Maya names and one at the house of a mestizo. However, 60 percent of the people who found infants on their doorstep were Hispanic men, and many of them were of high status. Seven were priests. Forty percent of the people on whose doorsteps children were abandoned were women, but only one was identified as a widow—that, in a city with plenty of widows.

This information suggests that children were not always abandoned in a random fashion. Perhaps houses headed by widows were seen as undesirable places to leave infants, while the houses of priests were seen as good drop-off points. In addition to the family connections that led some people to leave infants at the doorsteps of relatives, it is also possible that some of the people who received multiple foundlings were known to try to find adoptive parents for the infants or found a way to make them useful by passing them out to people who thought they might need servants in the not-too-distant future. Perhaps word of that got out, thereby encouraging others to drop off foundlings in the same places.

Lorenzo de Argaiz, at whose house eight children were left, may have been one of those. He belonged to one of two families in Yucatán that founded an entail (*vínculo*), although he does not seem to have been wealthy and he was not classified as an hidalgo.[55] He was also a member of the group of people who loaned money to Don Lorenzo de Ávila to buy the lucrative but expensive post of Escribano Mayor de Gobernación y Guerra. However, his participation—only 140 pesos—made him one of the least important of the moneylenders.[56]

Argaiz was the nephew, or perhaps even the illegitimate son, of Don Simón de Argaiz, the curate of the village of Mama (south of Mérida, almost to the Sierra region). Don Simón is likely to have been rather secular even for the secular clergy (the priests who did not belong to religious orders like the Franciscans or Jesuits). He was perhaps more businessman than priest. He was engaged in commerce, and his will reveals that he owed money to well-known people, including Juan del Castillo y Toledo (the father of Don Juan del Castillo y Arrúe). In addition, he had received money from his nephew Lorenzo to acquire an estancia near Valladolid—a long way from his parish. He kept an account book of 191 folios in which he kept a record of his business. An inventory of his property occupied the first 26 folios. All of his wealth was to go to his nephew. He owed money to his brother-in-law, Regidor Don Felipe de Ayora y Porras, who would be allowed to collect it from the income of his benefice, that is, from the Indians of the parish of Mama in the form of wax and cotton cloth. Finally, separate from the inventory in his book, he was the owner of six cows, one bull, fifty ewes—very rare in Yucatán!—and forty pigs of all ages. He named his nephew as executor of his estate.[57]

It is certainly possible that a priest like Don Simón de Argaiz was so secular that he did not adhere to the rules of the priesthood regarding chastity. It is within the realm of possibility that the priest was the father of one or more of the eight children left on the doorstep of Lorenzo de Argaiz or even of Lorenzo himself. However, in reality we can only speculate regarding the motives of the people who dropped off eight infants on his doorstep. Moreover, the above-cited cases of foundlings whose origins were later clarified suggests that some foundlings in Mérida were related not to the male head of the household but to a female relative of the wife. In truth, speculation is about all that can be done to explain the fate of so many foundlings in a city of mysteries as well as secrets.

But a question remains: why were there so many illegitimate children and foundlings in Mérida? They comprised 37 percent of the total children baptized between 1720 and 1729. In Spain and in Europe as a whole at that time, both civil and ecclesiastical authorities would have tried to identify the parents or the unknown fathers to make them responsible for the children and force them to marry. Certainly the Church tried to do the same in Mérida, and as we have already seen some marriages were hastily arranged and banns dispensed with. That suggests some social pressure.

Perhaps there was also pressure behind some of the sixty-five cases of Hispanic men who married Maya women. However, as always, class was significant: none of those men who married Indians was classified a member of the hidalgo class, while practically all of the people who married without banns, except for those who were dying, were classified as a *don* or *doña*, that is, hidalgos.[58] Staining the "honor" of an elite woman sometimes had consequences. On the other hand, anyone who could be pressured into marriage with a Maya woman was not a member of the elite. In any case, Mérida still had a high rate of illegitimacy. No matter how one looks at it, social and ecclesiastical pressure to marry pregnant women apparently did not work very well in colonial Mérida.

It is likely that there was such a large number of illegitimate children for the simple reason that the parents could not afford to get married. In places like Guadalajara this probably accounted for the very low rate of marriage and the very high rate of illegitimacy, while in Spain rates of marriage were much higher and illegitimacy was much less common.[59] In Mérida the sacrament of matrimony cost 8 pesos, which was more than poor people could afford. Moreover, as we have seen, perhaps one-fourth of the people classified as *españoles* were poor, and this would naturally have meant that the poor had children but not legitimate children.

If practically all of the *expósitos* were the result of extramarital sex, then from the Church's point of view Mérida was full of adulterers and fornicators, a city of sinners. But as already noted, it is certain that at least some of the foundlings were the children of married people who could not afford to raise their children and therefore gave them up for adoption. This was not sin but poverty. The large quantity of *expósitos* therefore was probably another sign that Mérida's Hispanic people were not infrequently poor.

Nevertheless, one suspects that a quantity of foundlings was the result of adulterous relationships. In modern times adultery is much more common among men than among women, and it is hard not to suspect that the same was even more true in the colonial period. Indeed, later in the century a bishop of Yucatán wrote to the king about the people in his diocese and complained that one of their most commonly committed sins was that against the Sixth Commandment ("Thou shalt not commit adultery").[60] If the illegitimate children were born as a result of adultery, then the fathers could not be forced to marry the mothers for the simple reason that they were already married.

The same holds true for many of the children identified as illegitimate. They represented fully 25 percent of all baptisms in the 1720s, which means that there were twice as many illegitimate children as foundlings. In the twentieth century many men of means maintained what was called a *casa chica* (little house) for their mistresses, who were usually of a lower status. These men frequently had children with their mistresses. Once again it is hard to imagine that the same did not take place in the colonial period, but at the same time the Church could not force these men to marry the mothers of illegitimate children because they were already married. Moreover, whether married or not, the fathers of illegitimate children or foundlings, unlike the mothers, usually suffered no social stigma or loss of honor as a result of what was immoral behavior in the eyes of the community.[61]

The greater incidence of illegitimacy and infant abandonment in Mérida and other places in America, as well as low rates of marriage compared with those in Spain, shows that conditions in Spanish American cities were somehow different from those in Spain. This is one more example of how Hispanic American communities were not like those in Spain. The social controls exercised by Church and family were apparently not as effective in America. Of course, as early as the sixteenth century the Spanish-born Franciscan Bernardino de Sahagún had written that in Mexico "the mildness and abundance of this land and the constellations that govern it encourage vice, idleness and sensuality."[62] We may doubt the influence of the stars and the climate on human behavior, but most Spaniards at the time did not. Spanish-born people for the rest of the colonial period argued frequently that the American-born Spaniards were degenerate. Leaving out value judgments, the evidence seems to show that many people, especially males, were sexually freer in America and may have had a less restrained sexual morality. The cities in Spain and America were different in part because the people in them behaved differently.

The priests who kept the records thus end up providing us with insight into the behavior of the Hispanic people in Mérida. At the same time, however, the sources show how colonialism was an important factor in that behavior. Many of the mothers of illegitimate children were Mayas, and since the colonial regime required indigenous women to perform labor services—called *servicio personal*—for Hispanic households, it is likely that many of these involuntary female workers were coerced into sexual relations with men of the house. Rape certainly occurred. Children would have sometimes resulted, and it is hard to believe that the Church would have tried to force unmarried young elite men to marry Maya women. Of course, in all Western societies the religious authorities would probably not have tried to force young noblemen to marry domestic servants, and the culture of colonialism would have made such forced marriages just as unacceptable to the elite of colonial society. The extreme social and cultural differences resulting from colonialism thus had an impact.

V. Material Culture and Identity

Since status and class were connected, Hispanic parents tried to maintain their social position by providing their daughters with dowries. It is important to note that in Hispanic societies a woman retained ownership of everything in her dowry, just as she did not change her name to that of her husband. If she predeceased her husband, then the widower had to restore everything to his late wife's family. If her cash had been invested in a business deal, then the profits were shared equally between her and her husband. This was a world that was quite different compared to that of English-speaking societies at the time. In Mérida, as everywhere else in Castile and Spanish America, women had more rights and more power because they were not necessarily dependent on their husbands.

They had that power, however, only if they had wealth. Of course not all parents had the resources to endow their daughters, and so some people married *"pobremente."* It is likely that the great majority of Hispanic women who married in Mérida were not endowed. When provided, the dowry in Mérida in the years between 1689 and 1692 typically consisted mostly of a trousseau, which combined luxury clothing and jewelry. Cash was much less important, and nothing but cash was uncommon. Houses and landed estates by themselves were even less common. Frequently included were normal household items like grinding stones, wash basins, beds, mattresses, quilts or bedspreads, pillows, sheets, etc. Quite common also were the small bowls made of hard wood in which a wooden pestle was used to pulverize cacao beans and then whip hot water with the powder to make hot chocolate. At a later time, those who could afford it would drink their hot chocolate in the late afternoon, and it is likely that the custom dates back to the colonial era.

The nature of dowries in Mérida was neither unique nor exceptional. Dowries in other parts of New Spain in the seventeenth and eighteenth centuries were roughly similar, although Mérida's relative poverty is revealed by the low value of what parents provided their daughters. In Guadalajara and Puebla, for example, in most cases cash and real estate were not the major components of dowries, although money was more important in the former than in the latter and in Mérida. Luxury clothing and jewelry were always included and frequently were the most valuable items. This was also true for the smaller dowries provided in the area around Mexico City in the second half of the seventeenth century, although the quantity of cash, as in Guadalajara, was once again greater.[63] This means that husbands did not necessarily benefit very much economically by marrying endowed women. They benefited socially, however, for their wives were well dressed, thus adding to their prestige and prominence in society.[64]

Women sometimes brought their own personal property into a marriage as a part of the dowry, thereby revealing that females engaged in their own business affairs. For example, when Doña María Carrillo de Albornoz married Don Martín de Salazar y Córdova in 1689, her dowry of 1,616 pesos consisted in part of the 1,142 pesos from her inheritance while the rest was in clothing "*que la dicha Doña María Carrillo adquirió con sus labores y grangerías*" (that the said Doña María acquired through her own work and enterprises). Yet the bride's brother, Captain Don Juan Manuel Carrillo de Albornoz, served as her "tutor and guardian" in the absence of her late father, and the brother had to certify the dowry.[65]

As has already been seen, property in the form of human beings could be included in dowries. When Doña Ignacia de Cepeda y Magaña, the daughter of Major Don Pedro de Cepeda y Lira (a Spanish-born soldier who was a knight of the Order of Calatrava) and Doña María de Magaña y Figueroa (a descendant of conquistadors), married Captain Don Íñigo de Mendoza y Vargas (the son of a Spanish-born soldier) in 1692, her dowry of 1,590 pesos included not just 500 pesos to buy a house but also a fourteen-year-old mulatta slave who was evaluated at 250 pesos.[66] When Doña Josefina Carrillo de Albornoz, the daughter of the politically important regidor Captain Don Nicolás Carrillo de Albornoz, married Don Gerónimo Salvador de Mimenza in 1720, her dowry consisted of a mulatto slave named Pedro Miguel Carrillo, whose monetary evaluation was 200 pesos.[67] That was all she got, suggesting that her father was not wealthy, did not like his daughter, did not approve of the husband, or was not very generous.

Dowries did not have to be large. Juan Romero de Salazar, a citizen of Valladolid, made his will in Mérida in 1690 and stated that his wife had a dowry of 130 pesos.[68] The lowest in value among citizens of Mérida in the documents was 150 pesos, provided to María Alcocer when she married Andrés de Salazar in 1692.[69] Because of incomplete records it is impossible to provide precise statistics, but in the relatively complete documents of one notary for the years 1689–1692, a total of eighteen dowries were either registered or acknowledged in wills. The total value was an impressive 269,587 pesos 4 reales, but most of this was in the form of clothing and jewelry, not cash. The average size was 1,497 pesos 6 reales, while the median was 1,377 pesos 4 reales. Not much changed in the first decades of the eighteenth century. Of the fourteen dowries mentioned or recorded in notarial documents between 1719–1723 and 1728–1729, the largest was 5,972 pesos, the smallest was 200 pesos, and half of them were 1,000 pesos or less.

Within the 1689–1692 sample, at the high end of the dowries was the 6,935 pesos promised to Doña Ana de Quiñones, wife of Captain Luis de Cabañas. However, most or all of this had been based on a future inheritance that never materialized, and when she made her will in 1692 she found herself too poor even to establish a chantry.[70] The next-most-valuable dowry was much smaller: 2,607 pesos 5 reales. This belonged to Doña Isabel Bojórquez, the daughter of Alférez Antonio Bojórquez and Doña Getrudis de Sosa, when she married Alférez Marcos Díaz de León, an immigrant from the Canary Islands. All of this was provided by the bride's uncle, Father Juan Gaspar de Bojórquez, the curate of Mérida's Maya parish of Santiago.[71] Only four dowries in the sample were valued at more than 2,000 pesos. However, at a later time, as we have seen, a very large dowry of 12,000 pesos in cash was provided to the granddaughter of the Count of Miraflores. She acknowledged this in her will in 1718.

The experiences of Doña Ana Quiñones, who had the largest dowry in the 1689–1692 sample, and that of Doña Antonia de Arrúe in the previous chapter show that the promises to deliver cash, goods, or real estate to women getting married were in fact just that: promises. Another example is provided by Doña Catalina Dorantes Magaña, the widow of Major Don Pedro Berzunza de Echeverría. When she made her will, she declared that she had provided a dowry for one of her daughters. However, she had promised a dowry to another daughter but had failed to provide it. Three other daughters were promised nothing and got nothing. Also left out was an adopted daughter.[72]

Presumably Doña Catalina failed to provide dowries because she lacked the resources to do so.

Dowries therefore were aspirational in nature. Other cases of failure to deliver undoubtedly occurred but did not show up in the surviving documentation. Again, we see that documents are not precisely accurate guides to a past reality.

Nevertheless, the detailed lists of clothing undoubtedly do provide insight into the late Hapsburg world in Yucatán. Luxury textiles were always by far the most important European export to colonial Spanish America,[73] and the dowries give an indication of Yucatán's commercial and cultural connections with the outside world.

Only rarely does the documentation of dowries identify the origin of the clothing. Some fustians were identified as coming from Rouen, the principal city in Normandy, which was one of the most important textile-producing regions of Europe. Thread identified as "Tangai" may have been Tangail silk thread from Bengal. Silk probably came from Granada or from China, on the *Nao de Manila* (Manila Ship) crossing the Pacific from the Philippines to Acapulco. What is known is that no Yucatán-made cotton cloth or thread is included in the dowries. Most of the clothing was of silk, linen, or cotton. The presence of a few woolen blouses shows that sometimes the cool temperatures of winter permitted the wearing of clothing usually considered more suitable to colder climates. After all, Yucatán was not always hot.

The cloth and thread were of the types manufactured in Spain, France, the Low Countries, England, Germany, and Italy. Most of these textiles undoubtedly were carried by ships departing from Seville or Cádiz and carried to Veracruz. After that, merchants sent the goods to Campeche and from there frequently to the secondary port of Sisal, just to the northwest of Mérida. Then mule trains carried them to the capital. They were the basis of the wealth accumulated in Campeche and Mérida by merchants, many of whom became rich by local standards and joined the ruling elite of the province. The large value of the clothing declared in dowries testifies to their importance in Yucatán's commercial economy. The imports also provided employment for tailors and hatmakers, since the cloth had to be handmade into clothing.

One presumes that the tailors kept up to date on European fashion and that the clothing they made was considered European in nature. Women must have dressed like women in Spain, France, and Italy—petticoats and floor-length dresses and all, despite the generally hot and humid climate of Yucatán.

The willingness of the people to wear such clothing demonstrates their determination to maintain their cultural identity. In Mérida, as elsewhere, clothing was one of the most effective ways to demonstrate social status within the Hispanic community and just as importantly to show that the person wearing the clothes was a Spaniard, not an "Indian." Indeed, the Hispanic people of Mérida, as well as all European immigrants, had an identity distinct from that of the indigenous population. That is why their baptisms, marriages, and last rites were recorded in books specifically for *españoles*. They called themselves Spaniards and certainly considered themselves to be Spaniards despite the different environment found in America.

The luxury clothing, however, was certainly used mostly in public, at Sunday Mass, religious holidays, baptisms, weddings, funerals, etc. Those were occasions when people had to display their status and identity. The upper class had to manifest "a certain decorum and an ethos, genuine or conventional, corresponding to the social model of the 'gentleman'" or lady.[74] Dressing properly was an essential part of that decorum and ethos. Such clothing, however, was very expensive, and continual use would have caused it to wear out quickly. Frequent replacement would have been beyond the means of many people. Behind closed doors, therefore, people certainly dressed at times in a more comfortable and affordable fashion. The large quantity of Maya-made cotton cloth readily available would have made it easy to do so.

There is little evidence for what happens in history behind closed doors, but an obtrusive and frequently annoying bishop, Juan Gómez de Parada, saw fit to intrude into the private world of the Hispanic people of Mérida. After several years in his position, and presumably after acquiring some information about the people, he issued new rules in 1722 regarding behavior in his diocese. He denounced the "pernicious" custom of Spanish women wearing "the dissolute and lascivious dress" of Maya women in their houses, which meant that they went around "almost naked" in front of everyone present. Therefore he ordered that such clothing should only be worn in front of husbands.[75] Of course, the bishop had no means of enforcing his rules, and the extramarital sexual relations that led to the birth of so many illegitimate children and the abandonment of foundlings in Mérida makes us suspect that, like much of what the Catholic Church preached about sexuality, people just ignored unwanted interference in their private lives.

When Hispanic women in the privacy of their homes dressed in clothing like that used by Maya women, they were not simply adapting to the hot and humid climate of Yucatán. They were also manifesting the cultural interaction that went on between the Hispanic and Maya people in a colonial society. Most Hispanic households had Maya domestic servants working and frequently living in the house, and the wealthy also had African slaves serving as domestic workers. This meant that Hispanic people in Mérida lived in a cultural environment different from that in small cities and towns in Spain. This was Spanish America.

Even people at the top of the Hispanic social scale manifested the results of cultural interaction with the Maya. Take the case of Don Juan del Castillo y Arrúe, regidor of Mérida, *alférez mayor* of the city council, colonel in the militia, and the most powerful local political figure for over twenty years. He was the son of Don Juan del Castillo y Toledo, a Spanish-born soldier, and three of his four grandparents were born in Spain. His father had worked to carry out the repartimientos of the governors, and to do that Castillo the father had lived with his wife and son in the large Maya village of Maní, in the heart of the Sierra, the region with the largest concentration of Maya villages in the province.[76] Castillo y Arrúe was probably born in Maní, for he does not appear in the baptismal records in Mérida. Eventually, however, he came to live in Mérida, where he pursued his political career at the top of society.

Some years later, while in Maní, he chanced upon a Spanish official carrying out the governor's repartimiento. That official was whipping some indigenous people for failure to deliver the wax that was due. According to the cacique of Maní, someone ran to find Castillo y Arrúe, who was in the village at the time, and begged for his help. He intervened to calm down the situation and stop the abuse. To do so, he communicated with the Maya "*en su lengua*" (in their tongue).[77] This most powerful leader of Yucatán's Hispanic people was bilingual.

The results sometimes upset outsiders. Bishop Gómez de Parada (a native of Guadalajara, New Galicia), the cleric who had complained about the way that Hispanic women dressed in the privacy of their homes, also disapproved of Spaniards learning the Mayan language. This happened, he said, because Spanish households included Maya servants and therefore the first language heard by Spanish infants was Mayan. He discouraged the use of Maya nursemaids, basing his opinion no doubt on the age-old assumption that human milk affected culture and behavior.[78] The bishop insisted that all infants learn Castilian as their only language.[79]

Again, one suspects that the bishop's orders were routinely ignored. Hispanic households depended on non-Hispanic domestic labor, and never was this reality made clearer than in 1722, when Gómez de Parada tried to abolish the right of Spaniards to demand domestic service from the Maya. That meant that no indigenous women would be available to grind corn. Yet that grain was essential to life because wheat does not grow in Yucatán, and therefore everyone—including Spaniards—had to eat the food made by grinding maize, using a *metate* (mortar stone), to get ground corn flour. A large number of Hispanic households was allocated indigenous female labor for that purpose, which explains the widespread and deep-seated outrage and vehement opposition to Gómez de Parada's reform program.

To defend their access to labor, the leaders of Hispanic society informed the king that "grinding maize is so natural to Indian women that ever since they reach the age of reason they are used to it." Meanwhile, it was alleged that the "*naturaleza débil*" (weak nature) of Spanish women made it impossible for them to perform that arduous task.[80] The bishop's attempted reform was soon stopped. The incident demonstrated clearly that Hispanic people in Yucatán would have had to work a lot harder, and been a lot poorer, had they not had Maya laborers to serve in their houses.

The controversy over domestic labor also demonstrates that Spaniards in America had to adapt to what they found. In this case they did so by eating food that is still not commonly eaten in Spain. Hispanic people had been forced to abandon the fear, common in the sixteenth century, that if they ate Indian food they would become Indians and cease to be Spaniards.[81] Therefore they ate what was possible and learned to like it.

Mérida, the "Spanish island in a sea of Indians," was very much affected by that surrounding sea. Cultural change was not a one-way street, for it flowed both from and to the Maya. As a result, Hispanic society, while remaining true to a certain extent to its Spanish cultural roots, was affected by the people it encountered, conquered, exploited, and lived with. Mérida therefore was fundamentally different from small cities in Spain. Inevitably, Hispanic society in America was becoming Spanish America.

FIVE

* * *

MIGRATION
People in Motion

I. Mérida as a Destination of Migration

Many of the people in Mérida had come in from elsewhere, and presumably some people from Mérida left for somewhere else. Society was dynamic, not static, and the inflow and outflow of people reveal another aspect of Hispanic society in America. These population movements meant that the building of a community entailed the acceptance or rejection of people from elsewhere.

Marriage records shed light on migration and immigration in early eighteenth- century Yucatán. That is because priests were expected to note the place of origin of the bride and groom. The Church was not very interested in that information when it came to baptism, because except in extremely rare circumstances the child being baptized had been born in Yucatán and the birthplace of the parents was irrelevant. When it came to the last rites, priests were even less interested in knowing where the people had come from. They were, after all, dead or soon to be. When it came to marriage, however, the Church was extremely interested. If someone was not from Mérida, then that person's marital status could not be immediately verified, and therefore to avoid bigamous marriages the Church tried to find out if the prospective bride or groom was already married. Bigamy, after all, was a serious, mortal sin, because it meant that the sinner was repudiating the sacrament of matrimony. That was not just a sin. It was heresy, and anyone caught committing bigamy fell into the hands of the Holy Office of the Inquisition.[1]

The Church may not have caught all such cases, but it did catch some. For example, in 1718 Nicolasa de la Cueva of Mérida married Nicolás Pérez

Monfante, a native of the Puerto de Santa María in Andalucía. He had already been married in Sanlúcar de Barrameda in Andalucía and was presumably a widower. However, in 1726 poor Nicolasa de la Cueva shows up in the records marrying again, her first marriage having been annulled. The Church discovered that before coming to Yucatán Pérez Monfante had married a woman in the Port of Trinidad, in Cuba, and that he was still married. Moreover, he was found to have used no fewer than three aliases, apparently in an effort to cover his tracks. He failed, and was caught by the long arm of the Church.[2]

The priests performing the sacrament of matrimony therefore almost always noted the place of origin of brides and grooms. Between 1697 and 1726 there were 1,351 marriages registered in the books for *Españoles*. Within Yucatán, Mérida possessed both centripetal and centrifugal qualities, for 153 people— some 11.3 percent of marriages in this time period—included a groom or a bride from one of the province's villages. Only twenty-three non-Hispanic people— fourteen Maya women, eight mestizos, and one mestiza—went from the villages and got married in Mérida and were registered in the *Libros de españoles*. They represented less than 2 percent of the total number of people in the books. Leaving out the Maya and mestizos, the data show that 129 Hispanic people from villages, representing 9.5 percent of the total, were married in Mérida.

There is no way of knowing the motives for migration from village to city, but the evidence suggests that proximity to Mérida was a contributing factor. Three villages closest to the provincial capital—Conkal, Tixkokob, and Umán—were the source of nineteen migrants, or 15 percent of the total. Moreover, the three *partidos* (administrative districts) closest to the capital— La Costa (to the east), La Sierra Alta (south), and El Camino Real Bajo (west and southwest)—were the source of seventy-four migrants, that is, 58 percent of the total.

Proximity to Mérida, however, was not the only factor that led Hispanic people to migrate to Mérida. Of the three closest *partidos*, only La Costa contributed a large number of people. The other two were not major sources of migrants. In fact, the rather distant district of La Sierra Alta contributed as many as the nearby Sierra Baja and Camino Real Bajo combined. The Sierra Alta was the region of the largest Maya villages and of the largest concentration of Maya people in the entire province. The twenty-six Hispanic people coming from the three largest villages in Yucatán—Ticul, Tekax, and Oxkutzcab— were in the Sierra Alta, and they represented more than 20 percent of the people whose origins were identified in the records.[3] Thus the two *partidos* of

La Costa and La Sierra Alta were the origins of 58 percent of all the Hispanic village people who got married in Mérida.

The arrival of Hispanic people from villages reveals the existence of non-Maya communities outside of the three Spanish cities in Yucatán. Legally only Maya people and priests were allowed to live in those places, but these people were living there anyway. The presence of Hispanic people from those villages getting married in Mérida probably demonstrates not just a push-factor causing people to leave the capital but also a pull-factor drawing non-Indians to the Maya villages. This is evidence of the ongoing trend for non-Indians to settle outside the cities. They were undoubtedly attracted by some economic opportunities not to be found in Mérida, Campeche, and Valladolid. By the late eighteenth century, the non-Maya population living in the villages would grow quite large.[4] The presence in the marriage records of Hispanic people from those places reveals a reverse flow, from rural areas to cities, but the outflow from Mérida, as well as from Campeche and Valladolid, may well have been even greater.

One of the results of the Spanish conquest of Yucatán therefore was not merely the establishment of Spanish cities—"islands in a sea of Indians"—but also the eventual emergence of Hispanic communities within the Maya villages. To be sure, these Hispanic people were even more likely to be affected by Maya culture than the people in the cities. However, they also tried to maintain their own separate cultural identity. Many must have succeeded to a certain extent, for as we have seen, some of the Hispanic females from the villages were recognized as women of higher status—as *doñas*—when they married in Mérida. These communities represented the vanguard of a culture that was beginning to displace or replace some aspects of Maya culture. They were outposts of the larger outposts of colonialism. In the long run, larger and larger numbers of people in the villages would speak both Maya and Spanish, and in modern times most of the villagers in Yucatán are bilingual. And language is not the only manifestation of acculturation outside the cities.

Migrants from Yucatán's other cities also show up getting married in Mérida. Valladolid and its hinterland had less economic activity and a much smaller population than the capital. One suspects, therefore, that the inflow of people from that eastern city was greater than the outflow of people from Mérida going to Valladolid. Indeed, three regidores of Valladolid eventually moved to the capital and became regidores of Mérida. One of these had been an elected official of the eastern city. Competition for wealth in the east was intense and as we have seen even reached almost literally cutthroat levels in the early eighteenth century, when two regidores of Valladolid were executed for having killed their political opponents. No city council member or elected official of Mérida moved in the opposite direction to take up a position in the eastern city.

We will never know much about migration into and out of Valladolid because of the complete destruction of the records in the eastern city during the Caste War in 1847–48. In any case, the people from Valladolid getting married in Mérida accounted for 4 percent of all marriages. Campeche, on the west coast, was a much more important city, for it carried out trade with Veracruz and, unlike most seaports in America, after 1718 it had direct contact with the Canary Islands and was the port of exit of Yucatán's products and of imports from Europe and the world economy. It was also the headquarters of the officials of the *Asiento*, the institution importing African slaves, and of the *Consulado de Negros* (the merchant guild that distributed the enslaved human beings to the rest of the Peninsula).[5] People from that city accounted for 2.9 percent of marriages in Mérida. Only future research in Campeche's ecclesiastical archives will reveal if the inflow of people from Mérida to the western port city was lesser or greater than the outflow of people going to the capital.

II. Migration and Immigration to Mérida

The Spanish cities were sites of cultural interaction between the Hispanic and Maya peoples, but to maintain Mérida's Spanish roots immigration from Spain and other places was essential. Among these migrants who came from elsewhere and married in Mérida were people from other Spanish colonies. They, like the others who were not from Yucatán, will be considered immigrants. In the time period under consideration, people from other Spanish colonies numbered only twenty-one individuals and made up just 1.5 percent of all marriages. They were more significant within the total of 207 immigrants. People from other Spanish colonies made up 10.1 percent of them and 10.2 percent of immigrant marriages. They came mostly from places with good maritime communications with the outside world, like Tabasco, Veracruz, Cuba, Santo Domingo, Caracas, and even the Caribbean island of Roatan.

Some people, however, came from Spanish colonies that did not have easy access to the sea or to Mérida. Places like this include Ciudad Real (modern-day San Cristóbal de Las Casas, Chiapas), Mexico City, Oaxaca City, and Santiago de Guatemala. One lawyer, Licenciado José Zavala, came from Peru (and founded one of Mérida's most prominent families that eventually produced one of Mexico's most important politicians as well as one of the country's most important historians), and one Mariano Rodríguez came all the way from Manila, on the other side of the world.

Rodríguez was not the only one in Mérida who had made the trans-Pacific voyage. Don Miguel de Zavalegui y Urzúa in fact had made a round trip. A native of Navarre, he had accompanied his uncle, Governor-Captain General Martín de Urzúa y Arizmendi, who after serving as governor–captain general of Yucatán was appointed governor–captain general of the Philippines. After crossing the Pacific from Mexico, he served as an infantry captain in Manila. When his uncle died, Zavalegui probably took the Manila ship back to Acapulco and from there made his way to Mérida. He may have been there before, when his uncle was governor of Yucatán, and chose to return, or he went to Mérida on the advice of his uncle. Something about the place must have attracted him. He became the captain of a cavalry company, and in 1724 he married into Mérida's colony of northern Spaniards. His wife was the daughter of the important Cantabrian captain Antonio de la Helguera, the commander of a company of heavy cavalry (*corazas*).[6] Zavalegui became an important rancher and member of the city council.

Some people from Spain had experience in other parts of America before settling in Mérida. Major Juan José de Castro, a native of Toledo, served as a common soldier in Venezuela and was promoted in Mexico City to captain when raising a company of soldiers for service in the Philippines. He apparently did not make the voyage across the Pacific but instead accompanied the newly appointed governor of Yucatán when the latter took up his post.[7] Castro, like Don Miguel de Zavalegui, became an important rancher and was elected city magistrate.

Of greatest significance for maintaining the Euro-American culture, identity, and nature of Mérida was immigration from across the Atlantic.[8] It is possible to identify 186 such individuals, who participated in a total of 176 marriages in Mérida. (Ten immigrants married fellow immigrants.) The numbers of people and of marriages involving immigrants may appear to be small at first glance, but it should be remembered that Mérida in 1700 had a "Spanish" population of only around 5,000 people. Moreover, the number of Europeans who settled in the capital of Yucatán was approximately the same as revealed in the marriage records in Guadalajara, which was twice as large as Mérida and was much wealthier.[9]

In Mérida, immigrants although small in number were therefore important relative to the total population. In the time period under consideration, in the Spanish parish of the city 13 percent of all of the 1,351 marriages—slightly more than one in eight—involved at least one person who was an immigrant.

Of course, with such a small number one cannot say anything definitive about immigration from across the sea. Not every immigrant got married, after all, and those who did not would not appear in the records.[10] Some may have come and gone within a short period of time. Others were already married before they got to America and did not get married in Mérida. Those who chose to stay were what might be called settler immigrants, who at first were called *residentes* (residents) and then became *vecinos* (citizens) once they had settled down permanently. Those who became citizens of Mérida would not necessarily have been representative of immigrants as a whole. Moreover, the information is for Mérida alone, not even for Yucatán as a whole, and it is certain that every town and city in Spanish America had its own unique experience.

On the other hand, the information for Mérida does give us at least a rough indication of patterns of immigration to the capital of Yucatán. Many of those who were not already married chose to stay and were likely to marry, even if, as sometimes happened, the local prospective spouse was not from the elite and would not contribute to improved chances of prosperity and upward social mobility. At all times, some information is better than none, and sometimes conclusions can be strengthened if corroborated by other sources. The data, after all, are derived from the records of 1,351 marriages, which is not an insignificant number. The context, then, suggests some validity at least for patterns of settler immigration in the case of Mérida itself if not for anywhere else.

Moreover, the apparently small number of immigrants does not mean that these people were insignificant or even irrelevant. Many of them came to have considerable importance in the economy, society, and politics of Mérida. Indeed, between 1695 and 1730, of the thirty-one *regidores* (city councilmen) of Mérida whose origins are known, fourteen were born in either Spain or the Canary Islands, and seven others were the sons of people from Spain. Two more were the sons of people from other places in New Spain. Only eight were born in Yucatán of fathers born in Yucatán. Immigrants also became ranchers. Overall, they had an impact much greater than their numbers would suggest.

With these caveats in mind, the data for 1697–1726 can be used to tell us something about the men and women crossing the Atlantic and marrying in

Mérida. Not all of them were Spanish, for among the group of immigrants were twenty-two men, and no women, from England (seven people), France (five), Italy (five), Portugal (two), Flanders (two), and Ireland (one). In at least one case, that of Miguel Roela from Antwerp, arrival in America had been preceded by prior settlement in the Canary Islands.[11] There seems to have been a tapering off of foreign immigration over time, for almost three-quarters of these people came in the first half of the period under consideration, that is, between 1697 and 1710, and only six foreigners showed up in the marriage records from 1714 on. That is noteworthy because for a large part of the earlier period Spain was at war with Great Britain. Peace seems to have led to diminished immigration.

Among Spanish immigrants as a whole, only 13 of 164 individuals—that is, 7.9 percent—were females who married in Mérida. This is to be expected, for in the eighteenth century 90 percent of all Castilian emigrants to America were male.[12] There may have been some men and women who were already married before getting to America, and these people of course would not show up in marriage records unless they were widows or widowers who were remarrying. Unfortunately, however, the priests did not record the origins of any of the people who remarried, since as far as the Church was concerned that was an irrelevant bit of information. Nevertheless, even allowing for married women among immigrants, it is still likely that transatlantic migration, even when from Spain, was overwhelmingly a male experience. While Yucatán's capital was undoubtedly quite different from those of many, and probably most, other Spanish American cities, it is clear that settler immigrants from Europe, involved in more than one in eight marriages, were of considerable importance in Mérida.

Data compiled by Peter Boyd-Bowman on Spanish emigration to America in the sixteenth century would suggest that the major region of origin of immigrants might be Andalucía.[13] Similarly, J. Ignacio Rubio Mañé demonstrated the predominance of *andaluces* among Spanish immigrants in Mexico City in 1689.[14] These conclusions are borne out by the information from Mérida, which is summarized in Table 5.1. Of the 163 Spaniards in the sample, 55—or 33.7 percent—were from that southern Spanish province with the major seaports having direct contact with America.[15]

Of great interest and significance for Mérida are the forty-two marriages, 3.1 percent of the total in Mérida, involving Canary Islanders, or *isleños*, as they were called. These people made up 30.1 percent of transatlantic immigrants, that is, a close second to those from Andalucía. The Islanders usually departed

TABLE 5.1: Spanish Immigration by Region

REGION	NUMBER	PERCENTAGE
ANDALUCÍA	55	33.7
CANARY ISLANDS	49	30.1
BASQUE COUNTRY*	22	13.5
CANTABRIA**	16	9.8
GALICIA	10	6.1
NEW CASTILE***	6	3.7
CROWN OF ARAGON	5	3.1
TOTAL	163	

* Includes people from Navarre.
** Includes one person from Asturias.
*** Includes one man from La Mancha.
Source: AGA, Matrimonios, Españoles, Libros 4–7.

for America not from Seville or Cadiz but from the Islands themselves and thus they do not appear in the emigration records kept by the Spanish *Casa de Contratación* (Board of Trade) in Seville or Cadiz. Boyd-Bowman's data, derived from that source, therefore show that *isleños* were insignificant as emigrants to America in the sixteenth century. Evidence compiled by Rubio Mañé for Mexico City in 1689 also shows virtually no presence of Canary Islanders among Spanish immigrants.

Nevertheless, there is good reason to suspect that people from the Islands would be present in some parts of America in the second half of the seventeenth century and early eighteenth century. That is because the Spanish crown carried out a project to colonize specific places in America with *isleños*. The Spanish population in the circum-Caribbean area was sparse throughout the sixteenth and seventeenth centuries because of the small number of indigenous people to exploit, opportunities for immigrants were better elsewhere, and the situation was made worse by pirate attacks on Spanish settlements near the Caribbean and the Gulf of Mexico.[16]

The Spanish government therefore found it difficult in places with small populations to maintain possession of its colonies in this region, and foreigners were trying to occupy or set up colonies in the circum-Caribbean area. The English took Jamaica from Spain in 1655 and almost took Santo Domingo as well. Furthermore, logwood cutters from England set up operations in the

Laguna de Términos, just down the Gulf Coast to the southwest of the port of Campeche. They were doing the same in what is now Belize, on the southeastern side of the Yucatán Peninsula. Meanwhile, in 1697 the French captured Cartagena and held on to it briefly, and after exploring the Mississippi River they founded their colony of New Orleans in 1718.

In the seventeenth century, Yucatán itself was frequently attacked by pirates. The small coastal town of Champotón, southwest of the city of Campeche, was the target in 1644 and 1672, and Campeche was attacked or sacked in 1663, 1672, and 1685. As a result, the crown made a major investment in the port's defenses to prevent such disasters from occurring again. People who were pirates, English, or English pirates landed on at least one occasion at Chuburná, on the coast just north of Mérida, thereby threatening the capital city itself.

All of this required the Spanish crown to strengthen its defenses. Yucatán's militia units were upgraded in importance, and the laws requiring all encomenderos to perform military service on demand were enforced. A heavy cavalry company was created in order to respond to an attack more quickly. The Spanish population of the Peninsula made voluntary or involuntary payments for the construction and upkeep of a flotilla of small coast guard ships to protect the coasts.[17] The situation in fact was serious.

To counter such threats in the Caribbean area, the Spanish government encouraged *isleño* settlement in regions with small Hispanic populations. The sporadic direct trade between the Canaries and America was sometimes made dependent on the willingness of merchants and wine producers on the Islands to recruit families to settle not only in the Caribbean area but also in Florida and Texas to discourage English and French expansion.[18] Furthermore, after 1718 merchants on the Islands were given permission to trade regularly with Campeche as well as with Havana and Caracas, and this also allowed Islanders to take advantage of opportunities in the region.[19]

There is almost no information available about commerce between Yucatán and the Canary Islands, but it is known that by the middle of the eighteenth century *isleños* and perhaps other merchants were exporting thousands of cowhides and deer hides to the islands. At the same time, *aguardiente* (rum) from the islands was arriving in Yucatán, and some people alleged that it was leading to drunkenness among the Maya.[20] It is known that some *isleños* were indeed selling rum, although probably not exclusively to the native people. In 1720 Jacinto Sánchez, a resident of Mérida originally from La Laguna in the Islands, had a store that included many barrels of *aguardiente* in its inventory.[21]

As a result of colonization programs and trade, some Spanish colonies received a small but significant flow of immigrants from the Canary Islands. The crown paid the transportation costs, and this made it much easier for these people to get to America. Since *guanches*, the original inhabitants of the Islands, were of Berber rather than Iberian origin, it is no accident that people from Yucatán have measurable genetic connections with people from Cuba, Venezuela, the Dominican Republic, and Puerto Rico.[22] This strongly suggests that the bulk of *isleño* emigration to America went to these Caribbean regions.

The records regarding colonization by Islanders are not complete, but it is known that in 1681 the crown dispatched a group of twenty-six families, each composed of between two and six people—that is, married couples with children—of *isleños* to Campeche. In the following year some seventy-seven soldiers, some of whom may have been married with children, from the Canary Islands were also sent to Campeche, presumably to garrison the fortifications that the crown was building to protect the city.[23]

The families were provided with animals and seed to get them started as farmers. However, upon arriving in Yucatán it is likely that the colonists found their seed to be useless, since wheat or whatever they were given would not grow in the province's hot and humid environment. They also would have found out that in an area with a significant number of Maya agriculturalists, the only people who worked the land were indigenous and mixed-race people. This might have encouraged them to abandon farming and find something else to do. It would not be unreasonable to suggest that some of these people who had left their homeland as children abandoned the port city and went to Mérida, and that some of them probably appear in the marriage records in the provincial capital.

Although many of the immigrants from the Canary Islands were undoubtedly poor, some *isleños* eventually set themselves up in Yucatán as merchants. As we have seen in a previous chapter, Leonardo Peneda Suárez was one of these. He left his wife and children in Tenerife and in 1720 is known to have owned a store in Mérida.[24] Other store-owning Islanders include Domingo Fernández Rico, Jacinto Sánchez, Pablo Romero, and the latter's brother Agustín.[25]

Since *isleños* were the only immigrants involved in an official community-founding project, it is not surprising to find suggestions of their special nature even in the meager data available about immigration to Mérida. Only thirteen unmarried women made the trip across the Atlantic and married in Mérida, yet nine of them were Canary Islanders, and they made up 18.4 percent of the immigrants from the islands. Moreover, in Mérida five of these women married fellow *isleño* men and two others married men who were probably Islanders. The proportion of unmarried females among immigrants from the Canary Islands was much greater than that among people from Andalucía, the region of greatest immigration, for only 5.5 percent of people from that region were women. No females at all came from the Basque Country, Cantabria, or Galicia, the other Iberian regions of significant immigration. The family nature of immigration by Islanders is supported by the information from Mérida: most of the females in the group had brothers or sisters who also show up in the marriage records.

Not all *isleño* siblings got married, and therefore they do not show up in the *Libros de Matrimonios*. However, proof of their existence sometimes shows up elsewhere. Agustín Romero, from Tenerife, got married in 1718, but his brother Pablo, also from Tenerife, apparently never married. The latter made his will in 1721, and in that document he makes no reference to a wife. Pablo Romero was a merchant and storekeeper, and one of his entrepreneurial activities involved selling goods at the Festival of the Virgin in Izamal. He left everything to his brother Agustín, who also was merchant.[26]

The importance of *isleños* demonstrates that immigration is almost never random in fashion. This is borne out by information concerning the other people from Spain who crossed the Atlantic and married in Mérida. After those from Andalucía and the Canary Islands, who made up 33.7 and 30.1 percent of immigrants respectively, came people from the Basque Country. They made up 13.5 percent of the total. Then came some people from Cantabria (9.8 percent) and *gallegos*—people from Galicia—who made up 6.7 percent. Relatively insignificant were people from New Castile (3.7 percent) and the Crown of Aragon (3.1 percent). The latter were not supposed to be in America at all, but laws restricting America to people from the Crown of Castile were not always rigidly enforced.

III. Settling in and Settling Down

The meager yet useful data show that immigration to Mérida was by no means like the emigration from Spain to America in the sixteenth century. Boyd-Bowman was able to identify the origins of the people emigrating before 1600.[27] However, he had no way of knowing where they ended up after crossing the Atlantic. Practically all of the emigrants gave either Mexico or Peru as their destination, but that was partly a function of the way that the passage to America worked, for the annual fleets that sailed in the sixteenth century always had either Mexico or Peru as their stated destination.

Auke Pieter Jacobs studied Spanish emigration and immigration in the early seventeenth century and found that a significant number of migrants gave places other than Mexico or Peru as their intended destination. Once again, however, there is no certainty as to where the people went after they got off the boat in Veracruz or Cartagena. Sometimes people in Seville missed the sailing of the first of the annual fleets and ended up taking the second, which took them somewhere else. Other times migrants may have landed at the correct port but chose not to proceed to their stated destinations.[28]

The lack of sources that distinguished between local people and immigrants makes it difficult to study these individuals.[29] Marriage records, however, usually identify people's origins and can give us some insight into what happened to the new arrivals. As we have seen previously, Thomas Calvo and Mariana Alicia Pérez used matrimonial documents to study immigrants in Guadalajara and Buenos Aires.[30] Those records allow us to do the same in Mérida.

One of the most important differences between emigration from Spain in the sixteenth century and immigration to Mérida in the early eighteenth century is the imbalance of males and females. In the earlier period, males outnumbered females more than two to one, but in Mérida in the early eighteenth century among the people getting married the ratio was eleven to one. That is what would be expected, however, since as we have seen Spanish emigration in the eighteenth century was 90 percent male. However, the data from Mérida leave out immigrants who were already married before arriving and so that imbalance was possibly somewhat exaggerated. If we leave out the Canary Islanders, the imbalance is even greater: only 4.3 percent of the unmarried Iberian immigrants were female, that is, only one in twenty-three. There was not one unmarried female immigrant from Cantabria, the Basque Country, or Galicia.

This means, of course, that newcomers marrying in Mérida almost always had to find American-born wives.[31] As a result, endogamy—intermarriage within the group—would have been virtually impossible. Any effort by an immigrant group to maintain an identity distinct from that of the American-born community as a whole would require the invention of a different definition of identity, one that somehow did not exclude people because of American-born wives or mothers.

A second difference between earlier emigration and later immigration concerns regional origins. As we have seen, in the sixteenth century emigrants from Andalucía were the single most important group of immigrants at a later time in Mérida. However, people from Extremadura, the second most important group among emigrants in the sixteenth century, were completely absent in Mérida (although some do appear in earlier records). As a result, people from southern Spain—Andalucía and Extremadura—were more numerous as emigrants in the sixteenth century than they were as immigrants in Mérida at a later time. Meanwhile, in the earlier period Basques, *gallegos*, and Cantabrians were less significant. As we have seen, Canary Islanders were very scarce in the sixteenth century, although that is because Boyd-Bowman's figures are derived only from those leaving for America from Seville, and he assumed that there was no significant emigration from the Canaries. If the *isleños* are excluded from the sample from Mérida, in order to focus just on Iberian immigrants and make the data comparable to those gathered by Boyd-Bowman, then Andalusians made up 48.2 percent. The data are summarized in Table 5.2.

These data about immigration suggest a good deal of validity to the marriage records. What is known about Spanish emigration in the sixteenth century suggests that Andalucía would be one of the most important regions of origin of immigrants, and this was reflected in the information from Mérida at a later time. Similarly, the history of official efforts to stimulate the settlement of families from the Canary Islands in the Gulf of Mexico–Caribbean region in the last half of the seventeenth century suggests that Yucatán would be a region affected by the immigration of Islanders, and this also was borne

TABLE 5.2: Iberian Immigration by Region

REGION	NUMBER	PERCENTAGE OF TOTAL
ANDALUCÍA	55	48.2
BASQUE COUNTRY	22	19.3
CANTABRIA	16	14.0
GALICIA	10	8.8
NEW CASTILE	6	5.3
CROWN OF ARAGON	5	4.4
	114	100

Source: AGA, Libros de Matrimonios de Españoles, Libros 4–7.

out by the marriage records in the capital of the province. Thus the conclusions drawn from the meager sources in Mérida are corroborated by sources from elsewhere.

Rubio Mañé's analysis of people in the *padrón* (registry of people) of Mexico City in 1689 suggests both similarities and differences compared to Mérida. The viceregal capital was of course much larger than Mérida, for the total non-indigenous and non-*casta* (mixed-race) population numbered approximately 57,000 people. That was probably eleven times larger than that of the capital of Yucatán. Immigrants from Europe numbered only 1,181 people, that is, 2.07 percent of the residents of Mexico City. Practically all of them were male. Since immigrants who married in Mérida numbered 208, there is the possibility that the newcomers in the capital of Yucatán were relatively more significant than in the viceregal capital. What is clear, however, is that Canary Islanders were important in Mérida but not in Mexico City, for in the latter *isleños* numbered only twelve people in 1689.[32]

What is also clear is that the proportion of the immigrants in Mérida who were from countries other than Spain was much greater than in the viceregal capital. There were only forty-eight such people in Mexico City in 1689, while in Yucatán's capital twenty-two such people got married between 1697 and 1726. On the other hand, the same foreigners—people from northern Italy, France, Flanders, and Ireland—found in Mexico City tended to be found in Mérida, with the exception of Englishmen, who were absent in the *padrón* of the viceregal capital. And whereas Mérida had its person from a Spanish colony in Asia—a Spaniard from Manila—Mexico City had someone who was Armenian, who almost certainly came to Mexico via Manila and Acapulco.[33]

Not all foreigners were of equal importance. In Mexico City the single most important group of foreign immigrants was from Genoa, while in Mérida the Genoese were in third place. There were twelve Genoese in Mexico City in 1689 and four who married in Mérida. A fifth Italian, from Milan, was also from northern Italy and may well have been connected to Genoa. This reflects the importance that Italy's most important seaport on its western coast had in Spanish expansion in America since 1492. It is possible that the Genoese people in Mérida were the commercial agents of merchants in Mexico City. But their presence in Yucatán is by no means unexpected and thus provides more support for the validity of the data regarding immigrants in Mérida.

David Brading has shown that in the last half of the eighteenth century, Basques and especially Cantabrians, both from northern Spain, were more important in Mexico than even Andalusians.[34] Santander and its mountainous hinterland in Cantabria, called *Las Montañas de Burgos*, were an important source of out-migration to other parts of Spain and to America during the first half of the eighteenth century.[35] One contemporary source from Santander lamented, "This excess of emigration is more frequent in this region than in any other part of the [Iberian] Peninsula and this shows that when so many people leave to seek professions and the means of subsistence, it is because of the lack of enterprises to employ them."[36] The main cause, then, was not so much poverty as it was the lack of opportunity.

The data from Mérida presented here are only from the late seventeenth and early eighteenth centuries and probably for that reason they do not support Brading's argument completely. Perhaps statistics derived from several decades later would do so. Nevertheless, the data do show a significant presence of Basques and Cantabrians.[37] If we leave out the Canary Islanders and concentrate just on immigrants from the Iberian Peninsula who show up in the marriage records, the data from Mérida show that people from the Basque Country and Cantabria made up 32.5 percent—almost one third—of all trans-Atlantic Spanish immigrants. That is still less than the proportion coming from Andalucía, but it is much greater than in Boyd-Bowman's data from the sixteenth century. Thus, Cantabrians and Basques were more important in Yucatán in the eighteenth century, as Brading has suggested for Mexico as a whole.

How is the presence in Mérida of a significant number of people from northern Spain—all of them men—to be explained? After all, they were almost absent in Guadalajara at the same time. Of course, it was much easier getting to Yucatán than to New Galicia at that time, and this is a partial explanation. Moreover, Yucatán's commerce, based on exports of cotton textiles to Veracruz and from there to the mining camps of northern Mexico, had existed for over a century, and Spanish merchants apparently found that trade to be moderately profitable while relatively risk-free. People from northern Spain were therefore simply maintaining a long-standing trade route. Indeed, the most prominent Basque immigrant—Pedro de Garrástegui, the Count of Miraflores—was one of the most important merchants involved in exports of cotton textiles to Veracruz.[38]

The Basque Country and Cantabria exported wool to the rest of Europe, but it certainly did not ship that product in any significant quantity to hot and humid Yucatán. Exports of iron products, the other traditional Basque export, would have been important, but it is unlikely to have been the basis of the accumulation of considerable wealth by merchants in Mérida. In fact, the most important source of the northern Spaniards' wealth was imported luxury textiles, which appear in almost all the notarized dowries of Hispanic people in Yucatán.

Basques could become wealthy as a result of this trade because they had a competitive advantage over all other Spaniards when it came to textiles imported from France, the Low Countries, and England. This was because of the special privileges (*fueros*) granted to the Basque Country before the European conquest of America. One of these privileges was the stationing of the customs collection post not at the ports on the coast but at a considerable distance inland. In medieval times that would not have been important, because almost all imported goods would have had to pass through customs on the way to markets in inland cities. After Spanish expansion into America, however, Basques discovered that they could import luxury goods duty free and ship them to Seville and Cadiz.[39] There, Basque merchants were ready to receive the goods and ship them to America, usually avoiding the taxes that other merchants in Spain had to pay. That was their competitive advantage.

Because of these special rights, the Basque seaports became "contraband paradises," in the words of some scholars.[40] This in turn would have opened up opportunities for merchants in nearby Santander, who lacking in opportunities at home could have gone to Bilbao, San Sebastián, or some minor Basque port to get a share of the contraband trade. It is possible that Basques and Cantabrians formed commercial partnerships with each other, just as they frequently worked in unison in Yucatán. When the Spanish government under the new Bourbon dynasty tried to remove this special privilege from the Basque Country in 1717 and put the customs collection post on the coast, there was a major revolt that forced the crown to back down. The northern coast of Spain thus remained a smuggler's paradise until the implementation of *Libre Comercio* (Free Trade within the Empire) in the 1770s. That measure eliminated the Basques' competitive advantage over the merchants of the rest of Spain.

The influx of Basque and Cantabrian merchants was not large in quantity, but the small size of Mérida resulted in their outsize importance in Yucatán. Unfortunately, little is known about the details of this emigration from Spain. A hint of what was going on is provided by the efforts to collect debts owed to Andrés Zamora, a Basque merchant in Mexico City. The debts were owed by Domingo Urgoitia, a Basque merchant in Mérida. In 1691, Urgoitia owed Zamora 1,300 pesos, the debt having been guaranteed by a Basque associate. The immigrant in Mérida had borrowed the money while he was still in Spain to pay for his passage from Cádiz to America. In addition, however, the funds were used for his provisions and trade goods that he brought with him.[41] That was a lot of money for a trip to America, which makes us wonder what those goods consisted of. There is no way of knowing, but it is likely that Urgoitia brought some merchandise with him to deliver to someone in America or to set himself up in business in Mérida. It also seems likely that few if any of the immigrants from northern Spain were well-off and that therefore they had to borrow money not just to get to America but also to arrive with goods to deliver or sell. Presumably Urgoitia and people like him knew in advance what was likely to sell in Mérida.

Data on Spanish emigration after Latin American Independence suggest that sometime between the sixteenth century and the nineteenth century a transition had occurred, as more and more people from Galicia and the Basque Country—hardly present at all in the early statistics—emigrated to America.[42] As we have seen, the information from late seventeenth- and early eighteenth-century Mérida reflects and confirms the growing importance of Basques and Cantabrians in the Spanish diaspora. However, the data also reflect the growing importance of immigrants from Galicia.

In other words, despite the small size of the sample of immigrants in Mérida, other sources tend to confirm, if not the precision, then at least the trends or suggestions found in the information derived from marriages in the capital of Yucatán between 1697 and 1726. This encourages some confidence in the general, if not specific, conclusions that can be drawn from the data.

A factor influencing migratory patterns to Mérida was close proximity to the sea. Almost four of five Andalusian immigrants (forty-three)—78.2 percent—were from Seville, Sanlúcar de Barrameda, Cádiz, Puerto de Santa María, Gibraltar, or Motril (a small port on the Mediterranean coast of Andalucía). All of the *isleños* (forty-nine) were of course also from islands tied into international trade, and if we add the people from maritime regions or seaports in the Basque Country (sixteen), Cantabria (eleven), Galicia (five), and Cartagena (one), we find that of 163 individuals, 125—76.7 percent—of all Spanish immigrants came from port cities or towns with seafaring traditions.[43] The maritime origin of immigrants was probably even more pronounced than that, for a few people from northern Spain simply stated that they were from Cantabria or Galicia. Some of them may have been from the coast, like most of the other people from those parts of Spain.

This pattern is reinforced even further when we consider the non-Spanish Europeans, for practically all of them came from seaports like Genoa, Livorno, and St. Malo, or from maritime regions like Brittany or islands like the Azores. Probably everyone from England and Ireland was from a place close to the ocean. All of this suggests that the experience of cities in the highlands of Spanish America like Oaxaca, Ciudad Real, and Santiago de Guatemala might have been markedly different compared to that of Mérida because they were so far removed from the sea.

Easy access to ships outbound from Spain for Veracruz from Seville or Cádiz, or from the Canary Islands to Campeche, must account for much of this. But one suspects that many of those who became immigrants found out about America and overseas opportunities by interaction with people who had already been there. Some of them may even have already made a trans-Atlantic passage themselves and went back to America to stay because of something that had attracted them. As José Moya puts it, "emigration embodies a process of diffusion ... of information, concepts, and behaviors."[44] And undoubtedly some seamen and others engaged in trans-Atlantic commerce just took the opportunity to jump ship while in port and stayed to become settlers. This would help account for the extreme gender imbalance in the case of immigrants in Mérida.

Finally, because these Europeans were arriving in a colonial society, upon arrival they would have discovered, or already knew, that being European in Yucatán automatically raised one's status to, or close to, that of gentleman. Being "white" counted, which is why all the Englishmen, Irishmen, Frenchmen, Italians, Flemings, and Portuguese were classified in the records as "*españoles*," that is, Spaniards.

The ease with which immigrants seem to have gotten married in Merida suggests acceptance of the newcomers by local society. That may have been the case, but the Spanish government was not quite so lenient. People from Castile and the Canary Islands were of course welcome, but those from other European countries presented the possibility of the spread of heresy or disloyalty. Therefore the government discouraged and even prohibited such uncontrolled immigration.

The crown addressed the problem on numerous occasions. In 1721 the Governor-Captain General of Yucatán, Antonio de Cortayre, received orders to expel all foreigners. He responded by explaining that those people were relatively few in number. Moreover, they were all Roman Catholic and were usually married to local women. In Mérida there were two Italians, three Englishmen, and three Frenchmen. Most of them appear in the marriage records. There was another Englishman who was married and lived in Valladolid.

Governor Cortayre provided more detailed information for Campeche, where no fewer than five men from Genoa resided. This demonstrates again the importance of the Genoese for the Spanish Empire and for Yucatán. Also living in the port were four men from France, one from modern-day Belgium, one from Portugal, and one from Ireland. Cortayre argued that these people represented no threat and indeed were useful to society. For example, Claudio Gaudet, from either Nantes or Nancy, was the only surgeon in the province at that time, and he had helped cure a previous governor.[45]

In 1738 the crown again ordered the expulsion of foreigners. Governor-Captain General Manuel Salcedo responded in 1739, providing the names of three foreigners: Don Alejandro Joseph de Guelle (Alexander Joseph Wells?), Don Patricio Maguier (Patrick McGuire?), and Don Gaspar Canahan (Casper Callaghan?). The latter was a Catholic Irishmen whose family had settled in the Canary Islands and who came to Yucatán in 1723. He lived in Campeche and was poor and disabled as the result of an accident. McGuire was also an Irish Catholic who had fled religious persecution and arrived with his wife and family in Campeche in 1731. The third man (Wells) was a Scott who had been living in Yucatán for thirty-six years, had a wife and family, and had received royal permission to live there. When he was baptized, as an adult, in Mérida in 1702, he was identified as the person "who winds the [city] clock," (and presumably set the time). Mérida, therefore, had a mechanical clock. He obviously had special skills.[46] Governor Salcedo suggested that they all be permitted to stay, and notably had placed a *don* before each man's name, thereby suggesting respectability.[47]

The fiscal of the Council of the Indies reported on the case, noting that McGuire had paid 200 pesos for residency status but that the other Irishman had not. The governor had reported that Callaghan was of upright morality and should be allowed to stay. The fiscal agreed, noting that Callaghan had been living in the Canaries or in Yucatán since an early age and was well behaved. The Council of the Indies went along with these recommendations but noted that the case should not be used as a precedent for future decisions. In short, they let the Irishman stay but did not want the decision to encourage other foreigners to immigrate.[48]

That such a small and apparently insignificant case got all the way to the Council of the Indies would suggest to some that colonial officials in Spain were busying themselves to an absurd degree with unimportant matters. But it also demonstrates just how important the presence of foreigners was to the Bourbon rulers of the Spanish empire. It should be remembered that at this time English traders were trying to gain control of the Laguna de Términos (Campeche) and Belize in order to acquire logwood to export. In response to these threats, in the 1720s Governor-Captain General Antonio de Figueroa y Silva led a successful military expedition that expelled the English from Belize.[49] Tensions were building up with Great Britain over the *Asiento* (slave trade) and British trading rights, and in fact later in 1739 full-scale war broke out. Foreigners therefore were possibly dangerous, and their presence required more attention than had previously been given by officials in the Hapsburg era.[50]

Nevertheless, these particular bureaucrats were not without feelings and made a humanitarian decision in the case. As Charles Nunn has concluded regarding the implementation of Spanish policy on foreigners at this time, "Legal practice stressed precedent rather than code; tolerance was more general than exceptional; and administration was more humane than inefficient."[51]

If three-quarters of Spanish immigrants came from the coastal ports and villages, then one-fourth of them was from inland places. Of course, the distinction between the two is arbitrary, for some immigrants came from towns that while in the interior still were not far from ocean-going ports. Some *andaluces*, for example, came from Marchena (close to Seville), Córdoba, Lebrija, Utrera, and Ronda. Only Granada was truly inland.

Those immigrants whose hometowns were not near coasts came from inland places in Navarre, Cantabria, Galicia, and New Castile. The only two unmarried female immigrants who were not from Andalucía or the Canary Islands were both from Madrid, which suggests a connection to government officials. Indeed, Governor-Captain General Fernando Meneses Bravo de Sarabia served as the matrimonial sponsor of Doña María Guzmán, a native of the Spanish capital, who in Mérida married Don Luis López Gayos, a man from the Kingdom of León, in 1709.[52] It is possible that the bride or the groom, or both, had come in the retinue of the incoming governor.

The same political connection does not seem to be evident in the case of Doña María Olaes, also a native of Madrid. She married a Basque immigrant in 1716.⁵³ Nevertheless, whether by personal choice or familial pressure, both women from the Spanish capital married fellow immigrants. As a whole, New Castile was relatively insignificant as a source for unmarried immigrants, for only six people—5.3 percent of the total—came from that part of Spain. Of the four male immigrants, one came from Madrid, two from Toledo, and one was from the Cuenca area in La Mancha (which for reasons of simplicity has been counted as New Castile).

The majority of unmarried immigrants to Mérida in the early eighteenth century were therefore from Andalucía and the Canary Islands. People from the Basque Country, Cantabria, and Galicia were of secondary importance, and those from New Castile and the Crown of Aragon were relatively insignificant in the total. The data from Mérida may be sparse, but they are supported by evidence from elsewhere and from other times. They are also bolstered by historical knowledge and even by common sense.

Mérida thus contained many people from Yucatán's villages and smaller cities, from other Spanish colonies, and from across the Atlantic. This does not mean, however, that the provincial capital was a melting pot of Mayas, *mestizos*, mulattoes, Africans, and Spaniards. It was that to a certain extent, of course, but the Hispanic population did not assimilate and become like the others. The Spaniards could maintain their separate identity because Hispanic society continually received reinforcements of people from across the Atlantic who were equally intent on preserving an identity distinct from that of everyone else.

The Spanish outpost of colonialism held out in part because of these reinforcements from across the sea. As a result, the Spanish-born people of Mérida remained distinct from most of the American-born *españoles*, as well as from the mixed-race and indigenous people of the city.

They were even more distinct from the colonized people of Yucatán. The difference between Spaniard and Maya was maintained long after the conquest and continually reinforced by Spanish immigration. As a result, the correlation of "race" (as it is now called), culture, and class continued to exist, survived into the twentieth century and beyond, and perpetuated a social structure characterized by extreme inequality.

SIX

* * *

IMMIGRANTS AND SOCIETY
Social Lives and Behavior

ANY GROUP THAT PARTICIPATED in 13 percent of marriages in a city cannot be considered insignificant. The small number of trans-Atlantic immigrants therefore must be put into the historical context of a relatively small city where one out of eight marriages is a lot. Immigration thus was important in the history of Mérida. In a place where mortality rates were high, the influx of people from elsewhere helped Hispanic society to grow faster than Maya society. Indeed, the size of the indigenous population was actually diminishing in the second half of the seventeenth century because of the yellow fever epidemic that began in 1648. With every year that passed, there was less of a chance that Hispanic people would be overwhelmed by the indigenous people and lose their identity.

Immigration therefore helped maintain Hispanic culture in America. This contributed to the belief among Hispanic people in America that they were in fact Spanish—and hence the title of the *Libros de españoles* for the recording of baptisms, marriages, and last rites. The influx of people from Spain allowed this Spanish outpost of colonialism to maintain some degree of its preferred cultural identity. That has persisted into the present, for in Mérida today the upper class and most of the middle class see themselves primarily as people of Spanish, not Maya, or even mestizo, descent and culture.

I. Immigrant Origins and Status

Immigrants were not simply important demographically in Mérida in the late seventeenth an early eighteenth centuries. The immigrant experience reveals aspects of the historical context of the time. The newcomers did not live in isolation, and their lives and their fate provide insight into Hispanic society in Yucatán and in Mérida.

Information from immigrant marriages in Mérida calls into question some common assumptions made about colonial Spanish America. It is often thought that people from Europe immediately experienced social mobility upward. In the terminology of the time, an immigrant automatically became an hidalgo, a lady or gentleman from the lower nobility. A majority of the Spanish residents of Mexico City, and certainly a large number of those in Mérida, were merchants or shopkeepers, and of them Viceroy Mancera wrote in 1673 that "the traders and dealers who in the Indies comprise a good part of the Spanish nation, approach the nobility very much, affecting their carriage and style. . . . It can be generally reckoned that in these provinces the gentleman is a merchant and the merchant is a gentleman."[1] Similarly, in the middle of the eighteenth century a Capuchin visitor who traveled to Mexico noted that "all *gachupines* [people from Spain] are addressed as *don* and are treated with great respect, all being taken for nobles, no matter what class they are since to be European suffices."[2]

Marriage records from Mérida in the late seventeenth and early eighteenth centuries do not support these broad generalizations. The priests who kept the records and who presumably reflected, to a point, the socio-cultural attitudes of the time and place, were not as liberal in their interpretation of social status. As noted in a previous chapter, the priests decided who qualified, and who did not, as a member of the hidalgo class, and although the records are sometimes inconsistent, the information derived from the *Libros de Matrimonios de Españoles* is useful and important because people at the time thought that the status distinctions were significant. In a colonial society the difference between a European-like person and someone else was of great importance. The priests may have made mistakes and errors of omission, but they (almost?) never assigned *don* or *doña* status to anyone thought to be undeserving. Therefore the records can be taken as a close proximity to a minimum number or proportion of ladies and gentlemen who got married in Mérida.

The data in Table 6.1 manifest the status of the immigrant men who married in the late seventeenth and early eighteenth century. At first glance, it would appear that most immigrants were not considered to be gentlemen, and that they did not move up to become hidalgos. However, further analysis reveals that the reality was more complicated.

TABLE 6.1: Status of Transatlantic Immigrant Men Who Married in Mérida, 1697–1726

REGION	% *DON*	% NON-*DON*	% NON-*DON* MARRYING *DOÑAS*
BASQUE COUNTRY	88.1	11.9	4.5
CANTABRIA	73.3	26.7	50.0
ANDALUCÍA	38.9	61.1	51.5
OTHER COLONIES	23.5	76.5	38.5
FOREIGN	21.7	78.3	27.8
GALICIA	10.0	90.0	30.0
CANARY ISLANDS	11.1	88.9	33.3

Source: AGA, Matrimonios, Españoles, Libros 4–7.

It is to be expected that the men most often classified as hidalgos would be Basques, and indeed that was the case in Mérida. It was widely known that for historical reasons practically everyone in the Basque Country claimed *hidalguía universal* (collective hereditary nobility), although that was not always accepted in other parts of the Crown of Castile.[3] Nevertheless, in America being of Basque origin counted for a great deal. In 1737 Governor Manuel Salcedo justified granting an encomienda to the daughter of a Basque immigrant because "his nobility is manifested by his surname." The grant had been made shortly before by the interim governor and Royal Treasury official Santiago Aguirre, who just happened to be a Basque.[4] Priests in Mérida apparently had little quarrel with assessments like that, and they registered 88 percent of Basque men as gentlemen. Clerical errors may account in part for the 12 percent who were not so classified.

People from Cantabria in northern Spain were sometimes recognized to be of hidalgo status in Mérida, but many others were not, at least not at first. That is because most of these immigrants were merchants, who in Spain did not have high status. In order to be accepted as someone of hidalgo status they had to accumulate wealth and serve as officers in the militia. Then their children would be considered to be members of the hidalgo class, for in Yucatán, as in Chile and many other places, "ranks in the militia acted as a means of ennoblement" for merchants in these societies organized for war.[5] This military function, after all, was the justification of the elite status of encomenderos and indeed of European nobility itself. The same process of "ennoblement" through military service also applied to some locally born people who were not hidalgos but whose children were accepted as members of that class. Social mobility upward therefore was frequently a two-step or multi-generational process.

On the other hand, no amount of cumulative clerical errors or carelessness can account for the extremely and consistently low status assigned to people from Galicia and the Canary Islands. In 1591 in Spain, only 5 percent of *gallegos* were classified as hidalgos.[6] It would seem that this low esteem was passed on in Yucatán. As for Canary Islanders, only 11 percent of *isleño* men who married in Mérida were registered as hidalgos, and those classified as a *don* possibly came from the Castilian conqueror class that took possession of the islands in the fifteenth and early sixteenth centuries. For example, Don Pedro Castro Illada married into a good family in 1695, for his wife's brother-in-law was Regidor Don Luis Magaña Dorantes. By the time he remarried in 1711 he held the position of *alférez* in the provincial militia, and his former brother-in-law, the city councilman, attended the wedding. Castro Illada was probably related to Juan González de Castro Illada, a seventeenth-century architect who designed many notable Baroque façades on structures in Tenerife and Gran Canaria. He must have been accepted as a gentleman, for in 1691 the bishop of Yucatán entrusted him with writing a report regarding an estancia's debts to the Church.[7]

Similarly, another high-status *isleño*, Major Don Cristóbal de Herrera y Córdova, was one of only two Canary Islanders who managed to serve on the city council as a regidor. High status had been achieved or recognized before he joined the ruling elite. The great majority of *isleños* did not have that advantage.

Most Canary Islanders were of a recognizably lower status and did not move up the social scale. There was something about most of the *isleños* that made the priests reluctant to assign them high status. Perhaps they were seen as less "civilized," since they had been Christianized only relatively recently. After all, Tenerife, the origin of many of the people marrying in Mérida, had only been conquered by Castile in 1496. However, no such reason existed to assign low status to the men coming from Galicia. Yet only 10 percent of the *gallegos* were considered gentlemen, and once again that cannot be attributed solely to clerical carelessness.

Marriage records, however, certainly conceal a process of social mobility that was taking place or had already taken place before the immigrants got married in Mérida. In Spain itself, literacy rates were relatively low, but the people from northern Spain who went to Mérida were mostly merchants and were probably literate before leaving their homeland. Then, in Mérida Basques and Cantabrians joined a Hispanic American society with a low level of literacy. This would have contributed to their success at claiming high status in America as well as to their capacity to amass wealth.[8] In the kingdom of the blind, the one-eyed man is king. This was another factor that helped contribute to the social mobility experienced by Basques and Cantabrians.

Between the two extremes of Basques and Cantabrians on the one hand and *gallegos* and *isleños* on the other were the *andaluces*, who made up the largest group of immigrants in the sample. Only about three of every eight people from Andalucía who married in Mérida were considered to be hidalgos. Somewhat surprisingly, even foreigners—people from England, France, Italy, Flanders, and Ireland—were more often accepted as gentlemen than people from Galicia and the Canaries even though the origins of many of these non-Spanish immigrants must have been dubious. They were more highly rated than even people moving to Mérida from other Spanish colonies. One presumes that those individuals could most easily be fitted into the preconceived categories that people in Yucatán used when judging people.

It should not be assumed, however, that being Spanish-born counted for nothing. The 38.9 percent of hidalgos among *andaluces* may be below that of Basques and Cantabrians but it was still a high proportion in the context of society in Castile at the time, where, as we have seen, the percentage of hidalgos was only between 5 and 10 percent.[9] It is certainly much higher than in Andalucía itself. It is known that some of the people from southern Spain came to Mérida as important government officials (lieutenant governors or treasury officials), and they were accepted immediately as hidalgos. Moreover, many of the non-hidalgos among the Andalusians were able to marry local women who were *doñas*, in a society that had very few immigrant women to marry. As shown in a previous chapter, one-third of the American-born women classified as *españolas* in the records were assigned hidalgo status when they married. Mérida simply had a number of *doñas* available to marry.

In the competition for women, therefore, the immigrant men may have done quite well. Over half of the non-hidalgo men from Andalucía, as well as those from Cantabria, succeeded in marrying American-born *doñas*. Even foreign Europeans, people from other colonies, *gallegos*, and *isleños* sometimes succeeded in finding higher-status women to marry.

It seems likely, therefore, that being from across the Atlantic, and especially from Europe, was a characteristic that allowed immigrant men to "marry up," that is, marry someone of a higher social class. In short, many people of transatlantic origins may well have experienced some sort of social mobility.

However, it should be remembered that the data are derived from marriage records and that not all immigrants got married. Some of them were already married before arriving in Mérida. To find a spouse, success and prosperity, even if moderate, gave some people an advantage over others, and those immigrants who did not experience success or prosperity would have had less chance of marrying anyone of higher status—or anyone at all. Illiteracy would have contributed to the lack of economic prospects. Many people like this would not show up in the records. In other words, lower-status people were less likely to marry and therefore would be undercounted in the sample. Nevertheless, while it is true that the majority of immigrants did not quickly, or even eventually, become hidalgos, the ability of a large number of the non-hidalgo immigrants to marry *doñas*—people of higher status—probably does signify some social mobility upward. This may have been possible in part, one suspects, by simply being European, that is, unequivocally not Indian or African.

II. Identities and Invented Identities

The experience of Mérida's Hispanic people also leads us to call into question the assumption that being born in America automatically gave people a consciousness of being American rather than Spanish. Technically, of course, being born in the Western Hemisphere made someone a "creole," although in Mexico as a whole in the colonial era such people were known first as *hijos de la tierra* (sons or children of the land) and later as American Spaniards (and the people from Spain were called European Spaniards). But did place of birth lead to American consciousness or a sense of identity?

There are some hints from the late seventeenth and early eighteenth centuries of a sense that Hispanic people born in Yucatán distinguished themselves from people born elsewhere. For example, in 1687 Don Lucas de Villamil y Vargas, whose father had arrived in Mérida from somewhere in New Spain, was identified in a governor's residencia proceedings as a captain of a "Spanish Infantry" unit that was made up "of the outsiders of the city" (*de los forasteros de la ciudad*).[10] These people were not referred to as foreigners (*extranjeros*) because in fact they were subjects of the king, as were all the inhabitants of

Yucatán. They were, however, perceived as being different from the people who *were* from Yucatán.

At the same time, the "outsiders" may not have approved of that distinction being made. Don Antonio de la Helguera, a Cantabrian who eventually joined Yucatán's upper class, was identified in one source in the late 1720s as a soldier who had served in Mérida as a member of "the [militia] Company that is vulgarly referred to as of outsiders" (*de forasteros*).[11] So, the distinction between outsiders and other people was being made, but no word was being used here for those who were in a sense insiders. Apparently, however, these insiders knew who the outsiders were.

And what about the sons and daughters of those "outsiders"? If the children of immigrants blended in seamlessly with all other Hispanic people born in America, then the immigrant experience in colonial Spanish America would have been completely different from that of practically all other immigrants in the Americas at a later time—including the Lebanese in Mérida. Elsewhere, as is well known, people from other continents usually tried to maintain some sense of identity and sometimes group solidarity, and hence the creation of the many urban areas known as "Little Italy," "Chinatown," "Little Tokyo," or some similar name depending on the group. (In early twentieth-century Mérida, the Lebanese lived everywhere but especially in the parish of San Cristóbal.) The most important difference between immigration in Mérida in the middle colonial period and immigration to North and South America in the nineteenth and twentieth centuries was the extremely small number of unmarried European females among the people who went to Mérida. Sex ratios were unbalanced in the later emigration from Europe, but not nearly as extreme as they were in colonial Yucatán.

Nevertheless, it is to be expected that immigrant groups would try to maintain their identity and have a preference for marrying within their group. However, in Mérida several groups were more likely than others to maintain their sense of identity. For non-Spanish Europeans this was all but impossible because of their small numbers. Nevertheless, some tried.

Italians in Mérida were all from northern Italy and were apparently merchants. In their case we actually can see attempts to marry other European, and occasionally Italian, immigrants. Juan Agustín Garibaldi, from Livorno, married a local woman in 1686, but in 1707 his daughter married an immigrant from Seville. The lack of Italians made it virtually impossible to marry within the group, and perhaps marriage with a European Spaniard was the next best choice.

Similarly, Don Bernardo Narich of Genoa, who had business contacts in Maracaibo (probably to import cacao) as well as in Campeche,[12] and who was the only man among the Italians accepted as a *don*, married a local *doña* in 1709. His daughter later married an immigrant gentleman from Utrera, in Andalucía. Francisco Gandulla, from Genoa, was apparently more determined to maintain ties of ethnicity. He married a local woman in 1688, but his daughter married an immigrant from the Genoa area in 1709. This was probably an arranged marriage along familiar lines: someone gets established in America and then writes home requesting someone to marry his daughter and take over the business. We have no information about the marital history of the descendants that the three other Italians in the sample may have had. However, we do know that only one of the four non-hidalgo Italians "married up," that is, found a wife recognized as a *doña*.

The immigrants from Spain and the Canary Islands were more numerous and had a better chance of maintaining their identity as people separate from the Yucatán-born. Nevertheless, the almost total absence of females among all immigrant groups except *isleños* made endogamy within each ethnic group impossible. Even the Canary Islanders, however, failed to achieve this, as would also be the case among *isleños* in San Antonio de Béxar in Texas.[13] The much larger number of immigrants in Mexico City made endogamous marriage possible among northern Spanish regional or ethnic groups in the Viceregal capital.[14] But not in Mérida. Any effort by an immigrant group to maintain an identity distinct from that of the American-born community as a whole would require the invention of a different identity.

Since the daughters of immigrants were apparently accepted as members of distinct Iberian ethnic groups, some immigrant men maintained their identity by marrying these American-born women. Or perhaps it would be better to say that the immigrant men who had married locally born women married their daughters to new immigrants. That worked for a few individuals, but there still were not enough American-born daughters of immigrants to go around. At most only 27 percent of Basques and 12.5 percent of Cantabrians found wives among the daughters of immigrants of their own group. Therefore, the pool was expanded by including females with the same social status. This allowed Basques and Cantabrians, the two groups with the highest average of hidalgos, to marry the daughters of high-status—and only high-status—Andalusians and the occasional Genoese or Flemish immigrant. This pool in effect included only European immigrants judged to be of high status. Left out were practically all *gallegos* and *isleños*. By necessity the latter married women who were not the daughters of European immigrants.

Therefore, if we consider European-born people *and* their daughters as a community, we can see what were in effect high rates of endogamy for some groups. Table 6.2 summarizes the data.

Canary Islanders are not included in the table because they were not Europeans. In any case, only 7.5 percent of male *isleños* married the daughters of European-born men. However, 33 percent of male and female immigrants from the Islands married either fellow Canary-born immigrants or the sons or daughters of *isleños*. They therefore displayed more endogamy within their own group than anyone else. The presence of just a handful of women made a difference.

This means that a quasi-European society was being re-created in America. Since immigrants and their sons made up a majority of the regidores of Mérida at this time, clearly this group was an important, and possibly dominant, part of the ruling elite and therefore of course an important component of the upper class. To be sure, the descendants of the original conquistadors and encomenderos were also an important part of that upper class. Nevertheless, as the marriage records show, Spanish people were continually arriving and reinforcing Spanish culture. Mérida thus retained to a certain extent its essence as a Spanish city in America.

This was made possible, however, only because Spanish immigrants and their wives could control the marriage of their daughters. It is impossible to believe that it was simply by chance that practically all of the daughters of immigrants married the next generation of immigrants. This pattern therefore is a rare example of real evidence for arranged marriages. But since nothing

TABLE 6.2: Endogamy* Among European Immigrants in Mérida, 1697-1726

GROUP	PERCENTAGE THAT MARRIED THE DAUGHTERS OF EUROPEANS
BASQUES	81
CANTABRIANS	62.5
ANDALUSIANS	22
GALICIANS	0

*Defined as marriage between European immigrants and the daughters of European immigrants.

Source: AGA, Libros de Matrimonios de Españoles, Libros 4-7.

at all is known about why anyone else got married in Mérida, it cannot be assumed that marriages were arranged only within the immigrant communities. It is more likely that many or even most matrimonial unions among upper-class people in Mérida were also arranged to one degree or another. On the other hand, non-immigrant parents would have had a much larger number of marital partners to choose from for their children and may have allowed their sons and daughters to have some veto power over the selection of prospective spouses. The daughters of immigrants must have had few, if any, options other than to do what they were told.

III. Enterprise and Matrimony

There were good reasons for European-born men and their wives to marry their daughters to new European immigrants. They wanted sons-in-law who were respectable and useful. Ironically, their own sons may not have been useful, because parents get the sons who are born, who may or may not have good character. But parents could choose their sons-in-law. They frequently selected men who had already proven themselves to be men of good character or had already begun to accumulate wealth.[15] They were important additions to the family.

Arranging the marriage of daughters to immigrant men was not merely a matter of maintaining social status or group identity. For many people there were commercial reasons for immigrant men to marry their American-born daughters to new immigrant men. This was inherent in the very commercial and marketing structure of the Spanish Empire. Many European immigrants, especially Basques and Cantabrians, came to America in this time period and set themselves up as wholesale merchants dealing in the import/export trade and selling to retailers. Sometimes they set themselves up in retail trade as well. They could do this because they had and maintained personal connections with merchants back in Europe. Trade in the world economy at the time depended to a great extent on trust, on previous connections between people who knew each other and may have been related to each other.[16] Some of the European-born probably had invitations to join up with merchants already operating in America.

Hillel Eyal argues that these networks lost their importance once the Bourbon kings got firmly established, implemented reforms, and cut down on smuggling, leaving immigrants in America with nothing but their merits to acquire wealth and marry well.[17] This would have been true to an extent for Mexico City, although John E. Kicza has argued that international commerce continued for most of the century to rely to a great extent on contacts or partners in Spain. This does not mean, however, that many immigrants came to be important merchants in the viceregal capital, as they did in Mérida.[18] There was, of course, a considerable difference of scale between the capital of Yucatán and the capital of the viceroyalty. The Hispanic population of Mexico City was eleven times larger than that of Mérida. The difference makes a comparison of the two cities problematic.

Moreover, most of the immigrants in Mérida in this study had arrived before the impact of the Bourbon Reforms later in the eighteenth century. They had come during the late Hapsburg period, when the Basque Country and neighboring Cantabria were smugglers' paradises.[19] People operating out of northern Spain could acquire valuable trade goods from northern Europe and undersell competitors. Personal contacts with people like that would have given people in Mérida an advantage over merchants whose contacts were only with people in Seville or Cádiz.

This entrepreneurial structure, however, presented what might seem to be a fatal problem: people died. They died in America and they died in Spain. That meant that the personal connections interwoven with the trust necessary to engage in long-distance commerce eventually ceased to exist. As a result, the people in the next generation in America might not continue as their fathers and had to find some other source of wealth.

However, in America immigrants with daughters could arrange marriages for them by bringing in the next generation of European-born merchants. By doing so, the fathers could establish new personal connections, and hence trust, back in Europe through their sons-in-law. In this way the entrepreneurial structure could continue to exist to the benefit of everyone involved. As a result, in the mid-colonial period overseas commerce continued to rely on trust based on relationships of kinship, regional or ethnic identity, fictive kinship (ritual God-parenthood and matrimonial sponsorship), and friendship.[20]

The experience of Captain Antonio Ruiz de la Vega demonstrates this historical process in action. He had come to Mérida from the Santander area and in 1683 married María Conde Pinacho, the daughter of Francisco Conde, a merchant from northern Spain. The second surname of the bride suggests that her mother may have been the daughter of an Italian merchant.[21] Neither bride nor groom was recognized as a member of the hidalgo class. However, Ruiz de la Vega was appointed as captain of the militia, and after that his children counted as hidalgos.

The couple had five daughters. Two of the daughters married Basque immigrants, one married a Cantabrian, and one married Don Andrés Vázquez Moscoso, an immigrant from Seville who was recognized as an hidalgo at the time of his marriage. The fifth daughter married someone born in Mérida, but her husband was the son of a Spanish-born high-ranking official in the Royal Treasury. Three of these sons-in-law joined with their father-in-law in posting expensive bonds for governors, and the connection to the treasury official could not have harmed the interests of any of them. It is likely that three or more of the sons-in-law had personal connections back in Spain that helped them prosper in business in America and that their father-in-law benefited as well. Thus we see three generations of immigrants—Francisco Conde, Antonio Ruiz de la Vega (who married Conde's daughter), and at least three of Ruiz de la Vega's sons-in-law—establishing or maintaining the personal connections with people in Spain that were necessary for success in long-distance commerce. Thus three, and possibly even more,[22] generations of immigrants worked together to engage in transatlantic commerce and presumably became wealthy by local standards.

Although we may be sure that not all of the resulting marriages were happy ones, it should also be noted that young females may have found good reasons to go along with their parents' wishes. Romantic notions certainly existed, but so too did the desire to have a comfortable life, and marrying men judged to be suitable by their parents was a good way of remaining prosperous. Women, after all, were probably no less concerned about class and status than men. Marrying high-status men was a way of preserving one's position in society. Marrying *gallegos* or *isleños* would have been a step down the social scale, as would marriage with any locally born non-hidalgo person.

Culture would have been another factor encouraging women to accept their parents' wishes. To a great degree their social life would have revolved around not just their family but also around their identity as daughters of recent Basque, Cantabrian, or Andalusian immigrants. The same was true for the lower-status *isleños*. In fact, a sense of a separate identity might have been preserved and maintained by the special languages that some groups probably spoke. Spanish-born Basques almost certainly spoke Basque, and it is likely that some or even most of the Canary Islanders could speak or understand the *Guanche* language of the Islands. Even Cantabrians may have had their own language, for the regional language, *cántabro*, continued to be spoken in northern Spain until the middle of the twentieth century and therefore may have been known or spoken by the immigrants two centuries earlier. When these groups got together for weddings, baptisms, funerals, religious holidays, and parties, the ties of community or identity were reinforced, and young, marriageable women would have been an important part of these society gatherings. It is likely that some or many of them wanted to marry within their group.

Back in Spain, Basques, Cantabrians, and Andalusians did not usually interact with one another because they lived in different places in a large country. They thus retained their separate identities and different languages. Regionalism was, and is, strong. In Mérida, however, the immigrants were too few in number to live in isolation from each other. They tried to maintain their original identity but had to interact with others in a similar situation. As a result they created in America a *Spanish* identity that barely existed in Spain itself outside of Madrid, Seville, and Cádiz.

IV. Weddings and the Reinforcement of Identities

Little is known about social life and behavior in much of colonial Spanish America. However, marriage records reveal aspects of the life of the Hispanic people living in Mérida. They can be used to show not just who married whom but also who attended weddings as matrimonial sponsors and witnesses. That broadens the scope of possible analysis by providing information about social behavior that otherwise could only be guessed at. That information demonstrates the existence of social networks of class, groups of people who tended to congregate with each other. These groups were not made up simply of family members. That, of course, would be expected at wedding ceremonies. They also consisted of people who had something in common: distinctive ancestry that united them into communities of individuals whom the families of brides and grooms invited to their weddings. Thus wedding "invitations" provide us with insight into colonial society and demonstrate the existence of immigrant communities. They were colonies within the colony of Yucatán and Mérida.[23]

THE SOCIAL LIFE OF A BASQUE
The unquestioned leader of the Basque community in Mérida was Don Pedro de Garrástegui, a native of Arrasate-Mondragón, Gipuzkoa, who came to Yucatán sometime in the second half of the seventeenth century.[24] In 1675 he

married Doña Micaela Rodríguez de Villamil y Vargas, whose father was a high-status soldier who had arrived in Yucatán from somewhere in New Spain and whose mother was from the local elite. That tied Garrástegui to the Vargas family, of the conquistador-encomendero class. He became rich as a merchant through his participation in the repartimiento business (the extension of credit or money to the Maya in return for repayment in kind), which allowed him to acquire cotton textiles and wax to export to central and northern Mexico. His purchase of the position as treasurer of the Santa Cruzada (the ecclesiastical institution that sold bulls of indulgence to raise money for crusades that no longer took place), previously held by his mother-in-law's family, made him richer because he found ways to sell bulls of indulgence on credit to the indigenous people.[25]

In 1689 Garrástegui was back in Spain probably to arrange the purchase of a title of nobility.[26] He became the Count of Miraflores, making him the only titled nobleman in Yucatán. He may also have spent his time in Spain trying to find suitable marriage partners for his suddenly high-class daughters, for soon after, in 1694, a native of Seville married Garrástegui's daughter Doña Francisca. She would have been about eighteen years old at the time. The wedding took place in Mérida, but the groom was not present. He was still in Spain or en route to Yucatán. The count himself stood in as the proxy.

Two years later another of the count's daughters, Doña María, married a native of Extremadura who was a Knight of the Order of Santiago. He had come to Yucatán in the 1670s as a hanger-on of a governor and had served as one of the governor's business agents. This marriage also was performed in absence of the groom. The groom must have been in his forties or even older at the time of the marriage, while the bride, born in 1683, would have been thirteen. Their first child was born a year later.

The fate of other Garrástegui women sheds some light on the social control exercised by parents. After the marriages of the first two juveniles, the remaining three sisters did not marry at early ages. In a double marriage in 1717, Doña Josefa Garrástegui and her sister Doña Nicolasa married Spanish-born gentlemen from Toledo and Castro Urdiales (Cantabria) respectively. Josefa must have been around thirty-one years old and her sister Nicolasa was around thirty-two. The last sister, Doña Ceferina, born sometime after 1686, married an hidalgo from Catalonia in 1721 and like her sisters must have been close to or over thirty.

These women married very late by local standards. How could three such cases happen in the same family? It is possible, of course, that the three women were so unappealing or unpleasant that no one wanted to marry them. It seems unlikely, however, that all three sisters had such characteristics. It is also possible that they did not choose to marry. However, this also seems unlikely, because Garrástegui and his wife would probably have married them off regardless of the wishes of their daughters.

The most likely explanations are either that their parents were waiting for appropriate suitors, who did not appear until later, or that they simply did not want their daughters to marry. Perhaps the count wanted to avoid having to provide dowries, or he wanted his daughters to stay home to take care of him. After the death of their father in 1712 all three sisters married, two in 1717 and the last one in 1721. Their mother may have exercised her power to delay their marriages until suitable husbands were found.

It is hardly a coincidence that all five of the Garrástegui daughters married Spanish-born men. It seems likely that there were not enough suitable immigrants from the home country to please the count. On the other hand, two sisters did not marry until five years after the death of their father and the youngest nine years after. That was also probably no coincidence. It is highly likely that their mother controlled the marriages of her daughters just as effectively as the father had done. This was parental, not patriarchal, power.

The conclusion is inescapable: being Spanish-born was a prerequisite for marrying the daughters of Spanish-born Don Pedro de Garrástegui and his American-born wife. On the other hand, none of the daughters married Basque immigrants. For the count and his wife, status, not ethnicity, seems to have been a prerequisite. Nevertheless, although the daughters were not marrying Basques, the women were maintaining ties to the Spanish immigrant community. Arranged marriages like these helped tie the immigrants together.

The value of marriage as a means of tying people of the European community together is revealed in attendance at the weddings of the Garrástegui sisters. The only people recorded as being present were Basques, Cantabrians, other Spanish-born people, or family members of the count's wife. And when there were no first- or second-generation immigrants available, the grandchildren of Spaniards were judged to be suitable witnesses.

At the same time, the count's family attended other people's weddings within the community. In 1698 his daughter Doña María and her husband served as matrimonial sponsors for a native of Vizcaya and his wife (either a Basque or of Basque descent). One of the witnesses was Captain Antonio Ruiz de la Vega, the most prominent Cantabrian in Mérida. In 1706 the count himself attended the wedding of a Basque and the daughter of a Basque. Also attending were his son-in-law from Extremadura and a Basque immigrant. The important role of *padrino de boda* was taken by a Basque, Governor-Captain General Martín de Urzúa, the Count of Lizarraga.

The social life and social network of Don Pedro de Garrástegui and his family thus demonstrate the impossibility of maintaining a Basque community in Mérida. As a result, there was frequent intermarriage and interaction with other Spaniards, especially Cantabrians.

THE SOCIAL LIFE OF A CANTABRIAN

The importance of women in maintaining the ties of community among Spaniards is revealed in the social life of Captain Antonio Ruiz de la Vega, from the Santander area. He became important in politics and eventually was elected as alcalde or *síndico procurador general* (procurator) of Mérida more often than anyone else. As we have seen, he had married the daughter of a merchant from northern Spain. He had five daughters, four of whom married Spanish immigrants while his fifth daughter married the son of an important Spanish-born official of the Real Hacienda. These women tended to marry young. The age of marriage of two of the daughters could not be determined, but the other three sisters married at sixteen, fourteen, and thirteen.

His participation, along with his first or second wife,[27] at weddings reveals the ties of community and the social network created and maintained among immigrants. He and his first or second wife served as the matrimonial sponsors of people from Granada, Cádiz, Seville, Sanlúcar de Barrameda, and, in one case, the Canary Islands. He and one of his daughters, who had married a Basque, served as *padrinos de boda* at the wedding of the daughter of a Basque.

The attendance at the weddings of the Ruiz de la Vega daughters gives insight into the social reproduction of the Spanish community. When his daughter Doña Tomasa Ruiz de la Vega married a Basque in 1701, the matrimonial sponsors were Governor-Captain General Martín de Urzúa y Arizmendi, a Basque, and the latter's Yucatán-born wife, Doña Juana Bolio, the daughter of a Genoese immigrant. The witnesses were the Extremaduran son-in-law of the Basque Count of Miraflores and Don Juan del Castillo y Arrúe, a rising political figure whose father was from Madrid and whose maternal grandfather was a Basque. The very same day Doña María Olaya Ruiz de la Vega, the sister of Tomasa, got married to Don Andrés Vázquez Moscoso, a high-status Andalusian, and these same people were the *padrinos de boda* and witnesses.

Continuing with the story of the daughters of Antonio Ruiz de la Vega, we see more examples of the ties of community. When Doña Petrona Luisa Ruiz de la Vega married the son of a Spanish-born official of the Real Hacienda in 1716, the matrimonial sponsors were a Cantabrian and his wife, who was the sister of the groom and therefore the daughter of Spaniards. One of the witnesses was the Andalusian Vázquez Moscoso, Ruiz de la Vega's son-in-law.

The latter also attended the wedding of others within the immigrant community. He was a witness at the marriage of the daughter of a native of Antwerp as well as at the wedding of a daughter of a *gallego*.

On the other hand, in 1706 Ruiz de la Vega was a witness at an elite wedding of someone not connected to recent immigration. His presence was a sign of his acceptance by local elite society. This, however, was the *only* time that he attended the wedding of people outside the immigrant community, and even then his fellow witness was a fellow immigrant, a man from Antwerp. His social life, therefore, was almost exclusively restricted to European-born people and their children.

THE SOCIAL LIFE OF A CANARY ISLANDER

The Canary Islanders were of the lowest status among immigrants, and it is no surprise to find that they rarely married the daughters of European-born immigrants. At the same time, the small number of female *isleñas* meant that most of the males from the Islands ended up marrying locally born and usually non-elite women who probably were not of *isleño* origin. Nevertheless, the Islanders belonged to their own distinct community, and the social life of their community leader manifests the existence of their group identity and their social network.

The most prominent of the Islanders was Canary-born Don Diego de Rivas Talavera, who became wealthy as a merchant, cattle rancher, and tithe collector. Despite his wealth, however, his social life took place to a great extent within the Canary Islander community. In 1686 he married Doña Ana Borreli de la Mota, who was probably the daughter of an Italian merchant. Although the couple had a least one son and one daughter, these children for one reason or another did not get married in Mérida. Nevertheless, Rivas Talavera and Ana Borreli had an active social life that reveals the presence in the provincial capital of a community of *isleños*.

Indeed, the two were community leaders when it came to social events like weddings among Canary Islanders. They served as the matrimonial sponsors at the 1699 wedding of a couple who were both immigrants from the Islands. Nineteen years later that couple's daughter married a merchant from Tenerife, and the *padrinos de boda* were none other than Rivas Talavera and his wife. The latter couple served again in 1721 as matrimonial sponsors of an *isleño* who married the daughter of an *isleño*. The groom had come from the Canary Islands accompanied by at least one brother and possibly his parents as well.

Rivas Talavera and his wife, however, did not limit their attendance strictly to the weddings of fellow Canary Islanders. In 1709 they served as the matrimonial sponsors at the marriage of a Genoese merchant, and two years later Rivas Talavera was a witness at the wedding of a Cantabrian immigrant. In this case a Basque served as the matrimonial sponsor. Only once, in 1712, did this prominent Canary Islander participate in the marriage of someone not clearly connected to Mérida's immigrant community, and in that case neither the bride nor the groom was identified as a *don* or *doña*. In other words, it was not a wedding of people of the hidalgo class. Apparently, members of Mérida's old elite did not invite him and his wife to serve as sponsors or witnesses at their weddings.

THE ANDALUSIANS: COMMUNITY AND ASSIMILATION

And what about the *andaluces*, the most numerous group of immigrants? Only three of the fifty-five immigrants from Andalucía who married in Mérida were women, and so the people from the southernmost part of Spain would have to follow the same matrimonial practice as everyone else: marry a locally born woman. The three immigrant women, however, did not have to marry local men, and they did not. Two of them married fellow Andalusians and the third wed a Canary Islander. Fifty immigrant male *andaluces* thus all married locally born women.

The marriage records reveal that the same patterns seen in the case of Canary Islanders and immigrants from northern Spain were repeated in the case of the Andalusians. For example, a man from Cádiz married a local woman, but one of that couple's daughters married a native of Gibraltar, while on the same day another daughter married an immigrant from the Andalusian town of Lebrija. So, both daughters of an *andaluz* married men who were *andaluces*. We have previously seen cases of double marriage of siblings. Perhaps when it came to weddings there were economies of scale. Similarly, in 1685 a native of Seville married a woman from Yucatán's eastern city of Valladolid, and twenty years later their first daughter married an immigrant from Sanlúcar de Barrameda. Three years later, in 1708, the couple's second daughter married a man from Gibraltar.

The tendency to try to maintain ties of identity is also revealed in the case of the daughters of Cristóbal Maldonado, an immigrant from Córdoba who married a local woman in 1681. In 1697 the couple's oldest daughter married Major Don Juan Joseph de Castro, a soldier from Seville with considerable military experience who two years later was elected as second alcalde of Mérida. The bride would have been about fifteen years old at the time. In 1714 another Maldonado daughter also married someone from Seville. This was Don Andrés Vázquez Moscoso, by then the widower of one of the daughters of Antonio Ruiz de la Vega. Thus locally born children of an *andaluz* married immigrants from Andalucía.

THE SOCIAL LIFE OF AN ANDALUSIAN

The most prominent of the immigrants from Andalucía was Don Andrés Vázquez Moscoso, who like his first father-in-law, Antonio Ruiz de la Vega, was one of the most frequently elected public officials of Mérida's city government. His behavior provides another example of an immigrant whose social life was closely intertwined with the lives of people within the immigrant community. This social network is seen in the following examples of his participation at weddings:

> After marrying the daughter of Antonio Ruiz de la Vega in 1700, he was a witness at the wedding of a Canary Islander in 1706, and he and his wife were the *padrinos de boda* of the marriage of his wife's sister in 1708. Sometime after that he was widowed and did not appear at weddings again until after remarrying in 1714.
>
> In 1716 he and his second wife, Doña Mariana Maldonado, were the matrimonial sponsors of an immigrant from Gibraltar.

In 1716 he was the witness at the double marriage of the Enríquez de Novoa brothers, the sons of a Spanish-born official of the Real Hacienda. One of them married the daughter and the other the granddaughter of Antonio Ruiz de la Vega; the granddaughter was the daughter of a Basque immigrant.

In 1717, when he was the alcalde, he and his fellow alcalde were the witnesses at the double wedding of the daughters of the Basque-born Count of Miraflores, who were marrying immigrants from Toledo and the Santander region respectively.

In 1718 he and his wife were the *padrinos de boda* of the wedding of a man from La Mancha and the daughter of Major Juan Joseph de Castro, from Seville, who also was the husband of his sister-in-law.

Finally in 1721, he and his wife were the marital sponsors of the wedding of still another daughter of the Count of Miraflores, of the wedding of the son of a regidor, and then of the wedding of a *gallego*. Only once—at the wedding of the son of a regidor—had he been a witness or a *padrino de boda* at a wedding not directly connected to immigrants or their children.

The lack of information prevents the identification of most of the local women who married men from Andalucía. Priests did not always record the names of brides' parents, especially in the case of non-elite people, making it impossible to know if they were the daughters of recent immigrants. As a result, only nine of the fifty local women certainly had Spanish-born fathers. One more woman was the daughter of a Canary Islander—perhaps another indicator of the perceived lower status of *isleños*. Three of the brides who married *andaluces* were the daughters of Italians; being members of the commercial community probably accounts for this. Five more women probably had Spanish or European-born fathers. Thus, thirty-three of the fifty local women seem to have belonged to families not connected to recent immigrants.

Why was there less propensity on the part of American-born daughters of immigrants to marry Andalusians as opposed to Basques or Cantabrians? This was probably the result in part of the perceived lower status of most of the people from Andalucía. While the small number of immigrants with commercial or governmental connections may have found it easier to choose wives from within the immigrant community, many of the Andalusians were probably people of lower status and were not merchants or government officials.

At the same time, prosperity as manifested in wealth was undoubtedly another factor of importance. People from Galicia and the Canary Islands, as well as those from Andalucía, who became prosperous would have had a better chance of marrying higher-status people in America. Perhaps prosperity was less common among these groups and thus their status did not rise in Mérida. Finally, some of the local women who married *andaluces* and were not of recent immigrant origins belonged to Mérida's old elite and in some cases were probably from prosperous families. They would have been desirable partners for immigrant men, and Spanish-born men, in turn, would have been somewhat desirable as husbands in the eyes of the old elite.

The marriage records thus reveal that *andaluces* married the children of immigrants much less often than *isleños*, Basques, and Cantabrians. Moreover, they interacted much less often with the immigrant community, judging by their participation in weddings. A few *andaluces* like Andrés Vázquez Moscoso served as matrimonial sponsors or witnesses at many weddings within the community, and others did so once or twice, but the great majority did not even do that.

One can only speculate regarding the causes of this behavior. So here are some speculations. First, as noted, people from Andalucía tended to be of lower ascribed or achieved status compared to that of Basques and Cantabrians. Moreover, as we have seen, they also were less likely than others to "marry up" with local women of the hidalgo class. This had to make them less desirable as matrimonial sponsors and witnesses of marriages. Second, some of the high-status *andaluces* married not just any *doñas* but women from the elite, the descendants of conquistadores and encomenderos from the sixteenth century. Instead of bringing their wives into the immigrant community it was just as likely that they were gradually brought into American society. In any case, the evidence from Mérida suggests that *andaluces* were assimilated into local society faster than any other immigrant group.

The social lives of Garrástegui, Ruiz de la Vega, Rivas Talavera, and Vázquez Moscoso show how weddings and the marriages of daughters of immigrants were the means used to tie immigrant communities together and to create social networks. The sons of the European-born people rarely married women within this group. That was because the daughters of Europeans were being allocated to new immigrant men. For the most part sons married locally born women of high status, especially those belonging to the traditional conquistador-encomendero class. Sons and daughters of immigrants therefore had radically different marriage patterns. This is more evidence for arranged marriages for the daughters of immigrant men.

Marriage records, and hence family history, also demonstrate the importance of women, especially marriageable females, as social capital. Nowhere was this truer than in the case of marriages involving immigrants from Spain. Teenage girls and women in general were valuable assets precisely because they were essential for the maintenance of social class and group identity. Therefore they had to be controlled and protected. Social stratification and Spanish identity relied on parental power. Mothers as well as fathers enforced the rules of their class and saw to it that their daughters married the right people.

Since women are usually entrusted with the task of imparting values and attitudes to children, and since these daughters of immigrants grew up in households originally headed by Europeans, it is hard to imagine that the families had no sense of belonging to a special group distinct from that of other American-born people of distant Spanish ancestry. As we have seen, it was impossible to maintain a Basque, Cantabrian, or Andalusian identity, so a new identity was created. They became Spaniards, people from Spain. This was an identity that barely existed in Spain itself. These were people who were not merely called *españoles*. They had close ties to Spanish-born individuals. These families probably believed themselves to be not "creoles" or "Americans" but genuine Spaniards. Mérida remained to an extent a semi-Spanish city in America.

V. Wealth, Poverty, and Power

Not all immigrants succeeded in acquiring wealth and power. The Englishman Guillermo Parca (William Parker?) was too poor to make a will when he died in 1698. Even gentlemen sometimes died poor. Such was the case of the *isleño* Don Gaspar Díaz Ruiz, a native of San Juan de la Rambla, Tenerife. Although classified as an hidalgo, "he did not make a will because he had no reason to, and he was buried out of charity," that is, using charitable funds. Juan González, of Sanlúcar de Barrameda, died in 1726, the year of an epidemic, but was so poor that he also could not pay for the last rites.[28] It is likely that many more immigrants died poor but left behind no record of that fact. Going to America probably did not raise the standard of living of many, perhaps most, people.

People who accumulate wealth and power tend to show up in documents, and in Mérida the evidence shows that many immigrants became powerful and relatively wealthy. Let us start with the encomienda, which in the past had been the basis of the wealth and status of the Spanish upper class. Many immigrants in fact succeeded in reaching the pinnacle of social status in Yucatán by being named encomenderos. The Count of Miraflores, Pedro de Garrástegui, was granted an encomienda because of his wife's ancestry. This was because the husbands of women who inherited or were granted encomiendas automatically became encomenderos and were expected to perform military service. It was assumed, of course, that females could not fulfill that obligation. Two of the count's sons and two of his daughters, and consequently his sons-in-law, all became encomenderos. So did several of his grandchildren.

Other important immigrants also succeeded in joining the ranks of encomenderos. One of these was Captain Antonio Ruiz de la Vega, who received one apparently because of the merits of his second wife, Doña María del Puerto, who was from the traditional encomendero elite. His daughter Petrona, from his first marriage, also was granted an encomienda. His son-in-law Andrés Vázquez Moscoso like his father-in-law did not acquire that status at first, but after his first wife died he remarried. His second wife was a member of an elite family of encomenderos. Two of the bride's brothers were in that group.

Once again, however, we find evidence suggesting the low status of Canary Islanders. Diego de Rivas Talavera, a leader in the community of *isleños*, did not become an encomendero, and apparently no one from that immigrant group did. On the other hand, the Canary Islanders may have done better when it came to the accumulation of wealth. At the same time, some immigrants from all places and their children ended up wealthy. They did so in part by becoming landowners, selling cattle in the city market, and producing cowhides, honey, and wax for domestic use and for export.

In this way the immigrant group in Mérida apparently differed from that of other places such as Oaxaca and other highland cities that were not mining camps. In Oaxaca City, unlike Mérida, practically all Spanish immigrants were merchants and few of them went into land ownership.[29] Two factors probably account for these differences. First, Oaxaca produced a large quantity of cochineal, which was Mexico's most important export to Europe after silver. It was so valuable that merchants were attracted to the region to get involved almost exclusively in the export business. Many of them never married in Oaxaca, either because they had already married in Spain and intended to return, or because they intended to return and find a wife at home after making money in America. Many of Campeche's merchants were probably similar, and that may have accounted in part for the significant quantity of rental properties in the coastal city. People who are thinking of leaving want to acquire liquid wealth, not real estate. In any case, Yucatán's cloth and wax exports were not as lucrative as cochineal, and the prospects for merchants in Mérida were probably even less promising than in Campeche. Moreover, economic prospects were more diverse than in the coastal city.

The second factor explaining the differences between Yucatán and places like Oaxaca was the existence in the area around Mérida of economic prospects that were more diverse than in Oaxaca and other mountainous areas. In the latter, land for agriculture or stock-raising was scarce, and many provinces in Mesoamerica were similarly inhabited by indigenous people who owned and used most of the land in the valleys. Spaniards found it far from easy to acquire property for stock-raising and agriculture. Some did, of course, but it was easier to do so in Yucatán, where a great deal of space for privately owned estancias existed, especially after the demographic decline following the conquest. There were no mountains to cramp the development of landed estates by limiting the quantity of usable land, most of which continued to be occupied by the indigenous people. In Yucatán ranches could be established almost anywhere where there was a cenote, and the ecology of Yucatán provided the region with hundreds of them. The only barrier to the growth of estancias was the difficulty of getting a license to raise cattle.

Moreover, while Oaxaca and other highland cities were distant from seaports and for that reason could only export goods of high unit value like cochineal, Yucatán could easily export cotton textiles, honey, wax, and leather to Veracruz or to the Canary Islands. Arriving Spaniards thus took advantage of what was available around Mérida and became landowners because they could earn money producing for the market in the provincial capital and potentially for export markets as well. Doing so usually implied permanent settlement in the province. Many, and probably most, immigrant merchants in Mérida apparently realized that it was better to have high status and prosperity in a small province than to return to Spain with only a modest or even a nonexistent fortune. And, of course, it was preferable to returning to live as paupers. Some undoubtedly wished they had stayed home.

Finally, when it came to political power, many immigrants succeeded in occupying the highest offices available to Mérida's upper class. Take, for example, the elective position on the city council of procurator, that is, the city attorney. He represented the city government, and by implication the entire province, before external authorities like the Audiencia of México and the King of Castile. These officials responded to crises. In 1677, 1689, and 1717, for example, the crown tried to abolish the encomienda. In addition, in the 1720s Bishop Juan Gómez de Parada tried to abolish the domestic labor services performed by the Maya for Spanish households.

The city council of Mérida acted vigorously to oppose change and reform. To succeed they needed the services of trusted members of the community to represent their interests in Spain and Mexico City. To whom did they turn when presented with threats to their interests?

They chose immigrants in their midst. During the crisis of 1677 they chose Major Pedro de Cepeda y Lira, a Knight of Calatrava, a native of Toledo who had settled in Mérida and served on the city council, to go to Spain to argue against the new taxes on encomiendas proposed by the crown.[30] In 1689 they chose the *Alférez Real* and regidor of the city council, Don Gaspar de Salazar y Córdoba, the son of an immigrant from elsewhere in New Spain, and Major Regidor Antonio Ayora y Porras, a high-status immigrant from Seville, to defend the encomenderos from new taxes (although it is not clear if they actually made the journey).[31] In 1720 they elected one of their fellow regidores, the Cantabrian Antonio de la Helguera, as procurator to be sent to Spain to argue in favor of the continued existence of the encomienda.[32] In 1722 the city council chose one of the regidores, Basque immigrant Don Juan de Zuazúa y Múxica, to go to Mexico City to argue before the Audiencia against the termination of labor services.

The regidores explained why they chose an immigrant to defend their interests: "Ever since he became a citizen of this City and Province [Zuazúa y Múxica] has demonstrated vigilance, activity, punctuality, and zeal in dedicating himself to His Majesty's service, attending to whatever has been his duty in the positions of infantry captain, alcalde, and currently regidor."[33] These were all signs of his dedication to his new home, and they tell us of the character demanded of those who eventually rose in society and politics.

And in the same year they elected Antonio Ruiz de la Vega as procurator in charge of making the case for the continuation of labor services, and he accompanied Zuazúa y Múxica to Mexico City.[34] Then the city council reelected

Ruiz de la Vega in 1723. They did the same in 1724 and again in 1725. After that, he stepped down, having served an unprecedented four consecutive times as procurator. The old Cantabrian who had gotten married in Mérida in 1683 when he was twenty years old had earned the respect of virtually the entire Hispanic community, both foreign-born and American-born, and was trusted to defend it before Audiencia and king.

It could not have been a coincidence that all but one of those who went to Spain or Mexico City to defend the interests of Hispanic society in Mérida were people from Spain. The elite may have known or suspected that Spanish-born Audiencia judges in Mexico City and the members of the Council of the Indies in Spain held low opinions of people born in America. Those attitudes had emerged in the sixteenth century, and ever since many people from Spain believed that "Spaniards" born in America were not like those born on the Iberian Peninsula. They had been corrupted by the easy living and slothful habits characteristic of the society in which they had been raised.

To protect themselves from such prejudice, the elite found it convenient to be represented by people whose accents would prove their identity as real Spaniards. The need to do so, however, revealed a fundamental reality: people born and raised in America were not like people born and raised in Spain. The *españoles* in America, who lived in the Spanish outpost of colonialism, may have tried to claim to be Spaniards, but the reality was that most of them were Spanish Americans. The environment they lived in transformed them into something that was not truly European.

SEVEN

SOCIAL STATUS
Class and Political Power

ALL SOCIETIES HAVE SOME form of social hierarchy, often in the form of social classes. The identification of those classes in the Hispanic community of colonial Mérida is made possible by analyzing the people according to the categories of capital/wealth, status, and political power.[1] A previous chapter identified the use of status distinctions, and it was clarified that the higher status people, categorized as hidalgos (people referred to as *don* or *doña*) made up approximately one fourth of the Hispanic community. That is probably too large to be considered an upper class, and therefore we must seek ways to identify stratification within that group. That will distinguish an upper class from a middle class.

One way of doing that is to study the exercise and distribution of political power. That is made possible to a certain degree through an analysis of office-holding in city government, for although a royal governor appointed by the king was the chief executive in Yucatán, the city of Mérida also enjoyed political power and exercised it through its city council. An analysis of the patterns of office-holding therefore will permit the identification of those within the group of hidalgos who possessed political power and those who did not or had less. That, in turn, will make it possible to distinguish between upper and middle classes.

I. Cities and City Government

Cities were a quintessentially Iberian form of European settlement in America. Most Hispanic people, including the elite, lived in urban centers rather than on landed estates or on farms scattered across the countryside. Technically non-Indians were not even allowed to live in the villages. Cities were also the focus of economic exchange, for urban markets had commercial hinterlands extending far out into the rural world. Finally, cities were sites of the concentration of political power.

In the most important urban centers, a royal government official exercised power over a wide area, and in all cities a cabildo also exercised power over the urban population and far out in the countryside. A city council therefore represented or ruled over not just a local city but also a hinterland that constituted a region. It was therefore the equivalent of a modern-day Mexican state legislature. It represented the region before the Audiencia (high court) in the capital of a kingdom, before the Council of the Indies in Spain, and before the king himself. It was a vital element of Hispanic American communities.

On the other hand, city governments in Spanish America were not always important. Such was the case, for example, in Guadalajara, where the cabildo inevitably was dominated by the Audiencia established in the same city. Moreover, the city was the capital of the Kingdom of New Galicia, which owed its existence to the silver and gold deposits found in northern Mexico. This meant that the opportunities to become wealthy were so great the people were not willing to waste their time and money on acquiring city council seats that offered few financial returns. Positions as regidor therefore were frequently left vacant.[2] Once again, the poverty of Yucatán played an important role in history. There were few economic opportunities available to people in Mérida, and political power helped to gain access to those scarce opportunities. City government, therefore, was important in colonial Yucatán.

One way of understanding political institutions is to show how they actually operated. Institutionally, cabildos are well studied.[3] To understand the actual functioning of the institution, however, knowledge of the real world and behavior of individual human beings is required. Several excellent studies of the cabildos of colonial Yucatán already exist and will help in the following analysis.[4]

We shall begin where the city councilmen themselves began every January 1: the elections. The municipal leaders met to elect people to the four, and usually five, elective offices that existed. These offices were the first magistrate or justice of the peace (*alcalde de primer voto*), the second magistrate (*alcalde de segundo voto*), the city attorney or procurator (*síndico procurador general*), the granary custodian (*mayordomo del pósito*), and the market inspector (*fiel ejecutor*). The latter position only began to be filled in Mérida in 1708 and after.

The Laws of the Indies, a legal code promulgated by the royal government, provided rules and procedures that all city councils in America were supposed to follow. However, as is usually the case, where there are rules there are ways to get around them. Ana Isabel Martínez Ortega has identified five ways in which the cabildo of Mérida, apparently like most cities in America, contravened or violated the rules:[5]

(1) Only permanent city council members—regidores—were allowed to vote, but in Mérida the practice was to allow the two outgoing alcaldes to vote even if they were not regidores.
(2) No immediate reelection was permitted but took place anyway.
(3) Royal government officials—such as treasury officials and military officers—were not allowed to be on the city council, but in Mérida some of them became regidores and were elected to office despite that prohibition.
(4) The cabildo was supposed to meet once a week but in fact meetings were more sporadic.
(5) No one with a vested interest in the economic activities monitored by the granary custodian or market inspector was supposed to be elected as *mayordomo del pósito* or as *fiel ejecutor*, yet most people elected to those posts in the mid-colonial period were the owners of cattle ranches.

Therefore, in Mérida the only people who were allowed to vote in city elections were the two alcaldes and the regidores. The latter varied in number between twelve and thirteen because of the special status of Don Pedro de Garrástegui, the first Count of Miraflores. He was the treasurer of the Santa Cruzada, a branch of the ecclesiastical administration that sold bulls of indulgence to pay for nonexistent crusades. This was an important source of money for the royal government and somehow he successfully claimed to be an *ex oficio* member of the cabildo. Some members of the city council objected to his claim, but for the most part the first count was successful in being admitted as a regidor until at least 1698. His son, Don Pedro de Garrástegui y Villamil, the second count, succeeded his father as treasurer of the Santa Cruzada and therefore also claimed to be an *ex oficio* member. He became a regidor in 1709. However, there was opposition to his claim, and he was denied preeminence. As a result, he refused to attend meetings after 1712.[6]

Therefore, the total number of voters in city elections in Mérida varied between a minimum of twelve (when both of the alcaldes were regidores and voted in that capacity and the count was not present) and a maximum of fifteen (when neither of the alcaldes was a regidor and the count was present). This naturally meant that the government served primarily the interests of the elite no matter how much these individuals tried to convince themselves and the public that they served the people as a whole.

There are no surviving city council records until 1747, so we do not know for certain how voting was carried out. However, there is no evidence in later documentation that anything had changed from previous decades, and therefore we will assume that the procedures used in the middle of the eighteenth century were roughly the same as those in use a few decades earlier.

On January 1 the governor presided over the meeting and the election, although he had no vote. The outgoing first and second alcaldes voted first. The remaining regidores then voted in order of seniority. Voting was not secret; every councilman's vote was announced in order, so everyone knew how everyone else voted. Experience from other times and places suggests that this was a formula for rancor. People knew who their friends were and perhaps more importantly who were not. So did the governor.

Whom did they elect? They did not elect anyone who was not a member of the hidalgo class or a militia officer. This means that there was close relationship between inherited status and access to political power, as we would expect in a society patterned on contemporary Europe. Only non-hidalgo men who were "ennobled" by military service were eligible for office, thus allowing a small number of non-hidalgo people to cross the class line and enter the higher social classes.

It is important to note that on many occasions the electors chose people from their own ranks—regidores—to fill city offices. As a result, regidores frequently served as elected officials. On other occasions the electors chose people from the community who were citizens (*vecinos*) but not regidores. There is no information about why particular people in the community were chosen, but many of them went on to become regidores, and therefore it would seem that holding an elective office was frequently the first step in a political career and the acquisition of power. Table 7.1 lists the people elected to office between 1696 and 1730 and shows that regidores frequently elected themselves to the executive offices of the cabildo.[7]

During this time period, a total of ninety-five different individuals were elected to serve in municipal offices. No less than seventy-two held the important elective offices of alcalde or procurator. These were the people who

TABLE 7.1: The Elected Officials of Mérida, 1696–1730

OFFICIAL	NUMBER OF TIMES ELECTED	POST(S) HELD
Antonio Ruiz de la Vega	10	alcalde, procurator, mayordomo
Juan del Castillo y Arrúe	8	REGIDOR, alcalde, mayordomo
Gregorio de Aldana	7	REGIDOR, procurator, mayordomo, fiel
Andrés Vázquez Moscoso	6	alcalde, mayordomo
Luis Magaña Dorantes	6	REGIDOR, fiel
Juan de Mendoza	5	REGIDOR, alcalde, fiel
Pedro de Cepeda y Lira	4	alcalde, mayordomo
Juan Ascencio Lazagavaster	4	alcalde, procurator, mayordomo
Juan del Campo	4	REGIDOR, procurator, mayordomo, fiel
Francisco Méndez Pacheco	3	REGIDOR, alcalde, procurator
Manuel Rodríguez Moreno	3	Mayordomo
Alonso de Aranda y Aguayo	3	REGIDOR, fiel
Domingo Urgoitia y Carrillo	3	REGIDOR, procurator, alcalde
Bartolomé de la Garma	2*	procurator, mayordomo
Antonio Casanova	2**	alcalde, procurator
Mateo Carlos de Cárdenas	2	procurator, mayordomo
Antonio de la Helguera	2	REGIDOR, alcalde, procurator
Juan de Fraga y España	2	alcalde, procurator
Pedro de Rivero	2	Alcalde
Alonso Chacón	2	Alcalde
Martín de Mezeta	2	Mayordomo
Pedro Ancona Hinostrosa	2	REGIDOR, alcalde
Juan Solís Casanova	2	alcalde, procurator
Ignacio Chacón y Ascorra	2	alcalde, procurator
Diego Méndez de Raya	2	Mayordomo
Pedro Castellanos	2	alcalde, procurator
Pedro Díaz Dávila	2	alcalde, procurator
Simón de Salazar y Villamil	2	Alcalde

(*Continued*)

TABLE 7.1: *(Continued)*

OFFICIAL	NUMBER OF TIMES ELECTED	POST(S) HELD
Miguel de la Ruela	2	procurator, mayordomo
Pedro de Lizarraga	2	Alcalde
Joseph Bermejo	2	REGIDOR, alcalde
Juan Francisco de Sosa	2	procurator, mayordomo
Iñigo de Mendoza y Vargas	1***	alcalde, procurator
Lucas de Villamil y Vargas	1****	REGIDOR, fiel
Francisco Solís Pacheco	1*****	REGIDOR, alcalde
Francisco Diez de Velasco	1	Alcalde
Juan Carrillo	1	Alcalde
Antonio de Barbosa	1	Procurator
Juan Antonio de Ávila	1	Procurator
Juan Joseph de Castro	1	Alcalde
Juan de Argaiz	1	Procurator
Diego Rodríguez	1	Mayordomo
Fernando Valdés	1	Mayordomo
Pedro Calderón y Robles	1	Alcalde
Pedro Calderón y Garrástegui	1	Procurator
Matías Soto Rubio	1	Alcalde
Nicolás del Puerto	1	REGIDOR, mayordomo
Gaspar de Salazar y Córdova	1	REGIDOR, alcalde
Alonso Chacón y Ascorra	1	Alcalde
Lorenzo de Ávila y Carranza	1	Alcalde
Cayetano de Herrera	1	Mayordomo
Joseph Carrillo	1	Alcalde
Juan Antonio de Zuazúa y Urquizu	1	REGIDOR, procurator
Clemente de Marcos Bermejo	1	Alcalde
Ignacio Solís	1	Alcalde
Cristóbal Herrera	1	REGIDOR, procurator
Simón de Evia	1	Alcalde
Jose Antonio del Campo	1	Procurator
Antonio de Ayora y Porras	1	REGIDOR, mayordomo

OFFICIAL	NUMBER OF TIMES ELECTED	POST(S) HELD
Juan Zuazúa y Múxica	1	REGIDOR, alcalde
Cristóbal de Herrera	1	Procurator
Felipe de Ayora y Argaiz	1	REGIDOR, fiel
Diego López	1	Procurator
Francisco Ortiz del Barrio	1	Alcalde
Francisco Sobrino	1	Alcalde
Miguel de la Paz	1	Mayordomo
Gaspar de Salazar	1	Alcalde
Rodrigo Chacón	1	Mayordomo
Juan Rodríguez Vigario Ortega	1	REGIDOR, alcalde
Andrés Fernández Blanco	1	Mayordomo
Francisco de Mendicuti	1	Alcalde
Carlos de Texada	1	Procurator
Francisco Lirimonte	1	Mayordomo
Diego de Ceballos	1	Alcalde
Nicolás Carrillo	1	REGIDOR, fiel
Ignacio González	1	Mayordomo
Bernabé Solís Barbosa	1	Alcalde
Pedro Garrástegui y Villamil	1	REGIDOR, alcalde
Miguel de Zavalegui y Urzúa	1	Alcalde
Ambrosio de Betancurt	1	Mayordomo
Antonio Solís Barbosa	1	REGIDOR, fiel
Santiago Bolio	1	Alcalde
Joseph de Betancurt	1	Mayordomo
Joaquín de Salazar	1	Alcalde
Joseph Perdomo Betancurt	1	Mayordomo
Gerónimo del Puerto	1	Alcalde
Jacinto de Salazar	1	Alcalde
Gerónimo Mimenza	1	Procurator
Manuel Díaz	1	Mayordomo
Eloy Clemente de Cuenca	1	Alcalde

(Continued)

TABLE 7.1: (*Continued*)

OFFICIAL	NUMBER OF TIMES ELECTED	POST(S) HELD
Joseph de Estrella	1	Mayordomo
Juan Ruiz Pérez	1	Alcalde
Alonso de Echanagucia	1	Alcalde
Diego de Aguayo	1	Procurator
Pedro Cabrera	1	Mayordomo

*Previously elected in 1690 and 1694
** Previously elected in 1686 and 1689
***Previously elected in 1690 and 1694
****Previously elected in 1688
*****Previously elected in 1692

Source: AGI, Escribanía de Cámara 321A, 321B, 321C, 322A, 322B, 323A, 324A, 324B.

ruled the city. The ninety-five people in total filled the 171 offices to which people were elected. (Many people were elected to office more than once.)[8] They would have comprised somewhere between one-quarter and one-third of the total adult male hidalgo population of the city.[9] This means that participation in city government was widespread among the hidalgo class. It demonstrates continued adherence to the Castilian tradition of a patrician class, a group that most members of the hidalgo class probably aspired to.[10] However, there was a marked concentration of power in the hands of a few men. Between 1696 and 1730 thirteen people were elected to office three or more times, and they were elected a total of sixty-six times.[11]

Nevertheless, a substantial proportion of the Hispanic population actually held political office, and this in turn demonstrates the existence of what can be called a middle class: people who frequently were descendants of conquistadors and encomenderos or of government officials and who were classified as members of the hidalgo class. This was a pool of people from whom was drawn those elected to office, and since movement upward into the ruling elite usually began with holding the less important political offices—Mario Góngora has compared this to a *cursus honorum*[12]—the line of separation between the middle class and the ruling elite was permeable and flexible rather than sharply drawn and rigid—as is in the nature of classes as opposed to castes. Nevertheless that line did exist and reflected a class difference because political power usually overlaps with social class. It is possible that the most important line of separation in the social structure of Hispanic society was that between hidalgos—some 20–30 percent of Hispanic society—and everyone else. In a sense, then, Mérida's rulers—the people who actually exercised power—were large in number, for they included both the relatively small number of people in the ruling elite and the much larger group of middle-class people who held office and had a chance of moving up.

The thirteen most often elected people, eight of whom were regidores, along with the rest of the regidores, were the true ruling elite of Mérida between 1694 and 1730.[13] The total number of people in this power elite therefore was twenty-eight (twenty-three regidores plus the five frequently elected men who were not city councilmen). The number, however, is misleading, for some of the men who were elected only once or twice after 1694 had held office in previous years but had ended their political careers by dying or retiring. Similarly, others who served only once or twice in the late 1720s were elected again several times after 1730 but were not yet prominent in the earlier period. Nevertheless, in the thirty-seven years between 1694 and 1730, the thirteen frequently elected men in question, plus fifteen additional regidores who joined the cabildo in 1694 or after, were the dominant people in power.

Who were these elected officials? Some information about them is summarized in Table 7.2. The origins of one of the thirteen—Francisco Méndez Pacheco—could not be certainly identified.[14] Of the remaining twelve, six were from Spain and six were born in Yucatán. At the same time, it should be noted that four of the American-born people were the sons of immigrants, that is, second generation.

The regidores were different in one fundamental way from those elected officials who were not permanent city councilmen: they purchased their positions and held on to them until they resigned or died. They were clearly members of the elite because only people with money could afford to buy these positions. Moreover, none of the regidores or elected officials received a salary. The selling price for a position as regidor was usually 200 pesos. However, if the post also included something extra—such as the position as marshal (*alguacil mayor*), treasurer (*depositario*), or royal standard-bearer (*alférez mayor*)—the price went up, sometimes as high as between 500 and 1,300 pesos. When Alférez Mayor Don Juan del Castillo y Cano, the son of Don Juan del Castillo y Arrúe (the previous *alférez mayor*), gave up his position in 1737, it was passed on for 266 pesos plus an additional fee—called a *media anata* (supposedly half a year's salary that was charged even if the post had no salary)—of 53 pesos.[15] The special duties of marshal and treasurer gave those officials legal ways to earn

TABLE 7.2: Geographical Origins of the Thirteen Most-Elected Officials of the City Government, 1696–1730

Antonio Ruiz de la Vega	CANTABRIA
Juan del Castillo y Arrúe	YUCATÁN (Second Generation)
Gregorio de Aldana	ANDALUCÍA (Seville)
Andrés Vázquez Moscoso	ANDALUCÍA (Seville)
Luis Magaña Dorantes	YUCATÁN, of parents born in Mérida
Juan de Mendoza	YUCATÁN, of parents born in Mérida
Pedro de Cepeda y Lira	YUCATÁN (Second Generation)
Juan Asencio Lazagavaster	BASQUE COUNTRY
Juan del Campo	CANTABRIA
Manuel Rodríguez Moreno	ANDALUCÍA (Granada)
Alonso de Aranda y Aguayo	YUCATÁN, (Second Generation)
Domingo Urgoitia y Carrillo	YUCATÁN (Second Generation)
Francisco Méndez Pacheco	UNIDENTIFIED

Source: AGA, Matrimonios, Españoles, Libros 4–7.

money from holding their offices. Especially valuable was the position as the city council scribe (*escribano*), who collected fees for certifying or recording anything.[16] Scribes, however, were non-voting members of city government.

A regidor could pass his post on to a designated successor. To do this he resigned and designated a successor, who could buy the position at half price. That allowed sons to succeed fathers and sons-in-law to succeed fathers-in-law, thereby perpetuating a family's political power. This means that the post of *alférez mayor*, passed on from Juan del Castillo y Cano for 266 pesos, would have cost an outsider 532 pesos. That was a lot of money at the time.

Martínez Ortega analyzed the regidores in the cabildos of 1705 and 1725 in terms of their geographical origins, ownership of estancias, and relationship to the encomienda system. She concluded that they were mostly people born in America and that the dominance of the American-born over the foreign-born increased throughout the eighteenth century.[17] However, because she could not consult marriage records, she could not identify the origins of all the regidores in the early eighteenth century. These documents, aided by petitions for encomiendas, allow for the identification of the geographical origins of all but two of the thirty-three persons who served as permanent city councilmen between 1694 and 1730.[18] The data are summarized in Table 7.3.

TABLE 7.3: The Origins of the Regidores of Mérida, 1694–1730

BORN IN YUCATÁN OF FATHERS BORN IN YUCATÁN (8)
    Nicolás del Puerto
    Juan de la Cámara Osorio
    Luis Magaña Dorantes
    Francisco Solís Casanova
    Nicolás Carrillo de Albornoz
    Juan de Mendoza
    Antonio Solís Barbosa
    Juan Rodríguez Vigario Ortega

SECOND GENERATION IMMIGRANTS (8)
    (BORN IN AMERICA OF FATHERS BORN IN SPAIN, PORTUGAL, OR NEW SPAIN)
    Alf. Mayor Gaspar de Salazar y Córdova
    Lucas de Villamil y Vargas
    Domingo Rodríguez Vigario Bohórquez
    Domingo Urgoitia y Carrillo
    Felipe de Ayora y Porras Argaiz
    Alonso de Aranda y Aguayo
    Juan del Castillo y Arrúe
    Pedro Garrástegui Villamil y Vargas

BORN IN SPAIN OR CANARY ISLANDS (15):

Pedro Garrástegui Oleaga, Count of Miraflores	BASQUE COUNTRY
Diego de Aranda y Aguayo	ANDALUCÍA
Cristóbal Maldonado Jurado	ANDALUCÍA
Antonio de Ayora y Porras	ANDALUCÍA
Martín de Echanagucia	BASQUE COUNTRY
Pedro de Ancona Hiniestrosa	ANDALUCÍA
Matías Beltrán de Mayorga	ANDALUCÍA
Cristóbal Herrera y Córdova	CANARY ISLANDS
Gregorio de Aldana	ANDALUCÍA
Juan Antonio de Zara y Urquizu	BASQUE COUNTRY
Antonio de la Helguera	CANTABRIA
Juan Zuazúa y Múxica	BASQUE COUNTRY

(*Continued*)

TABLE 7.3: (Continued)

Juan del Campo	CANTABRIA
José González de la Madriz	CANTABRIA
Juan Pardío Ordóñez	CANARY ISLANDS
UNIDENTIFIED (2)	
Francisco Méndez Pacheco	
Francisco de Zea Moscoso	

Source: AGA, Matrimonios, Españoles, Libros 4–7.

The table shows that sixteen of the thirty-one identifiable regidores were born in America, while thirteen were from Spain and two from the Canary Islands. Thus the American-born slightly outnumbered—sixteen to fifteen—those from across the Atlantic. This is similar to the pattern among the elected officials.

However, identity is always complicated. Marta Espejo-Ponce Hunt and Martínez Ortega perceptively chose to distinguish between "creoles," whose fathers were American-born, and those whose fathers were Spanish immigrants.[19] This is a relevant distinction, since as we have seen in the previous chapter, the sons of immigrants, especially the important ones, belonged to colonies-within-a-colony of the foreign-born. Almost always, three of the four grandparents of these American-born sons of immigrants were Spaniards who never came to America, and they were all tied into immigrant communities in Mérida. Some of them may even have learned to speak some Basque, *Cántabro*, or *Guanche*. These facts undoubtedly contributed to these people's sense of identity. All of this would also have applied to the three frequently elected second-generation officials as well.

It turns out that six of the regidores born in America were the sons of immigrants from Spain, one was the son of an immigrant from Portugal, and two others were the sons of newcomers from other Spanish colonies in America. It is hard to imagine that all the second-generation immigrants would have joined up with those born in Yucatán of fathers born in Yucatán to form a majority that would run roughshod over the interests of the foreign-born. For example, the father, maternal grandfather, and father-in-law of Don Juan del Castillo y Arrúe were from Spain, which made it unlikely that the most powerful regidor would consistently work against the interests of the

Spanish-born. Similarly, it is unlikely that the second generation would always join with the foreign-born to work against the other group. Moreover, as we have seen, when the upper class confronted a great threat to its interests in 1677, 1689, and the 1720s, it turned to the Spanish-born people to go to Mexico City or Spain to argue against the abolition of the encomienda or the reforms proposed by Bishop Gómez de Parada. The two groups worked quite well together when they had to.

The names of the regidores of Mérida between 1683 and 1730 are included in Table 7.4 in roughly the chronological order in which they joined the ranks of the permanent city councilmen. As noted, not all of the fifteen transatlantic immigrants were from Spain, for two were from the Canary Islands. The Spanish-born included six Andalusians, four Basques, and three Cantabrians, and as noted two other American-born people were the sons of immigrants from other places in New Spain.[20]

II. The Power Elite and the Transfer of Power, 1694–1729

As we have seen, the ruling elite of Mérida was composed of twenty-eight men (twenty-three regidores and five others who were frequently elected). No women were in the group for the simple reason that females could not hold public office. However, it would be misleading to conclude that women were unimportant. Men frequently listen to their mothers, wives, and sisters, and in this way the female members of Hispanic society may have exercised power indirectly. Of course, there is no way to know for certain.

It is known, however, that women sometimes did occupy positions in institutions. For example, Doña Magdalena Magaña, the widow of Accountant of the Royal Treasury Don Clemente de Marcos Bermejo, became the treasurer of the Tribunal de Indios upon the death of her husband, the former treasurer. She held on to that position for decades and regularly collected a large annual salary of 496 pesos 5 reales. She was even subjected to the usual residencia that all officials of the Tribunal had to undergo.[21] Similarly, Doña Micaela de Villamil y Vargas, the Countess of Miraflores, became the treasurer of the Santa Cruzada upon the death of her husband, the first count. Only later did her son, the second count, take up the post.[22] Both of these positions as treasurer were of the type that could be purchased, and they therefore could be passed on to an heir. It is possible that these women were mere figureheads who delegated the work to their sons, but their active participation can by no means be discounted.

TABLE 7.4: The Regidores of Mérida, 1683–1730 and the Year of Joining the City Council

(1) Alf. Mayor Gaspar de Salazar y Córdova (since at least 1683)
(2) Nicolás del Puerto (since at least 1683)
(3) Pedro Garrástegui Oleaga, Count of Miraflores (since at least 1683)
(4) Diego de Aranda y Aguayo (since at least 1683)
(5) Cristóbal Maldonado Jurado (since at least 1683)
(6) Martín de Echanagucia (since at least 1683)
(7) Antonio de Ayora y Porras (since at least 1683)
(8) Pedro de Ancona Hiniestrosa (since at least 1683)
(9) Matías Beltrán de Mayorga (since at least 1683)
(10) Juan de la Cámara Osorio (1688)
(11) Lucas de Villamil y Vargas (1688–91, again since 1694)
(12) Domingo Rodríguez Vigario Bohórquez (1695–1705, returned in 1706)
(13) Luis Magaña Dorantes (1695)
(14) Cristóbal Herrera y Córdova (1695)
(15) Alonso de Aranda y Aguayo (1700)
(16) Felipe de Ayora y Porras (1701)
(17) Francisco Solís Casanova (1705)
(18) Francisco Méndez Pacheco (1705)
(19) Juan del Castillo y Arrúe (1705)
(20) Gregorio de Aldana (1706)
(21) Nicolás Carrillo de Albornoz (1706)
(22) Juan de Mendoza (1706)
(23) Juan Rodríguez Vigario Ortega (1706)
(24) Juan Antonio de Zara y Urquizu (1709)
(25) Pedro Garrástegui Villamil y Vargas (1709)
(26) Antonio de la Helguera (1715)
(27) Juan Zuazúa y Múxica (1716)
(28) Juan del Campo (1720)
(29) Joseph González de la Madriz (1722)
(30) Antonio Solís Barbosa (1724)
(31) Domingo Urgoitia y Carrillo (1725)
(32) Juan Pardío Ordóñez (1726)
(33) Francisco de Zea Moscoso (1729)

Source: AGI, Escribanía de Cámara 321A, 321B, 321C, 322A, 322B, 323A, 324A, 324B.

It is also important to note that although many regidores rarely or never held elective office and therefore did not hold the reins of power as alcaldes or procuradores, they were nevertheless powerful in other ways. They participated in the approval or rejection of city council measures that affected the large hinterland of Mérida as well as the city itself. Also, along with the regidores who held office frequently, they were the ones who elected people to the important positions. Without their support, people did not get to hold the levers of power. Thus, like wives, mothers, and sisters, they were important people who participated, even if behind the scenes, in the exercise of power.

Since the number of people within this power elite was small, it is possible to explain in detail the process of political and social mobility by focusing on the men frequently elected to office and those who became regidores during the years from 1694 to 1730. There were only twenty-three men who joined the city council after 1694 and before 1730. In addition, five others who were frequently elected but who were not regidores have to be added to the group. An examination of these twenty-eight individuals will identify the characteristics that were necessary to get into the city's ruling elite. The analysis will allow us to observe the process of passing power on from one generation to the next.

Other scholars have demonstrated that a certain quantity of wealth was always a sine qua non for entry into the ruling elite. However, it is important to distinguish between wealth and status.[23] They do not always go together. It has already been shown that some people of the hidalgo class could not afford to pay for the last rites of the Church. Therefore it will be particularly important to demonstrate not just that wealthy people got on the city council, as is to be expected, but also that people of achieved, rather than inherited, high social status also became members of the political elite. The acquisition of a combination of wealth, status, and power will therefore be the primary focus of the analysis.

Table 7.5 summarizes information regarding inherited and achieved status, first of the thirteen most-elected men in city government, and second of the remaining fifteen regidores who served on the cabildo between 1694 and 1730. Descendants of conquistadors and/or encomenderos were counted as people who had inherited their positions. Two Andalusian immigrants who were government officials, another one who seems to have had hidalgo status even before he married and joined the political elite, and two Canary Islanders who were militia officers, as well as all of these people's Spanish-born sons, are also counted among those whose positions were inherited. Finally, the sons

TABLE 7.5: The Power Elite of Mérida, 1694–1730

OFFICIAL	NATURE OF ACQUISITION OF STATUS
Lucas Villamil y Vargas	Inherited
Antonio Ruiz de la Vega (Cantabrian)	Achieved
Juan del Castillo y Arrúe	Inherited
Gregorio de Aldana (Andalusian)	Inherited
Andrés Vázquez Moscoso (Andalusian)	Inherited
Luis Magaña Dorantes	Inherited
Juan de Mendoza	Inherited
Pedro de Cepeda y Lira	Inherited
Juan Ascencio Lazagavaster (Basque)	Achieved
Juan del Campo (Cantabrian)	Achieved
Francisco Méndez Pacheco (unknown origin)	Probably Achieved
Manuel Rodríguez Moreno (Andalusian)	Achieved
Alonso de Aranda y Aguayo	Inherited
Domingo Urgoitia y Carrillo	Inherited
Domingo Rodríguez Vigario Bohórquez	Inherited
Cristóbal Herrera y Córdova (Canary Islander)	Inherited
Felipe de Ayora y Porras	Inherited
Francisco Solís Casanova	Inherited
Nicolás Carrillo de Albornoz	Inherited
Juan Rodríguez Vigario Ortega	Inherited
Juan Antonio de Zara y Urquizu (Basque)	Achieved
Pedro de Garrástegui y Villamil,	Inherited
Antonio de la Helguera y Castillo (Cantabrian)	Achieved
Juan de Zuazúa y Múxica (Basque)	Achieved
José González de la Madriz (Cantabrian)	Achieved
Antonio Solís Barbosa	Inherited
Juan Pardío Ordóñez (Canary Islander)	Inherited
Francisco de Zea Moscoso	Inherited

Source: AGA, Matrimonios, Españoles, Libros 4–7; AGI, México 888, 892, 998, 1020, 3083.

of people who had achieved their position were included among those who inherited their position, because that is exactly what they did.

All Cantabrians are counted among those who achieved their position. This is because they were merchants, and as such they did not have high status in Spain but acquired it in Mérida once they possessed wealth and served as officers in the militia. Basques are also counted as people who achieved their position, because although they were supposedly hidalgos in Spain, they had to acquire wealth in America in order to join Yucatán's ruling elite.

This table shows that entry into the power elite was twice as likely the result of inheritance rather than of accomplishment. Nevertheless, at least eight men—and nine if we count Francisco Méndez Pacheco, who probably achieved his position—did succeed in getting into the group without being born into it. At the same time, what is striking is something that apparently did not happen very often: social mobility upward for men born in Yucatán who were not born into the hidalgo class. There is only one possible example of native-born social mobility—that of Francisco Méndez Pacheco—but his origins are unclear and therefore we cannot be sure that he was born into the non-hidalgo class. Even if he were not originally of hidalgo status, however, his case would be the exception that proves the rule: a man who was not considered worthy of being called *don* had little chance of becoming a member of the power elite.

It has often been assumed that in colonial Spanish America those in higher social classes tended to perpetuate themselves within that class and to exclude everyone else. The evidence from Mérida confirms that in two-thirds of the cases. Social mobility upward in fact did take place, but it usually involved merchants who had become wealthy after arriving in Yucatán and had held officer rank in the militia. Then their children became members of the hidalgo class. The same process of "ennoblement" through military service also applied occasionally to locally born people who were not hidalgos but who acquired wealth and became militia officers in this "society organized for war."

The information presented in Table 7.1 suggests that some degree of power sharing took place among the members of the large hidalgo class. As we have seen, ninety-five different individuals served in elective office in Mérida between 1696 and 1730, and that might have been as much as one-third of the total number of adult male hidalgos. Of course, the people in the power elite received the lion's share of offices, but an extraordinary number of others were allowed or enjoyed some participation in government. Perhaps some of them were people whose families had fallen out of the top of the elite, while others may have been experiencing limited upward social mobility as a result of the accumulation of some wealth. If the latter married women with elite ancestors, then their chances, as well as those of their sons, of moving further up were enhanced. Indeed, by this point in history the number of people who were descendants of conquistadors and/or encomenderos was large and growing. Anyone who married into this group had a chance of moving further up the social scale, and their children would have been even more favored— if the family managed to hang on to wealth. Otherwise, social mobility was downward.

Another striking feature of social mobility and political power revealed in the table, as already noted, is that a significant number of outsiders came to Yucatán and quickly joined the local elite. This did not make Mérida unique, however, for seventeenth-century Santiago de Guatemala had the same experience of the importance of immigrants, especially merchants, in the city council.[24] Presumably many Spanish American cities were similar in this respect.

In the case of Mérida, it must be noted that not all of these outsiders who joined the elite experienced social mobility. That is because some of the immigrant regidores were already men of high status before they stepped off the boat in America. But non-elite immigrants certainly had to achieve economic success and acquire some wealth before they could acquire higher status and political power. Only then could they be accepted as suitable members of the upper class.

Of course, the immigrants who achieved social mobility and acquired political power had started with important advantages over other Hispanic people. It is likely that they were all literate, while many people in Mérida, even people classified as españoles, were not. In many cases, the outsiders quickly joined already existing commercial establishments and even married the daughters of the owners. In some cases it seems that these connections were the motivating factor behind the decision to leave the home country and settle in Yucatán. Upon arrival they associated with people who had capital, and they soon prospered through their connections. American-born men could not do this as easily. Many of them must have lacked such connections. In other words, people with social capital had access to resources that helped them accumulate economic capital.

III. Social Networks and Genealogies of Power

Because Mérida had a relatively small Hispanic population in the late seventeenth and early eighteenth centuries, it is possible to carry out a class analysis in the way suggested by Francisco Chacón Jiménez: "to know the processes of social reproduction by bringing to bear social genealogies that explain social mobility and the networks that constitute and integrate individuals through families."[25] This reveals the reality of social classes. The family histories of the regidores and elected officials show how the ruling elites sometimes perpetuated their hold on political power and kept their families within the group and within the upper class. Table 7.6 summarizes some of this information. Six of the regidores in the group[26] had sons who became regidores, although the sons did not always succeed or replace their fathers immediately. At least one regidor[27] was the son of a regidor from a previous generation (before the time period being considered), and several others were probably in a similar situation. Still others[28] had sons who became regidores in the next generation (beyond the time period being considered). Furthermore, many of these city councilmen were chosen to serve in elective offices, which probably meant that many had voted for themselves or for their sons. Still more regidores were the sons of the elected officials of the cabildo,[29] and many of the elected officials of the cabildo were the sons of regidores. Finally, some of the elected officials who were not regidores had sons who also became elected officials.

This information demonstrates the process of social reproduction, that is, how it was possible in many cases to maintain the ruling elite by passing power and wealth on to the next generation. However, it was not always possible to pass power on from father to son. Demographic factors were an important cause of this apparent discontinuity. Some regidores and elected officials had no children or no male children. Others, like Don Luis Magaña Dorantes and Don Pedro Garrástegui y Villamil, had no surviving legitimate sons to inherit their positions. The high death rate in Yucatán meant that not all male children survived long enough to replace their fathers.

Social factors also contributed to the failure to produce suitable successors. Some surviving sons for one reason or another left Mérida or did not go into political life. They did not join the ruling elite. Some of these may have married women judged to be of unacceptable character or status. Other sons

TABLE 7.6: Family Power: The Generational Transfer of Power From Regidores and/or Elected Officials to Relatives

PERSON AND POSITION	FAMILY CONNECTIONS
Gaspar de Salazar y Córdova, Regidor, alcalde	Brother of alcalde
	Father of alcalde
Francisco Solís Casanova, Regidor	Son of regidor
	Father of regidor
	Brother of alcalde
Francisco Antonio de Ancona, Regidor	Father of regidor
Diego de Aranda y Aguayo, Regidor	Father of regidor
Juan del Castillo y Arrúe, Regidor, alcalde (elected 8 times)	Grandson of alcalde
	Son of alcalde
	Father of regidor
Martín de Echanagucia, Regidor	Father of alcalde
Pedro Gárrastegui y Oleaga, Regidor	Father of regidor, alcalde
Nicolás Carrillo de Albornoz, Regidor	Father of regidor
Domingo Urgoitia y Carrillo, Procurator, Alcalde	Father of regidor
Alonso Chacón, Alcalde (2 times)	Father of alcalde (2 times)
Clemente de Marcos Bermejo, Alcalde	Father of regidor, alcalde
	Father of alcalde (other son)
Juan Rodríguez Vigario Ortega, Regidor	Son of regidor
Pedro Calderón y Robles, Alcalde	Father of regidor, procurator

Source: AGA, Matrimonios, Españoles, Libros 4–7; AGI, México 888, 892, 998, 1020, 3083.

became priests, thereby removing themselves from legitimate procreation. And surely some men lived lives of dissipation and thereby disqualified themselves for consideration as city fathers.

This helps explain why the ruling group in Mérida was part of an upper class but not of a caste. Classes are maintained and characterized by the admission of new people and the exit of others. The importance of the entry of new people is demonstrated in Table 7.7, which summarizes the geographical origins of the grandparents of twenty-six of the twenty-eight men who made up the power elite—twenty-one regidores and five others who were elected three times or more to the important posts of alcalde and procurator in

TABLE 7.7: The Grandparents of The Power Elite

PERSON IN ELITE	NUMBER OF GRANDPARENTS BORN IN YUCATÁN
Nicolás Carrillo de Albornoz, Regidor	4
Luis Magaña Dorantes, Regidor	4
Juan de Mendoza, Regidor	4
Antonio Solís Barbosa, Regidor	4
Francisco Solís Casanova, Regidor	3
Juan Rodríguez Vigario Ortega, Regidor	3
Lucas de Villamil y Vargas, Regidor	2
Alonso de Aranda y Aguayo, Regidor	2, 3, or 4*
Pedro de Cepeda y Lira	2
Domingo Urgoitia Carrillo, Regidor	2
Domingo Rodríguez Vigario Bohórquez, Regidor	2
Felipe de Ayora y Porras, Regidor	2
Pedro Garrástegui y Villamil, Regidor	2
Juan del Castillo y Arrúe, Regidor	1
Antonio Ruiz de la Vega	0
Andrés Vázquez Moscoso	0
Gregorio de Aldana, Regidor	0
Juan Ascencio Lazagavaster	0
Juan del Campo, Regidor	0
Manuel Rodríguez Moreno	0
Cristóbal Herrera y Córdoba, Regidor	0
Juan Antonio de Zara y Urquizu, Regidor	0
Antonio de la Helguera, Regidor	0
Juan de Zuazúa y Múxica, Regidor	0
José González de la Madriz, Regidor	0
Juan Pardío Ordóñez, Regidor	0
Francisco Méndez Pacheco, Regidor	?
Francisco de Zea Moscoso, Regidor	?

* The mother of Alonso de Aranda y Aguayo, Doña María Mijangos Cabrera, could not be identified as born in Yucatán or born somewhere else.

Source: Valdés Acosta, *A través de las centurias*; Archivo General del Arzobispado, Libros de Bautismos de Españoles; Libros de Matrimonios de Españoles.

Mérida between 1694 and 1730. (The ancestry of two of the twenty-eight people in the power elite could not be identified, and the maternal grandparents of one of the remaining twenty-six also could not be identified.) This group was clearly upper-class in nature, for fifteen of them were encomenderos. If these twenty-six people were the product of perfectly endogamous marriage practices, then all 104 of their grandparents would have been born in Yucatán.

At most 39 of the 104 grandparents—37.5 percent—were born in Yucatán. At least 63 of the 104—60.6 percent—were born in Spain (53–55), the Canary Islands (4), Portugal (3), Italy (1), or somewhere in New Spain other than Yucatán (2).[30] It is therefore inaccurate to argue that the conquistadors and early colonists established themselves as a caste that practiced endogamy and remained as the upper class throughout the colonial period and even after.[31] Stephen Webre has also shown this to be inaccurate in the case of Santiago de Guatemala.[32] Far from practicing endogamy, people in the upper class in Mérida displayed a high tendency toward exogamy, that is, the opposite. The upper class did not reproduce itself socially from one generation to the next without admitting outsiders. One suspects that the same was true elsewhere in Spanish America.

Outsiders or their children therefore moved in and sometimes moved up into the upper class. Social mobility was upward for some but downward for others. It is likely that in these latter cases the Spanish system of partible inheritance—all children had the right to a share of the inheritance—caused the fragmentation of wealth, making downward social mobility a stark reality. Similarly, as we have seen, wealthy families could afford to found capellanías, and the need to pay for them would have reduced family wealth. Eventually this could have resulted in social mobility downward, as some families no longer had the wealth to stay in the upper class. Moreover, not everyone was eligible to move into the upper class. Entrance through marriage was carefully controlled by parents, who to a great extent had the power to select their children's choice of spouse. As we have seen, parental power was a mechanism for maintaining the upper class.

The absence of sons to replace them meant that daughters were assets that fathers used to maintain their family's place in the upper class and thereby maintain the class structure. The marriage of daughters was probably the most significant way in which the upper class admitted new members to its ranks. This explains the large proportion of foreign-born men on the city council. Of course, most male immigrants did not enter into the upper class, but a surprising number of them did and—especially in the case of Basques and Cantabrians—did so quickly. This was accomplished through marriage, for practically all of the foreign-born regidores had married well, and as we have seen in a previous chapter, they almost always married the daughters of previous immigrants who had experienced success. Women as social capital were valuable to acquire from the point of view of men who were not from the upper class, for they provided entry into the elite. They also paid dividends, from the point of view of parents, because they brought high-quality sons-in-law into the family.

This reveals the great importance in Hispanic society of social networks resulting from marriage. Among the most important of these, as we have seen in previous chapters, was that between fathers-in-law (*suegros*) and sons-in-law (*yernos*). In twentieth-century small-town Andalucía—which probably shared many cultural characteristics of other Hispanic societies in the past—daughters-in-law did not seem to be particularly important, because social life tended to be oriented more around the family of the wife than of the husband. The other side of the coin, of course, was that a son-in-law was drawn into the family of the father-in-law. It was said that through marriage a father did not lose a daughter but gained a son.[33] The same thing was and is said in many societies, but in a matrifocal Hispanic society, especially in a family of wealth and high social standing, this was more of a reality than an irrelevant expression of consolation at a wedding. We have already noted the experience of Captain Antonio Ruiz de la Vega, who married four of his daughters to Spanish immigrants and then collaborated financially with at least three of his sons-in-law. His family serves as a good example of this in practice.

Sons-in-law certainly had many functions other than helping out in business. In some cases they could be trusted to be fair executors of someone's estate if no close blood relative was at hand. The *isleño* merchant Don Pedro Cabrera Calderón named his son-in-law, fellow Canary Islander Don Domingo Fernández Rico, as executor when he made his will in 1728. Cabrera Calderón had two daughters, one of whom had married Fernández Rico, but women were not permitted to serve as executors. His other daughter and his two sons were not married, which probably means that they were too young to take up important roles in society.[34] Then, when Cabrera Calderón's other daughter married, Fernández Rico and his wife served as the matrimonial sponsors.[35]

Another important relationship resulting from marriage was that of matrimonial sponsors. Usually these people were a married couple some years senior to the people getting married. For immigrants such sponsors were very important and potentially useful; after all, their baptismal godparents (*padrinos*) were useless because they were on the other side of the ocean. An important step for most newcomers was to get married, for by doing so they were declaring themselves to be members of local society. They were no longer simply *residentes* (residents) but *vecinos* (citizens or permanent residents). By joining the community they were recognized as being committed to that community, and that commitment was manifested through marriage.

In Mérida, as in twentieth-century Andalusia, marriage thus brought the groom into a relationship with a matrimonial sponsor as well as with a father-in-law.[36] The groom and the *padrino de boda* were expected to help and support each other. In many cases, both incoming immigrants and locally born men moved into the ruling elite with the help of their matrimonial sponsors as well as that of their fathers-in-law. Establishing such relationships was not just a way for people on the way up to enlist important supporters. It was also a way for people already in the elite to gain new supporters.

The importance of such social networks is evident in the case of Don Juan del Castillo y Arrúe. For his first marriage in 1691, his matrimonial sponsor was Major Juan Antonio Chacón, who was the alcalde at the time. After the death of his first wife, he remarried in 1711, and his second *padrino de boda* was Captain Francisco Solís Casanova, a fellow regidor. In turn, Castillo y Arrúe served as the matrimonial sponsor of no fewer than sixteen married couples. He sponsored people of high and low status: members of the locally born elite, humble people connected to his household, and immigrants from Spain and England.

The social network that tied many members of the power elite together into the upper class is demonstrated in Table 7.8. Eight of the regidores who served during this time period—one-fourth of the total—were the sons-in-law of previous regidores, while three other regidores were the sons-in-law of alcaldes. Moreover, nine regidores were the fathers-in-law of people elected to the important offices of alcalde and/or procurator.

Matrimonial sponsorships were also of significance as social and political relationships within this social network: seven regidores had *padrinos de boda* who were previous or fellow regidores. Eleven regidores, alcaldes, or procurators had matrimonial sponsors who were also regidores, alcaldes, or procurators.

TABLE 7.8: Social Networks of Political Power in Mérida, 1690–1730: Fathers-in-Laws, Sons-in-Law, and Matrimonial Sponsors (*Padrinos De Boda*)

Gaspar de Salazar y Córdova, Regidor
    Father-in-law of alcalde/procurator (Ignacio Chacón Ascora)
Pedro Garrástegui y Oleaga, Regidor
    Father-in-law of alcalde (Pedro Calderón y Robles)
    Father-in-law of regidor (José González de la Madriz)
    Padrino de boda of regidor (Lucas de Villamil y Vargas)
Diego de Aranda y Aguayo, Regidor
    Father-in-law of regidor (Matías Beltrán de Mayorga)
    Father-in-law of regidor (Lucas de Villamil y Vargas)
Cristóbal Maldonado Jurado, Regidor
    Son-in-law of regidor (Pedro de Lara)
    Father-in-law of alcalde (Juan José de Castro)
Matías Beltrán de Mayorga, Regidor
    Son-in-law of regidor (Diego Aranda y Aguayo)
    Father-in-law of regidor (Felipe de Ayora)
    Father-in-law of regidor (Zara y Urquizu)
    Father-in-law of a regidor (Del Campo)
Juan de la Cámara Osorio, Regidor
    Father-in-law of procurator/mayordomo (Juan Francisco de Sosa)
Lucas de Villamil, Regidor
    Son-in-law of regidor (Diego de Aranda y Aguayo)
    Son-in-law of regidor (Pedro de Cepeda y Lira)
    Padrino de boda of regidor (Felipe de Ayora)
    Padrino de boda of regidor (Nicolás Carrillo de Albornoz)
    Padrino de boda of regidor (Juan del Campo)
    Padrino de boda of regidor (José González de la Madriz)
    Sponsored by regidor (Pedro Garrástegui y Oleaga)
    Sponsored by governor (Juan José de Vértiz y Hortañón)
Domingo Rodríguz Vigario Bohórquez, Regidor
    Father-in-law of procurator/mayordomo (Mateo Carlos de Cárdenas)
Cristóbal Herrera y Córdoba, Regidor
    Son-in-law of lieutenant governor (Francisco Antonio de Ancona)

(Continued)

TABLE 7.8: *(Continued)*

Alonso de Aranda y Aguayo, Regidor, Elected 3 times
    Sponsored by regidor/alcalde (Juan del Castillo)
Felipe de Ayora y Porras, Regidor
    Son-in-law of regidor (Matías Beltrán de Mayorga)
    Sponsored by regidor (Lucas de Villamil y Vargas)
Francisco Solís Casanova, Regidor
    Padrino de boda of regidor, alcalde (Juan del Castillo)
Francisco Méndez Pacheco, Regidor
    Father-in-law of alcalde (Gerónimo del Puerto)
Juan del Castillo y Arrúe, Regidor, alcalde, mayordomo, fiel (elected 8 times)
    Father-in-law of regidor (Antonio Solís Barbosa)
    Padrino de boda of regidor (Alonso de Aranda y Aguayo)
    Father-in-law of alcalde (and future regidor [1731]) (Joseph de Marcos Bermejo)
    Sponsored by alcalde (Juan Antonio Chacón)
    Padrino de boda of alcalde (Juan José de Castro)
    Sponsored by regidor (Francisco Solís Casanova)
Gregorio de Aldana y Malpica, Regidor, Elected 4 times (Procurator, mayordomo, fiel)
    Father-in-law of mayordomo (Ignacio González)
Nicolás Carrillo de Albornoz, Regidor
    Sponsored by regidor (Lucas de Villamil y Vargas)
    Father-in-law of procurator (Gerónimo de Mimenza)
Juan Antonio Zara y Urquizu, Regidor
    Son-in-law of regidor (Matías Beltrán de Mayorga)
Pedro Garrástegui Villamil y Vargas, Regidor
    Son-in-law of alcalde (second marriage)
Antonio de la Helguera, Regidor, Elected 2 times, alcalde, procurator
    Father-in-law of procurator (Pedro Calderón y Garrástegui)
    Father-in-law of regidor (Miguel de Zavalegui)
    Padrino de boda of procurator (Francisco Ortiz del Barrio)
Juan del Campo, Regidor, Elected 4 times, procurator, mayordomo, fiel
    Son-in-law of regidor (Matías Beltrán de Mayorga)
    Sponsored by regidor (Lucas de Villamil y Vargas)

José González de la Madriz, Regidor
    Son-in-law of Regidor (Pedro Garrástegui y Oleaga)
    Sponsored by Regidor (Lucas de Villamil y Vargas)
Antonio Solís Barbosa, Regidor
    Son-in-law of regidor (Juan del Castillo)
    Sponsored by alcalde (and future regidor) (Joseph Bermejo)

FREQUENTY ELECTED OFFICIALS WHO WERE NOT REGIDORES

Antonio Ruiz de la Vega, Elected 10 times, Alcalde, procurator, mayordomo
    Father-in-law, padrino de boda of alcalde elected six times (Andrés Vázquez Moscoso)
    Father-in-law of alcalde (elected twice) (Pedro Lizarraga)
    Father-in-law of alcalde (elected once) (Juan Ruiz Pérez)
    Padrino de boda of mayordomo (elected three times) (Manuel Rodríguez Moreno)
Andrés Vázquez Moscoso, Elected 6 times, alcalde, mayordomo
    Son-in-law of alcalde/procurator (Antonio Ruiz de la Vega)
    Sponsored by alcalde/procurator (Antonio Ruiz de la Vega)
Pedro de Cepeda y Lira, Alcalde, mayordomo (elected 4 times)
    Son-in-law of regidor (Diego de Aranda y Aguayo)
    Father-in-law of regidor (Lucas de Villamil y Vargas)
Manuel Rodríguez Moreno, elected three times (mayordomo)
    Sponsored by alcalde/procurator (Antonio Ruiz de la Vega)

Source: AGA, Matrimonios, Españoles, Libros 4–7; AGI, México 888, 892, 998, 1020, 3083.

Despite the frequent inheritance of political power or the acquisition of positions through the help offered by fathers-in-law, not all regidores got into power merely through such connections. Some of the locally born rulers in Table 7.4 moved into the ruling elite without powerful fathers or fathers-in-law. They did so because they were already members of the hidalgo class and presumably possessed or had acquired enough wealth to make themselves people of consequence. Don Luis Magaña Dorantes is a good example of an hidalgo descended from conquistadors who moved into the ruling elite without the support of a powerful father or father-in-law. Thus the power elite was not closed to new members—as long as those new members came from the right social class.

Of course, it is to be expected that members of the elite would intermarry with each other. Marrying outside of one's class was certainly frowned upon, as is proved by the manifest matrimonial solidarity among hidalgos. This discernable pattern was not accidental or something that happened at random. Daughters, once again, made this possible, for without them parents would not have been able to attract the right kinds of men to join their family. Parents must have chosen their sons-in-law carefully, for otherwise many of the latter would not have had the ability or wealth to join the political elite. It is likely that in most cases parents chose their daughters' husbands for them, and the daughters married them whether or not they wanted to. This was essential to maintaining the integrity of class and group. All of this contributed to the successful social reproduction of Hispanic society in Mérida.

The social network helps explain how the upper class was able to hold on to its superior status and political power. In some cases, sons inherited the positions of their fathers. In others, sons-in-law moved up or in presumably with the help of their wives' fathers. Sometimes entry was eased or facilitated through the help of matrimonial sponsors. At the same time, Yucatán's Hispanic society kept growing and so too did the number of people who were descendants of the conquistadors or of encomenderos. As a result, there was a number of eligible women accepted or classified as *doñas* who could marry men on their way up, and the sons of immigrants frequently married them. Their sisters, as we have seen, usually found husbands among high-quality immigrant men. Marriage, therefore, was the institution that brought about social reproduction, that is, a social order of classes.

Finally, a significant number of men of hidalgo status participated in politics through election to municipal office even though they did not succeed in joining the ruling elite. The number of these people kept expanding. They were distinguished from the people below them by their hidalgo status. They were a middle class, and they were an important part of Hispanic society in colonial Yucatán.

IV. Political Power and the Encomienda

As the upper class took in new members, the latter usually wanted to decorate their status, as well as gain more income, by acquiring status symbols of upper-class Hispanic society. The most import of these was an encomienda.

It has been argued that encomenderos dominated political life in Mérida, for at any given moment in time the majority of the regidores were encomenderos.[37] Of course, the encomenderos could be seen as dominating political life if they had moved into the ruling elite by assuming the elective offices and purchased/inherited positions as regidores. However, a different process seems to have been at work.

Focusing on a given moment in time is a static approach to the study of a society characterized by change. It does not take into account the lives of people before and after that moment. Therefore, to understand the relationship between the encomienda and the ruling elite, it is better to examine a longer time period. Looking at a thirty-five-year period (1696–1730) provides a larger pool of individuals to analyze. Of course, this still ignores what people did before and after that time period. Nevertheless, bearing in mind the arbitrary nature of any choice of time period to study, a larger pool of people is better than a smaller one.

An examination of the lives lived by two generations of upper-class, politically important people shows, as we would expect, that a large number of the elected officials and regidores of Mérida—sixteen of thirty-three regidores—was made up of encomenderos. One of the most frequently elected persons who was not a regidor was an encomendero. However, in at least five of these cases people became encomenderos only *after* having been elected to office or having become a regidor. Moreover, some of those who were not at first encomenderos married women who either were encomenderas or who became encomenderas shortly thereafter. These men, as we have seen, automatically became encomenderos because of the requirement to perform military service. They were not, however, the sons of encomenderos. Only two of the people who were encomenderos before they became regidores were the sons of encomenderos.

In other words, the majority of the people in the ruling elite either were never encomenderos or had become politically important *before* becoming encomenderos. These men were already powerful or were becoming powerful, even if immigrants, and that is why they could marry into the encomendero class and become encomenderos themselves. Usually this was the result of a second marriage. It was a minority of people therefore who were encomenderos before they took political power into their hands, and very few second-generation encomenderos became regidores.

In any case, since an encomienda stayed in the same family for only two generations, people who wanted to be encomenderos had to request an encomienda that had become vacant. They had to petition the governor, and the governor's decision had to be approved by the royal government in Spain.

The reality is that in a city as small as Mérida, a very large proportion of the people in the hidalgo class were descendants of conquistadors and as such were eligible to receive encomiendas. Governors therefore had *many* candidates to choose from. In other words, Mérida was a city run mostly by descendants of conquistadors and encomenderos whether or not the regidores were in fact encomenderos at the time when they joined the cabildo.

Political power therefore usually preceded encomendero status. To be sure, upon becoming regidores or being elected to offices, these rulers always acted to prevent the abolition of the encomienda—which the crown contemplated on numerous occasions—and therefore to preserve a basis of upper-class wealth and status. They did the same when the bishop tried to abolish the "personal services" that the Maya were required to perform for the city's Spaniards. Indeed, the royal government's attempts to eliminate the encomiendas and the "personal services" probably contributed greatly to the strengthening of the solidarity of everyone in the hidalgo class. Moreover, the members of the middle class would have joined with the upper class in the political struggle because they were frequently descendants of encomenderos and aspired to be granted encomiendas in the future. All these people united in defense of their interests. Historically, that is what we would expect of people like this, whose wealth was based to a certain extent on the resources and labor of a conquered people.

EIGHT

. . .

CLASS AND WEALTH
Ranchers and the Urban Market

DIFFERENCES IN WEALTH ARE always important elements in the determination of social classes. Of course, not everyone who becomes wealthy is accepted as a member of the upper class, at least not at first, but clearly having money helps in the process of social mobility upward. Unfortunately, measuring wealth among the Hispanic people of Mérida in the late seventeenth and early eighteenth centuries is difficult because of the lack of sources. There were no property tax records or censuses, and consequently real estate and commercial wealth are great unknowns.

Nevertheless, some insight is provided by records from the 1720s that provide details regarding the allocation of market days for the sale of cattle in the city.[1] The number of days received by individuals are the equivalent of market shares. An analysis of the distribution of those market shares demonstrates differences in wealth, in the form of cattle, at that point in time. Since cattle ranching was the only productive economic activity that Spaniards engaged in, the distribution of market shares can be used as an indicator for measuring at least one form of property ownership and thereby provide insight into one of the bases of social stratification.

I. Ranching and the Economy

By 1800 landed estates had become the most important source of wealth for Hispanic society, and this remained true in Yucatán until the agrarian reforms of the 1920s and 1930s. Even before, however, ranching was one of several sources of income for Maya and Spaniard alike, and therefore people wanted to become estancieros.[2]

Estancias produced hides for export and beef-on-the-hoof for urban markets within the province. In the mid-colonial period, the estates around Mérida rarely engaged in commercial agriculture, since the Maya produced enough food to feed themselves and provision the urban centers as well. Around Campeche, however, some estancias engaged in maize production because that region was not as densely populated with indigenous people as that around Mérida and thus could not produce enough food for the port city and its people. Finally, most estancias possessed donkeys and mares to breed mules, which were the basis of commercial transportation. They were used on the estate and also sold to teamsters and to the indigenous people for transporting their goods to market.

The Maya did not consume much of the beef processed from the cattle of Spanish-owned estancias. This was because villages and village-owned *cofradías* (religious brotherhoods) had their own estates producing what was needed by the indigenous people. This meant that Mérida was the only significant market for beef for most of the ranchers around the provincial capital. With such limited demand, the market could easily be flooded, resulting in low prices and few profits. In these circumstances, opposition from existing ranchers meant that setting up new estancias was by no means easy.

Had there been no sedentary surplus-producing indigenous society nearby, the situation would have been completely different. In San Antonio (Texas), for example, the absence of such a society meant that for Hispanic people land was plentiful and available at no cost. Ranchers did not even bother to claim ownership; they just rounded up the cattle they wanted.[3] In Yucatán, however, the Maya were large in number compared to Spaniards, and their production provided valuable income, in the form of taxes and tribute, for the Royal Government, the Catholic Church, and the encomenderos. Had the indigenous people lost their land, they could not produce a surplus and pay their tribute. The colonial regime at this point in history depended on Maya ownership of the means of production. The acquisition of land by non-Indians threatened powerful vested interests.

II. The Distribution of Market Shares

In the area around Mérida there certainly was a large number of estancias. In the detailed records of the allocation of market days to ranchers between 1723 and 1726, between 59 and 75 individuals received days, the equivalent of market shares. The number shot up to 112 in 1727 because of the famine, which caused the depletion of the herds of many estancias. Many of these individuals owned two or more estates, and so it is quite likely that the number of estancias in the countryside near Mérida was 125 or more, as was argued at the time by a rancher, Don Nicolás Carrillo de Albornoz.[4]

With such a large number of cattle-producing estates, it is easy to see how the city's cattle market could be flooded. This prompted a response from the ranching elite. In the late seventeenth century the city council of Mérida changed the way in which market days were allocated. Formerly, an individual would offer to carry out the allocation by himself with the promise that beef would be sold at a fixed price. This was arranged through an auction: the person who offered the cheapest price became what was called the *obligado*, the one who allocated the market days. However, sometime in the 1690s the regidores threw out the auction system and carried out the allocations on their own. This innovation was used on and off until sometime after 1728.

What was the motive for making this change? After all, the previous manner of giving the task to an individual was required by law and had been in existence in Castilian cities since medieval times. Cities in America were expected to do the same. For decades, therefore, residencia judges in Mérida from the 1690s through 1728 charged the regidores with violating the law. The regidores claimed that their system of allocating market days was always done "in conformity with what the people who raise [cattle] are allowed and with attention to the number that they have."[5] They defended themselves by arguing that frequently no individual would agree to carry out the task because the fixed price of beef was too low and that therefore they had no choice but to do it themselves. The residencia judges always exonerated them.

Is this explanation by the regidores to be believed? It is of course possible that what they were saying was true, and that no individual was willing to allocate the market days and guarantee the fixed price of beef. However, once the traditional system had been restored after 1728, there was always someone willing to take on the responsibility of allocating market days and selling at the lowest price offered at the auction. It is hard not to suspect that earlier in the century the city council took the job on itself so that it could set higher prices and please the ranchers—and themselves.

And that is exactly what they did. The prices set during the time when the city council itself carried out the allocation were higher than those set after 1728, when the old system was restored. Only later, when food shortages were becoming more common, did the price of beef regularly rise higher than at the beginning of the century.[6]

Whatever the case, the flagrant violation of the law drew the attention of the royal government, and there followed an investigation into the city council's administration of the allocation of market days before the restoration of the old system. The investigation provided extraordinary details of how the city council had controlled the marketing of cattle, and this information provides insight into the relationship between regidores, ranchers, and markets in the early eighteenth century. The information covers the years between 1723 and 1727, that is, five successive years.

Culture shapes all human activity, and this clearly shows up in the records of the allocation of market days. Catholicism prohibited the sale of meat during Lent or on Fridays or Holy Days. (Usually Thursdays were excluded as well.) As a result, during five years there were 1,100 market days, only 60 percent of the 1,826 days in the five years. On average, 219 of 365 days were market days. The distributions followed the religious calendar, for each allocation year began on the day after Easter (usually in March) and carried over into the following year until the day before Lent (usually in February). Thus the 1723 year ran from March 1723 through February 1724, and so on.

Since political power was not distributed equally, it is no surprise to find that the allocation of market days was unequal. Some people received many days, that is, market shares, while others received very few. Three people got fifteen days annually on two or more occasions. These men were among the thirty-eight individuals who received four or more days in at least one of the years. These elite ranchers got a large part of the market. As Table 8.1 shows, this group, made up of twenty-six people in 1723, received 66 percent of the market days. Thereafter the elite's share declined, as did their number, but the big ranchers continued to get 42 percent or more of the market days until 1727, when the number of people in the elite group fell to only nine and they received only 21 percent of the days. That was the result of the great famine of 1726–27.

Meanwhile, the small ranchers—those who received one day or only part of a day—received obviously a smaller number of days. That was until 1727, for the famine apparently opened up the market to a large number of small ranchers—seventy-two in total—who together received over 28 percent of the days. That was more than the elite received and is a sign of the impact of the famine. Table 8.1 shows that while the number of elite ranchers diminished,

TABLE 8.1: Ranchers and Their Market Shares (In Percentages)

	1723		1724		1725		1726		1727	
	No.	%	No.	%	No.	%	No.	%	No.	%
BIG RANCHERS	26	66.1	17	54.7	16	42.9	15	45.8	9	20.9
MEDIUM RANCHERS	19	19.2	28	30.4	29	30.1	25	28.7	31	36.0
SMALL RANCHERS	30	12.6	28	12.6	14	6.0	26	12.3	72	28.4
COFRADÍAS	3	2.1	3	2.3	20	21.0	14	13.2	26	14.7
NUMBER OF INDIVIDUALS	75		73		59		66		112	

Big ranchers: people who received four or more days.
Medium ranchers: people who received more than one day but less than four days.
Small ranchers: people who received one day or less.

Source: AGN, Tierras, 483, Exp. 2 (1728), fols. 1–39.

the number and importance of middle-sized producers—people who received more than one day but less than four—increased.

As noted, there were probably 125 or more estancias in the Mérida area in the early eighteenth century. However, as Table 8.1 makes clear, the elite made up a large proportion of the total number of ranchers. They constituted 34 percent of the ranchers in 1723, but thereafter they were a smaller part of the total. Their estates must have been badly depleted during the famine, for they comprised only 8 percent of the total ranchers after the famine. Smaller ranchers also suffered, although their workers probably suffered even worse. Atanasio de la Cruz Gómez, who was given one market day in 1723 and 1727, two in 1724 and 1725, and none in 1726, remembered the crisis well when he drew up his will in 1737. He stated that his estancia, San José Ool, was virtually destroyed in 1726, for not only were the cattle sold off entirely or stolen, but many of his Maya indebted workers died in the epidemic and famine.[7]

At the same time, the food crisis forced the city council to open up the market to more people. As a result, the small ranchers made up 64 percent of the total in 1727. Moreover, the cofradías continued to receive market shares, and the city council even allocated days to three caciques (one day to each one). These people may have been ranchers in their own right, for many village leaders used their positions to acquire private property. It is also possible, however, that they simply represented their villages and organized the local people for a cattle run to the provincial capital.

Even before that, however, other changes had been taking place. Significantly, the estancias owned by cofradías were becoming more important over time. Unfortunately, it is impossible to determine precisely how many of these indigenous brotherhoods participated in marketing cattle in Mérida, because the Hispanic people of the city also had cofradías and it is possible that some of them also owned ranches that provisioned the market. Before 1725 the documents simply list the names of the administrators of the ranches and do not specify whether the brotherhood was of a village or of Spaniards. Then, the record-keepers began to get more specific, and between 1727 and 1728 no less than twenty-five cofradías identified as village-owned were recorded as participating in the cattle market.

The importance of the ranches belonging to religious brotherhoods, whether of Spaniards or Mayas, increased over time. In 1723–24 only three were given market shares, and they were allocated only slightly more than 2 percent of the market days. The allocation of 1724 was virtually the same. Then, for reasons that we would like to know more about, the city council in 1725 gave market shares to twenty cofradías, which received 21 percent of the market days. Some of this seems to have come at the expense of the small producers, who in that year received only 6 percent of the market while their numbers declined by half. But the changes also affected the big ranchers, for their share of the market fell to about 43 percent, and their numbers declined to sixteen (from twenty-six two years before).

The surviving records do not reveal why the abrupt change in 1725 took place. The allocations for that year were made by Regidor Juan Pardío, an *isleño* immigrant, and Procurator Antonio Ruiz de la Vega, a Cantabrian immigrant. These two men also drew up the allocations for 1726. In the following year, in the midst of the famine, Regidor Nicolás Carrillo de Albornoz and Procurator Juan de Sosa were in charge. It is unlikely that these individuals were solely responsible for the changes, for the procurators were elected by the regidores and therefore presumably represented the wishes of the majority of the city councilmen.

For some unknown reason, then, the city council apparently felt the need to open the system up by giving the cofradías a greater share of the market. The decision in 1727 to allow a much larger number of people, especially small ranchers, to have access to the market was certainly motivated in part by the need to provision the city during the famine. The ranching elite could no longer provide as much beef to the market for the simple reason that their herds had been depleted by increased sales made in response to the elevated demand for food, by the need to feed their own workers and families, and by their inability to prevent the theft of cattle by starving people in the countryside. Unfortunately, there is no way of knowing if this broader pattern of market participation continued very long. Future regidores would be able to change it at will.

The documentation does not permit a precise count of the number of individuals who received market shares during these five years. The people who drew up the schedule may have lacked information. For example, in 1723 three market days were allocated to "los Ricaldes" and their mother. How many people was that? Possibly four, for three years later Francisco, Carlos, and Juan Ricalde together were allocated three days, but their mother was not. In 1727 one day was assigned to "los Rodríguez de Izamal," but again we do not know how many people that was.

Despite the shortcomings in the data, a count of the people known to have received market shares gives a total of at least 171 individuals. Many of them appear in the records only in 1727, once the system was opened up in a desperate measure to feed the city. On the other hand, nine people received market days in all five of the years. The vast majority of the ranchers, therefore, did not receive market days every year.

Death was a major cause of this lack of continuity even among the largest of the ranchers. The records show the dynamism of human society, for death removed some people, thereby opening up opportunity for others to replace them. For example, the oft-mentioned Regidor Lucas de Villamil y Vargas received ten market days in both 1723–24 and 1724–25, putting him among the five most important ranchers. Then he died, and in the next year the city council allocated five days to the executors of his estate and five more to his widow, Doña Josefa Sánchez de Aguilar, for 1725–26. The following year, the widow received five days; and the next year her new husband, Lieutenant Governor Manuel Socobio Ceballos, got three, but Doña Josefa got none. The gradual diminution of the days allocated to the heirs of Lucas de Villamil y Vargas allowed other people to get more.

Other big ranchers died too. Doña María Barbosa, given five days in the 1723–24 schedule, died in 1724. Francisco Mendicuti received four days in 1724 and five in 1725 and 1726, and then he died. His son Joseph then got two in

1726 and one in 1727. A big rancher's shares were thus given to others. Two additional people in the elite group probably died as well. So too did small ranchers. Regidor Luis Magaña Dorantes was given one day in 1724 but died before the end of the year. Regidor Felipe de Ayora was allocated one day in 1723 and one in 1724, and then passed away in 1725.

As people entered and exited the group of ranchers receiving market shares, women were constant, although relatively unimportant, participants. Only eight or nine women received market days in each year between 1723 and 1726. The number jumped to sixteen in 1727, which means that female ranchers doubled in number once the system opened up to many new people. Even then, however, the women only received about 8 percent of market shares. There were three women who were members of the elite group that received four or more market days in a single year.

Priests were relatively unimportant in the marketing of cattle. This is somewhat unexpected, since it is known that clergymen frequently owned estancias. Only four priests show up in the allocations of 1723. The number rises to eight in 1725 and ten in 1727. But there were none at all in 1724 and 1726. Three of the priests allocated market shares between 1723 and 1727 were among the group of big ranchers. The most notable of these was the Señor Deán Doctor Don José de Aranda y Aguayo, third in the hierarchy of the Cathedral Chapter (after the bishop and the vicar general). He also was the brother of Regidor Alonso de Aranda y Aguayo.

The big ranchers—those receiving four or more market shares in at least one year in the five-year period—totaled thirty-eight people. They are listed in Table 8.2, which also shows their political connections, if any. Twenty-six of them were present among those who received market days in 1723. After that, as noted, several people died, while new people were added to the group.

Most immediately striking about this elite are the connections that these ranchers had with the city council. Twenty-five of the thirty-eight people had those connections. Eight of the twenty-five were in fact regidores themselves. Eleven others were elected as alcaldes or procuradores on at least one occasion. One more had been elected only to the politically less important position of mayordomo del pósito, although his father-in-law was a regidor. Others were the sons or sons-in-law of regidores or alcaldes. One person had one of the most powerful men on the city council—Juan del Castillo y Arrúe—as his matrimonial sponsor. Finally, not counted among those with political connections was a priest who was probably, but not certainly, the son of a previous regidor.

TABLE 8.2: Big Ranchers (38 people) 1723–24 (26)

RANCHER	YEARS OF MARKET DAYS	POLITICAL CONNECTION
Martín de Noguera (2nd)	1723–27	-
Alonso de Aranda y Aguayo (2nd)	1723–27	Regidor
Lucas de Villamil y Vargas (2nd)	1723, 1724	Regidor
Pedro de Lira (2nd)	1723–27	Son of Alcalde (4)
Francisco Pérez	1723–27	-
Manuel Ricalde	1723, 1725, 1727	Sponsored by Regidor Juan del Castillo
Cristóbal de Herrera y Medina (1st)	1723	Procurator
Simón de Salazar	1723–27	Alcalde (2), nephew of Regidor
Francisco Ramírez	1723	-
Juan Rodríguez Arce	1723, 1725	-
Juan Nieves	1723	-
Andrés Vázquez Moscoso (1st)	1723	Alcalde (3), mayordomo (3)
Juan del Castillo (2nd)	1723–27	Regidor, Alférez Mayor
Antonio de la Helguera (1st)	1723–27	Regidor
Juan de Zuazúa (1st)	1723, 1727	Regidor
Antonio Ruiz de la Vega (1st)	1723–26	Alcalde (1), Procurator (8), mayordomo (1)
Juan de Mendoza	1723–1724, 1726–1727	Regidor
Ignacio González	1723, 1724	Mayordomo (1), son-in-law of Regidor
Francisco Solís Casanova	1723–1727	Regidor
Juan Joseph de Castro (1st)	1723, 1724, 1726, 1727	Alcalde (1), son-in-law of past regidor

(Continued)

TABLE 8.2: *(Continued)*

RANCHER	YEARS OF MARKET DAYS	POLITICAL CONNECTION
Doña María Barbosa	1723	Mother of Regidor Wife of alcalde (1)
Bernabé Mésquita (1st)	1723, 1724, 1725, 1726	-
Br. D Lucas de Meseta	1723	-
Miguel de la Ruela (1st)	1723, 1727	Procurator (2)
Juan Perez	1723	-
Gaspar de Salazar	1723, 1724	Alcalde (1)
Juan del Campo (1st)	1723, 1724	Regidor
Diego de Rivas (1st)	1724	-
Doña Magdalena Magaña	1724, 1725	Mother of alcalde Widow of alcalde (1) Treasurer of the Tribunal de Indios
Francisco de Mendicuti (1st)	1724, 1725, 1726	Alcalde (1) Son-in-law of alcalde
Br. D Juan Maldonado	1725	(Prob son of previous regidor)
Doña Josefa Sánchez	1725, 1726	Widow of Regidor Wife of lieutenant governor
Francisco de los Santos	1723, 1725	-
Sr. Dean Dr. D José de Aranda y Aguayo (2nd)	1725	Son & brother of Regidor
Lorenzo Ávila	1726	Alcalde (1), son of Escribano Mayor son-in-law of previous regidor
Miguel de Zavalegui (1st)	1726	Alcalde (1)
Alonso Echanagucia (2nd)	1726	Alcalde (1), son of previous regidor
Joseph Fernández de Estrella	1727	-

(1st) = first-generation immigrant (twelve in all)
(2nd) = second-generation immigrant (seven in all)
Number in parenthesis is the number of times elected to that political office.

Source: AGN, Tierras, 483, Exp. 2 (1728), fols. 1–39.

Even the women in the group of elite ranchers had political connections. Doña María Barbosa was the wife of a former alcalde (Ignacio Solís). Doña Magdalena Magaña was the widow of an alcalde (Clemente de Marcos Bermejo) who had also been the accountant of the Royal Treasury. She also just happened to be the mother of one of the alcaldes in 1723 (José Bermejo) who served as alcalde again in 1729 and would become a regidor in 1731. Still another of her sons (Bernardo Bermejo) would be elected alcalde in 1731. And as we have seen in a previous chapter, she held the salaried position of Treasurer of the Tribunal de Indios. Finally, as already noted, Doña Josefa Sánchez was the widow of the powerful regidor Lucas de Villamil y Vargas, and her second husband was the lieutenant governor (Manuel de Socobio y Ceballos).

Unfortunately, there is of course no record of the conversations that these women had with their sons or husbands regarding market shares. It is possible that this was a simple case of the men favoring their wives or mothers. But it is also possible that the men did what their mothers or wives told them to do. It cannot be assumed that women had no influence over male family members.

The close overlap of political power and economic benefits derived from political power is clear evidence that people used their political positions to benefit themselves economically. The rulers of the city were a dominant part of the upper class. That is why getting into the political elite was so useful, and of course, as always, political conflict frequently involved the clash of economic interests. It has been argued that positions on city councils in Spanish America yielded no economic benefits and hence were frequently not worth the purchase price, and in some cities positions as regidor were vacant for years.[8] That may have been true elsewhere, but it clearly was not the case in Mérida at this time in history.

Nevertheless, it is easy to overlook something else that the records reveal: not all members of the political elite benefited economically from their positions in the form of market shares. For example, Regidor Nicolás Carrillo de Albornoz, on the city council since 1706, received only two market days in 1725, two in 1726, and one in 1727. In 1723 and 1724 he got nothing at all. Regidor Luis Magaña Dorantes, on the city council since 1695, got nothing in 1723 and one day in 1724. He then died, but his daughter and son-in-law got nothing after that, and his widow got only a half of a day, in 1727. Regidor Felipe de Ayora, on the city council since 1701, received one day in both 1723 and 1724. He then died, but nothing went to his widow or son. Regidor Gregorio de

Aldana, who joined the city council in 1706, got nothing at all in the whole period, and neither did either of his wives or his children.

It is unlikely that these important people were being punished for political reasons. After all, during the political crisis of the previous decade, Luis Magaña Dorantes was a strong supporter of the pro-governor faction led by Juan del Castillo y Arrúe, while Nicolás Carrillo de Albornoz was one of the leaders of the opposition. The most likely explanation is that these people simply were not important ranchers. They had been politically active for some time but did not develop their rural estates as many of their colleagues on the city council had done. It will be remembered from an earlier chapter that Carrillo de Albornoz did not seem to be wealthy enough to provide his daughter a significant dowry when she married.

Some of the regidores who had been on the city council for only a few years also failed to benefit significantly from their positions by significant grants of market shares. Antonio Solís Barbosa, a regidor since 1725, received no market days in 1725 or 1726 and only one day in 1727. José González de la Madriz, on the city council since 1722, received two market days in 1726 but nothing in any other year. Domingo Urgoitia Carrillo and José Pardío, regidores since 1725 and 1726 respectively, were given no market days at all. Once again, it is likely that these men were not important ranchers at the time. Political power, in short, did not always lead to prominence as landowners.

Also notable in the records of the allocation of market days between 1723 and 1727 is that a number of people without known political connections received a significant number of market shares. Francisco Pérez and Martín de Noguera are good examples. Neither man was ever elected to anything, and neither had married a woman related to people on the city council (although Noguera's second wife was the former mistress of the governor).

Francisco Pérez is an example of a person of somewhat modest origins who acquired enough wealth to become a member of the ranching elite. When he married in 1690 he was identified as a native of Campeche, which suggests a mercantile background, and indeed when he testified at a trial in 1716 he said that he knew about the repartimiento business in the villages because he used to be a *tratante*, that is, an itinerate peddler. Neither he nor his wife, Nicolasa Galaz Rangel, was recognized as a member of the hidalgo class when they married, further confirming their non-elite origins. The priest did not even bother to record the names of their parents. Nevertheless, the wife brought to the marriage a respectable dowry of 800 pesos, mostly in the form of luxury clothing.[9]

Pérez eventually improved his status by being named alférez in the militia, a position he had acquired by 1703. He held that subaltern officer rank until being promoted to captain, sometime before 1715. Meanwhile, his participation in weddings as a matrimonial sponsor was always limited to people who were not of the hidalgo class. This was still another sign of his modest background. After promotion to captain, however, he had become respectable enough to be invited as a witness at the wedding of the half-brother of Juan del Castillo y Arrúe. Pérez was one of the few persons during the period who agreed to serve as the *obligado* and provide meat at an agreed-upon low price by allocating market days among the ranchers. He is also known to have been a moneylender, which makes sense given his mercantile background. He loaned 500 pesos at 5 percent interest in 1719 and was repaid in 1728.[10]

Little or nothing is known about the other people in the group of important ranchers without known political connections. For example, all that is known about Juan Pérez (possibly related to Francisco Pérez) is that he was a resident of Izamal. Yet these unidentifiable people were important landowners who received significant market shares. Normally in Western societies, people of importance show up in records. Most of these people did not, or else appeared infrequently. That suggests that they were not particularly important. However, when it came to stock-raising, they were important. It is possible that some of them were people who had taken up residence in villages to be closer to their estates and that as their ranching activities became economically significant they were given entry to the largest urban market in the province.

In short, the identifiable ranching elite of Mérida did not or could not monopolize the stock-raising economy in Yucatán. The members of that elite clearly were dominant, but they did not control all the resources. Other people could and did become ranchers. Some accumulated capital and made themselves important.

This is proved by a characteristic of many of the important ranchers, including all of those in the ranching elite: no less than twelve of the thirty-eight were first-generation immigrants, and another seven were second-generation immigrants. Exactly half of the big ranchers therefore were people who had moved into the elite or the sons of people who had moved into the elite. It would have been impossible for so many newcomers to become so important so quickly if the traditional upper class had truly monopolized the resources necessary to enter stock-raising. Of these nineteen men, fifteen had held political offices, and indeed six of them were regidores, while two others were among the most frequently elected people in city government at the time.

In a previous chapter it was shown that first- and second-generation immigrants held a majority on the city council as regidores. Here we see that their prominence was almost as great among the ranching elite. It is likely that in many cases the immigrants who were merchants first acquired wealth through trade and then acquired both political power and estancias that already had licenses to raise cattle. Antonio Ruiz de la Vega and Francisco Pérez are examples of that process. Others, especially those about whom there is little documentary evidence, became prominent ranchers but did not acquire, or had not yet acquired, political power. Some of the people who could not be identified were probably in that group.

The ability of a number of people to acquire economic power through ranching meant that economic opportunities existed. The system was not closed to all outsiders. And in fact, as members of the ranching elite died, they had to be replaced, and that meant that there was some room at the top. We can get an idea of how the dead were replaced by identifying the six new people who became members of the elite after the death of several important ranchers in 1723 and 1724.

(1) Doña Josefa Sánchez joined the group, but only after the death of her husband, Regidor Lucas de Villamil y Vargas, who had been one of the most important ranchers. She therefore inherited membership.

(2) The Dean of the Cathedral Chapter, Señor Doctor Don José de Aranda y Aguayo, got in presumably with the help of his brother Alonso, who was a regidor. José and Alonso Aranda y Aguayo were the sons of a previous regidor. Thus these people were already in the upper class.

(3) Lorenzo Ávila was the son of the former Escribano Mayor de Gobernación y Guerra (an important, and lucrative, public office that cost over 20,000 pesos to buy). He was also the son-in-law of a previous regidor. Thus, like the previous two new people, he was already a member of the upper class.

(4) Miguel de Zavalegui was not born into the political, economic, or social elite. He was a Basque immigrant and almost certainly had connections

to commerce. He was soon recognized as someone eligible to join the elite, for in 1724 he married the daughter of Regidor Antonio de la Helguera, a Cantabrian immigrant and one of the important ranchers. Zavalegui was elected alcalde in 1725, the year before he first received market shares. Thus he entered the ranching elite presumably by acquiring wealth through trade and then by marrying someone in that elite.

(5) Alonso Echanagucia, like the Aranda y Aguayo brothers, was the son of a previous regidor. His father was a Basque immigrant merchant who had become a rancher. Thus the son was already in the upper class at the time of the allocation of market shares.

(6) José Fernández de Estrella was not identified as an immigrant when he married in 1704, although he was identified as a merchant when he testified at the residencia of a governor in 1709.[11] He was one of the nineteen merchants who signed a letter to the king in 1723 requesting the restitution of the personal serviced demanded of the Maya.[12] He married Doña Micaela Caballero y Salgado, a respectable but not upper-class woman. At the ceremony he was not recognized as an hidalgo. Twenty years later, however, he had moved up in the world and was identified as an *alférez*. Military service as an officer, as we have seen, was a step toward social acceptance and social mobility upward. Fernández de Estrella apparently is an example of someone without significant political or social connections, that is, someone not already in the upper class, who succeeded in joining the ranching elite.

What is certain is that the upper class in Yucatán did not prevent social mobility, and thus some outsiders became insiders. Once again we see that the upper class was a class and not an endogamous caste. The presence of so many first- and second-generation immigrants among the large ranchers, as well as the entry into the ranching elite of people originally of non-hidalgo status, are further manifestations of this. There were enough economic resources available to allow new people to acquire them and eventually, with good luck and a bit of work, move up. This does not mean that it was easy to establish a landed estate and get a license to raise cattle. Anyone who tried that inevitably ran into the opposition of very powerful people. However, it was easy for someone with money to acquire both land and a license by buying an existing estancia that possessed the necessary license. This helps explain why so many Basque and Cantabrian immigrants and other merchants became landowners so quickly. These were people of commercial backgrounds who undoubbtedly chose to diversify their enterprises by investing in stock-raising.

III. Merchant Ranchers

It is important to note that people involved in the import-export economy who became landowners did not necessarily abandon commerce. Lucas de Villamil y Vargas acquired exportable goods by loaning money to encomenderos.[13] He and fellow regidor Juan del Campo, a Cantabrian immigrant, loaned 4,000 pesos to the governor's teniente in Valladolid in return for cotton cloth and wax.[14] These two important men therefore were moneylenders as well as ranchers who continued to be involved in commercial activities.

Regidor Antonio de la Helguera, another Cantabrian merchant who became one of the big ranchers of Mérida as well as a regidor, also did not abandon commerce. In fact, he continued to be deeply involved, for in 1728 he joined a commercial company operating out of Veracruz. To finance his participation, he mortgaged all four of his estancias as well as the income from his encomienda. Thus Helguera wore several hats: after arriving in Yucatán he got connected to other northern Spanish immigrants as a merchant, became a captain in the militia and then captain of heavy cavalry, and then a landowner. At the time of his joining the company in Veracruz, all of his estancias were free of debt.[15]

Antonio de la Helguera's family was also involved in commercial activities. On the first day of 1729, his daughter Angela bought some stores in Mérida from Doña Susana Iguala, the widow of Regidor Luis Magaña Dorantes, for 4,000 pesos less debts of 1,300 pesos. Iguala had inherited the stores from her regidor-husband.[16] Doña Angela de la Helguera's husband was Miguel de Zavalegui, a Basque merchant who was one of the big ranchers of the 1720s. In the previous year he had loaned 610 pesos to an encomendero and another 1,500 to a resident of Valladolid, in the heart of Yucatán's cotton-growing region, demanding repayment in wax, cotton cloth, and cloth bags. Once again, the lender wanted export goods.[17] The day before his wife bought the stores from Susana Iguala, Zavalegui had borrowed 700 pesos from the same person.[18] Perhaps that was used to help finance Angela de la Helguera's purchase.

Other big ranchers continued to be involved in commerce and moneylending. In 1719 Francisco Pérez, one of the biggest of the big ranchers, loaned 500 pesos at 5 percent interest to a prominent citizen of Mérida. Fernando Martín Tenorio, an immigrant from Sanlúcar de Barrameda, who was allocated market days in the 1720s, owned a store in Campeche. And the most important rancher and regidor of Mérida, Juan del Castillo y Arrúe, the son of a Spanish immigrant involved in a former governor's export business, owned a store in Mérida, which he gave to his wife in 1729.[19]

It is likely that many members of Mérida's elite were both ranchers and merchants. In a letter to the king signed by nineteen merchants in Mérida in 1723, six of the signatories were among the ranchers who received market days between 1723 and 1728.[20] Apparently for many merchants, entry into the ranching business did not separate them from commerce. The two businesses worked perfectly well together.

The mixing of commercial and landowning interests in Mérida was by no means rare. Merchants in Mexico City and in various cities in Chile also invested in landed properties.[21] This in fact was common throughout Spanish America. Merchants did not do this for reasons of any prestige attached to owning land. It was simply good business, and in addition it was a way to diversify income and survive the upturns and downturns of the colonial economy.

Land ownership and the allocation of market days in the 1720s provides more insight into the nature of Hispanic society in Mérida in the early eighteenth century. Cattle ranching and market access were concentrated in the hands of a ranching elite, and since many members of that elite had close connections to the people on the city council—indeed some of them were regidores or men frequently elected as alcaldes or as procurators—possession of political power seems to have been useful for accumulating wealth through cattle raising. Political power overlapped with economic power and membership in the ranching elite.

However, there also existed a considerable number of lesser ranchers as well, and they managed to get a share of the market. Concentration did not mean monopolization. Access to resources was restricted but not closed to newcomers. The evidence therefore demonstrates again the existence of a Hispanic middle class as well as an upper class. Some of these middle-class people were among those who served in minor ways in the less important elective offices of city government, as seen in a previous chapter. In this way the overlap of political and economic power reveals the existence of social stratification within the hidalgo class.

To be sure, as everywhere else in the Western world, and indeed almost everywhere in the world, money counted for a lot. The possession of capital helps explain the ease with which immigrants, especially those from northern Spain, moved from commerce into landowning, cattle raising, and political power. At the same time, the widespread practice of cattle ranching on a small as well as on a large scale allowed some non-elite people to move eventually into the ranching elite, thereby laying the basis for possible future social mobility and possession of political power.

On the other hand, those without money would not have been able to restock a deeply indebted estate. They could have acquired land cheaply and then tried to get a license to raise cattle, but that was not easy. As we would expect, the road into the upper class was usually closed for people without resources. Entrance into that class was reserved for those with capital or for medium and small ranchers who already had licenses and good luck. Meanwhile, because of chantry debts and the division of inheritance among all the children, many families lost the property or wealth needed to stay in the upper class and thus experienced social mobility downward. The latter may have been just as common as movement in the opposite direction. Social classes, far from being rigid and closed, were flexible, open, and always changing.

NINE

. . .

RIVAL FACTIONS
Political Conflict in Mérida

ALL SOCIETIES HAVE SOME form of political conflict. Chapter 1 discussed the people involved in the struggle between political factions in 1714–15. That conflict did not lead to violence in part because only a small number of people, all in the upper class, was involved. It was not the result, therefore, of class conflict. That would take place later in the history of Yucatán, in the Maya uprisings of 1761 and 1847–48.

The events described in that chapter nevertheless reveal a great deal about the nature of politics in Mérida in the early eighteenth century. A detailed analysis of the conflict can thus help explain the political side of life among the Hispanic people. It shows immediately that the conflict was not the result of the famous rivalry between the American-born and the European-born members of the elite. Both sides in the dispute had supporters among both groups. So how can the conflict be explained?

The simplest explanation is probably the correct one: money. That should surprise no one. After all, it is known that throughout the Spanish empire economic motives were frequently behind the disputes that went on in cathedral chapters.[1] If priests fought over access to resources in a manner that was often ruthless, unethical, and even violent, we would not expect civil governments and the people in them to be any different.

I. Hard Power

The very structure of the Spanish empire naturally led to conflict between royal officials and local rulers. The crown could not afford to pay its bureaucrats salaries adequate to keep them honest. Therefore, underpaid governors made up for low salaries through illegal but tolerated practices like the repartimiento.[2] That yielded profits by extracting commercial goods produced by the native people. However, other people were also living off the surplus extracted from the Maya and there was always the potential for rivalry, as people struggled to see who got what.

Underpaying officials was not the only feature of the imperial system that encouraged ministers to engage in illegal activities. The crown also sold positions like that of governor. The governorship of Yucatán sold for 9,000 pesos in 1707 and for 12,000 in 1711.[3] This meant that an incoming governor not only had to exploit the native people in order to provide himself with income sufficient for his own needs and for his retirement, he also had to repay the people who had loaned him the money to purchase his office.

To make matters worse, Governor-Captain General Fernando Meneses Bravo de Sarabia (the brother of Alfonso, who would become governor after his brother), suffered misfortune, and his response to misfortune precipitated the political conflict in Yucatán in the early eighteenth century. Pirates captured him and his family on their way to Yucatán, and the governor had to pay a ransom of 14,000 pesos.[4] The new governor found himself in desperate straits, and he had to find ways, some of them novel, to get money as fast as possible. Therefore, he paid himself an exorbitant salary for carrying out the residencias of three previous governors. He possibly engaged in smuggling. He created new regional posts called captaincies and sold them to people who used their political power to extort money from the indigenous people. And instead of carrying out the repartimiento twice per year, as had been the custom, he did it three time per year.

Another money-making ploy of Governor Fernando Meneses was to change the weights and measures of the goods that the Maya had to deliver to repay their repartimiento debts. For example, a pound of wax, formerly 16 ounces, was declared to be 19 ounces, thereby requiring the native people to deliver more. He similarly increased the size of the sheet of cloth (called a *manta* or a *patí*) that the Maya women had to weave. A bale of cotton was increased from 32 to 40 pounds.

The Maya of Yucatán did not take this lying down. They dragged their feet and resisted payment. The governor's business agents therefore used heavy-handed measures to force payment. They jailed village leaders and whipped anyone who refused to pay. The governor's business manager, Francisco

Medina Cachón, had a hand in this, and there is little doubt about what the local agents were doing. Eventually, practically all the witnesses at the residencia of Fernando Meneses testified that the governor's debt collectors had abused the native people. As we have seen in a previous chapter, even Juan del Castillo, the leader of the political supporters of the governor, felt compelled to intervene to protect the villagers of Maní from mistreatment perpetrated by the governor's repartimiento agent.

At the same time, Governor Meneses was hoping to increase his income by taking a larger share of the products of the indigenous economy. The first Count of Miraflores had come up with the idea of using his position as treasurer of the Santa Cruzada to sell indulgences to the Mayas on credit and requiring repayment in cloth and wax. This was extremely lucrative, and therefore the governor tried to take the position of treasurer away from the count. The bishop refused to go along with that, but in 1712 Meneses succeeded in getting the first count's son, Pedro de Garrástegui y Villamil, the second count, excluded from the city council on the grounds that no official from the Santa Cruzada had the right *ex oficio* to a seat on the cabildo. When the regidores voted to exclude Miraflores from the city council, those who voted in favor of throwing him out were Juan del Castillo, Luis Magaña Dorantes, Alonso de Aranda y Aguayo, Francisco de Solís, and Juan de Mendoza. This was the dominant pro-governor faction in the cabildo, which a few years later would thwart the plan to get the count elected first alcalde on January 1, 1715.

Although no one at the time explained why the regidores belonged to one faction or the other, motivations are not hard to find. First, the governor was the person who decided who would get encomiendas when they became vacant. Also, as the captain general he made appointments to salaried military positions (such as coast watchers) and to pseudo-military positions (*capitanes a guerra*) with opportunities to extort export goods from the Maya. He also made all appointments to positions as militia officers, and as we have seen serving as an officer was a way for people who were not hidalgos to raise their status and aspire to political power. Some members of the elite thus owed their position in part to the governor, and would-be members of that elite felt that they would benefit from the captain general's support. Finally, he had veto power over appointments to salaried positions on the Cathedral Chapter. Being on the side of the governor, no matter how bad or unpopular he was, increased the chances of the regidores, their family members, their friends, and of course their supporters to acquire lucrative positions and status.

People who were passed over for those positions were certainly disgruntled. Since there were more aspirants than positions available, there must have been some disgruntled regidores. The attack against the financial interests of the counts of Miraflores certainly motivated hostility among their supporters. There is also the real possibility that ethics or morality motivated some people to oppose the governor, who was clearly carrying out policies that were injurious to the Maya. Still others may have feared that the governor's abusive policies would provoke an indigenous rebellion, which would have been bad for all members of the Hispanic community. Finally, it is obvious that certain regidores despised each other, thereby worsening hostility. Meanwhile, once political antagonism grew heated, three regidores apparently stopped participating in city council affairs. They therefore played no role in resisting or supporting the governor. It is possible that they were keeping their heads down because they wanted to avoid ending up on the losing side.

In any case, after the bishop refused to take the post of Santa Cruzada treasurer away from the count, Governor Meneses ordered an investigation into the Cruzada indulgence business. He alleged that the counts had been enriching themselves for years and had been avoiding the payment of import and export duties the whole time. As is to be expected, charges led to counter-charges, as the count defended himself and charged the governor with multiple abuses of power.

The bishop got involved by ordering his own investigation into the governor's repartimiento abuses. In 1711 he tried to send a letter to the king criticizing the governor, but Meneses stopped the letter from reaching its destination by preventing ships from leaving Campeche. To accomplish this, he declared a state of emergency, the equivalent of martial law, thereby depriving the alcaldes of the port from exercising their normal jurisdiction. To make the emergency look real, he called up the militia in Mérida and Campeche on the pretext that an English invasion was imminent and then kept the militia under arms for an extended period of time. Meanwhile, he apparently found and destroyed the bishop's letter. (He was later charged with illegally reading confidential correspondence.) The bishop in turn sent a letter to the cabildo of Mérida complaining about the governor's abuses in carrying out the repartimiento. The governor then criticized the cabildo for receiving the letter, since the king had ordered bishops to stay out of politics.[5]

The governor's investigation of the Santa Cruzada provided a lot of useful historical information. The Cruzada's exports to Veracruz of cotton thread, cloth, sacks, wax, and combs between 1704 and 1714 were worth between 187,000 and 255,000 pesos in Campeche and were sold in Mexico City for 345,000 pesos. The bulls of indulgence cost 80,000 pesos, which was paid to the Church, which then had to share them with the crown. After purchasing the cotton to be distributed to the Maya women spinners and weavers, the count and his agents made annual profits of around 15,000 pesos. That helps explain how Miraflores was able to provide good dowries for his daughters and find men willing to marry them. It also explains why the count and his allies fought so hard against the governor. They had a lot to lose. The investigation also revealed, however, that customs duties had been properly paid on all the merchandise.

The conflict also brought other people into the struggle. When Fernando Meneses decided to go back to Spain before finishing his term in office, he passed the position of governor on to his brother Alonso and asked the city council of Mérida to authorize his absence. Two regidores, Gregorio de Aldana and Felipe de Ayora y Porras, refused to go along with this. Since the law required the governor to stay in Yucatán until after his residencia, Aldana and Ayora y Porras refused to attend the city council meeting or vote on the request. Governor Meneses had both regidores arrested and exiled to Campeche. It is not known when they returned, but they were both back in Mérida for the events of December 31, 1714, and for the election the next day. They were members of the opposition to the governor and his supporters. But they were on the losing side, of course. The incident was brought up at the residencia, and Fernando Meneses was charged with arresting Aldana and Ayora y Porras without just cause.[6]

The dispute continued after Fernando Meneses left office in 1712 and was succeeded by his brother. Meanwhile, the latter had borrowed 50,000 pesos from a merchant in Mexico City and then another 21,000 from merchants in Veracruz and Campeche. The debts had to be repaid in one year.[7] Miraflores alleged that the money was used by Alonso Meneses to buy the governorship from his brother. The size of the debt would have put a lot of pressure on the new governor, like his brother, to acquire money quickly. Fernando, in the meantime, had gone back to Spain, in flagrant violation of a specific order and of the law requiring all officials to stay in place for their residencias.

The conflict between the governor and his backers on the one hand and the count and his supporters on the other continued into the administration of the second Meneses brother. The city council apparently tried to get on the good side of the new governor by praising him. On the other hand, the regidores also "exhorted" him not to act like his brother and engage in extortionate and abusive activities at the expense of the Mayas.[8]

The new Governor Meneses realized that he had to clean up the mess left by his brother. Francisco Medina Cachón, his brother's business manager, had died and Alonso Meneses replaced him first with Francisco Ortiz del Barrio and then with Juan del Castillo. Most of those who testified at his residencia asserted that the new business managers stopped the abuses and carried out the repartimiento in the normal way.

Nevertheless, dislike of both Meneses brothers was strong. It was manifested in a very symbolic way in church. Many regidores refused to rise when Alonso Meneses entered the cathedral to attend Mass. The governor was of course furious over the lack of respect accorded him as a representative of the king.[9]

The governor also got himself involved in a conflict between members of the elite, and the results were not good for him. The dispute had begun at the end of the administration of Governor Martín de Urzúa, the Count of Lizarraga. In 1708 that governor had intervened to prevent Juan Manuel Carrillo de Albornoz, the Escribano Mayor de Gobernación y Guerra (the person who was well paid for certifying all royal documents and who in this case happened to be a relative of Regidor Nicolás Carrillo de Albornoz) from passing the position on to his chosen successor, as had been the custom in the case of all purchased posts. Governor Urzúa had secured it for Francisco Méndez Pacheco, a member of the city council who became even more important by becoming the escribano mayor.

Juan Manuel Carrillo de Albornoz, however, took his case to Mexico City, and there the Audiencia ruled in his favor. It issued an order requiring the governor to return the post to its previous holder. Carrillo de Albornoz and the royal order arrived in Campeche when Alonso Meneses was governor. The latter, however, not only refused to recognize a writ from the Audiencia but also had Carrillo de Albornoz arrested in Campeche, where he died while incarcerated. This certainly made governor Meneses quite unpopular in certain circles, and at his residencia he would be charged for disobeying an order of the Audiencia.[10]

Miraflores meanwhile was planning on taking his case to the Audiencia in Mexico City. To avoid that, someone in the count's circle came up with the idea of getting him elected first alcalde for 1715, which would have given him some political power behind his personal opposition to the governor. We have seen the failure of that strategy, and the election of that year surely antagonized the governor's opponents even more. Miraflores then took the long trip—lasting more than a month—to Mexico City to make his case before the Audiencia. He eventually submitted a long list of charges against the Meneses brothers, detailing the abuses carried out at the expense of the indigenous people.

The count did not refrain from character assassination. He accused Alonso Meneses of deflowering virgins and of keeping a lover (*amazía*) in his house. The lover escaped, however, and was put under the protection of a priest. Then, when the priest died, the governor took her back to his house. According to Miraflores, Governor Meneses seduced or tried to seduce the wives of men whom he exiled for the purpose of getting access to the women. Regarding one of the husbands, for reasons of propriety the count said that "I cannot give his name." But he did give the names of some of the women who had been seduced.[11]

Miraflores also tried to settle scores with Juan del Castillo, who had participated in the decision to deprive the count of his seat on the city council. Castillo had become the manager of the governor's repartimiento business and used his house and store for receiving the province's caciques as they arrived to deliver their goods. If someone failed to pay, the count alleged, then it was Castillo who sent out debt collectors to the villages. Moreover, according to Miraflores, Castillo refused to convene city council meetings in order to avoid criticism of the governor by members of the cabildo.[12]

Alonso Meneses responded in kind. He alleged that the count believed himself and his family to be exempt from secular authority because of his position as treasurer of the Santa Cruzada, and when secular authorities tried to enforce the law, Miraflores got the bishop to excommunicate the officials involved. Moreover, the count behaved outrageously when he received official confirmation of his noble title (after the death of his father). According to the governor and Manuel Alarcón, his henchman who appeared as a witness, the count held a large celebration in the streets announced by bugles. He and his wife rode around in their coach accompanied by the buglers, and everyone who turned out to see them was likely to receive some of the money being thrown out to the crowd. The city was overwhelmed by "merriment, hurrahs, bulls, and parties for a period of days, causing a general and manifest scandal." (It is not clear if this refers to bull fights or to the running of bulls through the streets.) Why was this bad behavior? Because it was taking place after news had been received of the death of the queen (María Luisa Gabriela of Savoy), and the whole Spanish Empire was in mourning. It was not a time for celebration and mirth. To make matters worse, important members of the local elite, including Lucas de Villamil y Vargas, alcalde Domingo de Urgoitia, and militia commander Colonel Francisco de Salazar y Córdova (a longtime supporter of former governor Fernando Meneses), participated in the festivities.[13]

II. Cover-up and Reconciliation

As Alonso Meneses neared the end of his term in office, the issue of the residencias of the two brothers came up. Someone with influence somehow managed to get the viceroy to appoint someone in Mexico City named Juan Francisco Medina Cachón to serve as the judge. This Medina Cachón just happened to be the son of the Medina Cachón who had been Fernando Meneses' business manager. The fix was in.

When this news arrived in Mérida, the factions geared up for more combat. The regidores in those factions were aligned as follows:

PRO-GOVERNOR REGIDORES	ANTI-GOVERNOR REGIDORES
Juan del Castillo y Arrúe, leader	Lucas de Villamil y Vargas, leader
Alonso de Aranda y Aguayo	Nicolás Francisco Carrillo de Albornoz
Luis Magaña Dorantes	Felipe de Ayora y Porras
Juan de Mendoza	Gregorio de Aldana
Francisco de Solís	

(The Count of Miraflores, formerly on the cabildo, of course supported the anti-governor faction in their efforts.)

A special meeting of the city council was held on November 4, 1715, to discuss what should be done. Clearly the viceroy had not known about the relationship between Medina Cachón father and son, but the latter showed up with the proper credentials as residencia judge. Before the city council could vote on whether or not to accept Medina Cachón's papers, Regidor Nicolás Carrillo de Albornoz spoke, demanding that regidores Juan del Castillo and Luis Magaña Dorantes leave the room and recuse themselves from voting. Both men had served Fernando and Alonso Meneses and would be tried for their conduct along with the governors, and therefore there was a conflict of interest if they participated in choosing the man who would be their judge.

However, both regidores refused to leave, for in fact it was normal during a residencia to judge all members of the city council and all members of the government in addition to the governor. Castillo and Magaña Dorantes stayed and voted with the majority to accept Medina Cachón as the residencia judge.[14] Two of the regidores—Magaña Dorantes and Juan de Mendoza—along with Francisco de Salazar y Córdova were chosen by Fernando Meneses to represent him during the trial. The latter was a guarantor of the governor's bond, posted when he had taken office to guarantee payment of any fines that might result from his residencia.

Medina Cachón began the proceedings, and in Mérida the first witness called was Captain Ignacio Chacón, the first alcalde. This was the same man elected as alcalde on January 1, 1715, by the governor's supporters on the city council, thereby defeating the opposition's candidate, the Count of Miraflores. He had married into the Salazar family and thus was tightly tied into the former governor's circle. He could be expected to deny any abuse by Fernando Meneses, and that is exactly what he did. He was followed by others who did the same.

Apparently, some witnesses were afraid to say what they thought. Juan Ascencio Lazagavaster, who although not a regidor was one of the men most often elected to public office, did not denounce the governor, but he did not praise him either. A few years later, in different circumstances, Lazagavaster was to be one of the most strident critics of the governor. Other witness said that they had heard about abuses but had not seen them personally. The judge would be able to dismiss that testimony as hearsay.

The trial was proving to be a cover-up. But then the new governor, Juan Joseph de Vértiz y Ortoñón, showed up in Mérida with orders to carry out the residencias of the Meneses brothers if Medina Cachón had not finished doing so.[15] Since the latter had not finished, the law was on the side of Governor Vértiz. Supporters of the former governors, however, resisted and tried to continue with the cover-up. Particularly resistant was Manuel Alarcón, a supporter of the governor and of Juan del Castillo, who was in charge of taking testimony in Campeche.[16] Eventually, however, Medina Cachón and his supporters were forced to yield, and the new governor took over the residencia. Then Vértiz was ordered to wait until his own term in office was over before proceeding against the Meneses brothers. As a result, the definitive residencia did not begin until 1721. That was thirteen years after Fernando Meneses had begun his term in office.

Once Alonso Meneses was out of office, his opponents began a counterattack. Regidor Juan del Campo was elected procurator in 1716 and started to bring charges against the Meneses brothers. The delay of the residencia, however, led to the postponement of the legal process. It began again in 1721 under the direction of Carlos de Texada, the procurator at the time.[17] The charges were then added to the residencia proceedings.

Meanwhile, it had apparently become clear to Juan del Castillo that it was time to change course as the political winds were shifting in the opposite direction. Shortly after the notorious election of 1715, he paid 400 pesos to Regidores Gregorio de Aldana and Felipe de Ayora in return for not bringing charges against Governor Alonso de Meneses for having exiled them to Campeche.[18]

Then, in 1717, someone tried to effect some sort of reconciliation between the political factions. In that year Lucas de Villamil y Vargas, the leader of those aligned with the Count of Miraflores, got married for the third time. His bride was Josepha de Sánchez Aguilar, a member of the encomendero elite. The wedding presented a political opportunity. Governor Vértiz and his wife served as the matrimonial sponsors. The witnesses of the wedding were Juan del Castillo and Nicolás Carrillo de Albornoz, enemies and notable members of the opposing factions.[19] Indeed, Castillo had led the cabildo in the successful attempt to throw Villamil's nephew, the Count of Miraflores, off the city council, and Carrillo de Albornoz had tried to exclude Castillo from the cabildo meeting that discussed the residencias.

Somehow someone got the major antagonists together in the same room. This could have been the initiative of the governor, since it was in his interest to lessen or eliminate political conflict within the elite. It could also have been an effort made by Castillo, who had already begun to move away from his position of antagonism to the faction led by the count's family and Villamil y Vargas. Finally, the person behind the effort could even have been the dowager Countess of Miraflores, Doña Micaela de Villamil y Vargas—the sister, of course, of Lucas, the groom at the wedding. She was reported to have made a nighttime visit to Castillo's house in around 1714 and therefore it is probable that the two were on speaking terms.[20] It is not known if the wedding resulted in any reconciliation between the factions.

Perhaps tensions diminished somewhat over time. This is suggested by the city elections of 1719. The old Canary Islander Cristóbal de Herrera y Córdova was elected as procurator, but shortly afterward he asked to be permitted to resign because he was old and sick. Who would replace him? Regidores Luis Magaña Dorantes and Alonso de Aranda y Aguayo, both members of the pro-governor party that had voted to throw the Count of Miraflores off the city council and to defeat him in the 1715 election, actually argued against accepting the resignation. This was probably because they feared what would happen if someone else were procurator. In any case, Antonio Ruiz de la Vega was suggested as a candidate. Since the latter was not a regidor, he could not vote in city elections, but he had already served as procurator in 1700, as first alcalde in 1705, and as *mayordomo del pósito* in 1708. Eventually, as we have seen, he was to be the most frequently elected city official between 1690 and 1730. In 1719, however, his career was not even half over.

Someone on the city council put forward his name, which suggests that at least some people trusted him. The city council voted, and voting for him were Juan del Castillo, Francisco de Solís, and Juan de Mendoza—all members of the faction that had supported the governor and had expelled the count from the cabildo. Joining with them were the formerly dissident anti-governor regidores Gregorio de Aldana and Nicolás Carrillo de Albornoz. The two factions at least temporarily buried the hatchet and worked together. But Magaña Dorantes and Aranda y Aguayo were recalcitrant and voted for Simón de Salazar, from a family known for its service to the governors.[21] Some reconciliation seems to have taken place, but not everyone was conciliated.

Even Alonso Aranda y Aguayo and Gregorio de Aldana seem to have come around somewhat to the idea of getting along with former enemies. This was achieved through a wedding. In 1721 Petronila de Ayora, the daughter of Felipe de Ayora (the dissident regidor who had been exiled to Campeche by Governor Alonso Meneses), married Nicolás Bermejo, the son of Magdalena Magaña (the woman who held the position of treasurer of the Tribunal de Indios). Serving as matrimonial sponsors were Regidor Alonso de Aranda y Aguayo and his wife. The witnesses were Juan del Castillo and Regidor Gregorio de Aldana (who had been exiled along with Felipe de Ayora).[22] Thus people from opposite sides in the political conflict seem to have found a way to get along, or at least get into the same room.

Meanwhile, however, Governor Vértiz had come to Yucatán with special instructions. The viceroy ordered him to investigate the abuses and "tyrannical acts" that the Meneses brothers had been perpetrating against the Maya and against the Hispanic people of Mérida. Apparently either the Count of Miraflores or someone of like mind had communicated with the viceroy and convinced him of the need to carry out a special investigation of the Meneses brothers. On the other hand, the new governor also inherited the investigation begun by Alonso Meneses of the abuses carried out by the Santa Cruzada under the administration of the Count of Miraflores. Thus Governor Vértiz would be investigating the former governor as well as the latter's principal enemy.

Vértiz had to wait to proceed against the former governor, but he began to investigate the count and his business in 1716.[23] He sent notaries out into the villages to question the indigenous people. No one complained about the sale of bulls of indulgence and no new evidence was turned up. Once again the investigation showed that the count had paid all of the relevant taxes and had done nothing illegal. Eventually Governor Vértiz was ordered to stop the investigation.

Sometimes the dispute had entertaining moments. For example, in 1716 Governor Alonso Meneses had found out that a ship, probably engaged in smuggling, had been wrecked on the coast. Some English crew members had gone to Mérida and taken refuge in the house of the dowager Countess of Miraflores. The governor sent Manuel Alarcón—his henchman who would soon be in charge in Campeche of the spurious residencia carried out by Medina Cachón—and other officials to arrest the Englishmen. For Protestants, arrest could have led to serious problems with the Inquisition. However, the countess refused to hand the men over, alleging that as treasurer of the Santa Cruzada—she had inherited the post upon the death of her husband—her household was exempt from secular authority. The governor therefore sent the local official of the Inquisition and two others to the house to inform the countess that her household was not exempt from royal jurisdiction and that she had to hand over the alleged smugglers.

When these officials got to the house of the countess, however, they found that she had taken the Englishmen to the cathedral. These men must have had an epiphany: they decided to convert to Catholicism. All five of the Englishmen were baptized and thereby saved from the Inquisition. The episode suggests that the countess and her family may indeed have been involved in smuggling, for once ashore the Englishmen knew where to go for help in the capital.

III. Justice

The definitive residencia of the Meneses brothers began in 1721 with former Governor Vértiz as judge.[24] The first witness called in Mérida was Antonio Ruiz de la Vega. His testimony set the tone for the rest of the witnesses. He mentioned the exile of the two regidores and reported in detail what he knew about the abuses carried out in the villages by the repartimiento agents of Governor Fernando Meneses. The Maya villagers were required to deliver more wax and cloth than normal because Francisco Medina Cachón, the governor's business agent, ordered his men to change the weights and measures. When there was a shortage of cotton in the Valladolid area, the villagers had trouble paying in kind the quantities demanded by the governor. Therefore, seeing commercial opportunity, the agents bought cotton elsewhere and then sold it to the Mayas at high prices so that they could deliver the quantities demanded. The most abusive of the governor's agents was Francisco de Arostegui. On the other hand, Ruiz de la Vega said that the abuses ceased during the term of Alonso Meneses because Juan del Castillo took charge and carried out the repartimiento in a fair way. When run properly, according to the witness, the system was good for the Mayas because it allowed them to acquire the money that they needed to pay their taxes.[25]

When Juan Ascencio Lazagavaster testified, he severely criticized Governor Fernando Meneses for what had happened during his governorship. Lazagavaster stated that repartimiento debts were collected "with great rigor, tyranny, and cruelty."[26] Many other witnesses were also extremely critical of Fernando Meneses.

Luis Magaña Dorantes, however, defended both brothers and revealed the details about the efforts to influence his vote in the election of 1715. His son-in-law also testified, supporting his father-in-law's account of the attempt to bribe the regidor by giving gifts and money to his daughter.

After hearing the testimony of many residents of Mérida, it was the turn of the Maya village leaders to speak. They provided eyewitness accounts of the whipping carried out by the governor's repartimiento agents to force the villagers to deliver the goods. The cacique of Maní provided details of the abuses carried out there and in the nearby village of Tipikal by Francisco de Arostegui and of how Juan del Castillo had intervened to protect them.[27]

The judge then brought twelve charges against the Meneses brothers. Among these were allegations regarding the refusal to obey an order from the Audiencia in the case of Juan Manuel Carrillo de Albornoz (charge #1 against Alonso Meneses), the arrest and exile of the regidores (#2 against Fernando Meneses), trying to interfere in the city elections by bringing in soldiers to intimidate the regidores (#3, against Alonso Meneses), carrying out an abusive repartimiento system (#5, against both), forcing the Mayas to pay to have their village leaders confirmed in office (#7, against Fernando Meneses), smuggling with a French ship in Campeche (#8, against Fernando Meneses), reading other people's confidential correspondence (#9, against Fernando Meneses), and paying a ransom to pirates (#10, against Fernando Meneses). The judge also brought charges against several other people, including Juan del Castillo (for carrying out the repartimiento while serving on the city council) and Francisco de Arostegui (for mistreating the villagers).[28]

Alonso Meneses defended himself and his brother in person as follows:[29]

> He had refused to obey the order from the Audiencia regarding Carrillo de Albornoz's claim to the post of secretario mayor de gobernación y guerra because Francisco Méndez Pacheco's claim had already been approved, and besides Carrillo had disobeyed an order closing the port of Campeche by taking a ship needed to repel the English landing in Laguna de Términos.
>
> He had arrested the regidores because they had refused to follow orders.
>
> The testimony of Magaña Dorantes justified his use of soldiers to insure the validity of the election of 1715.
>
> He denied the abuses perpetrated by his brother, pointing out that if the indigenous people had any complaints, they would have brought them before the governor. Moreover, spinning thread and weaving cloth of the required size was so easy that "even the laziest Indian woman" could do it easily in less than six days. Moreover, priests, encomenderos, and merchants also carry out repartimientos with the Mayas. Finally, although the repartimiento was prohibited by law, "it is universally tolerated all over the Indies, especially in this province, in consideration of the low salaries of the governors, who are not paid enough to pay for their expenses and cost of living in decency."[30]
>
> Therefore, he argued that, as in the cases of previous governors, he and his brother should be absolved of guilt.

Witnesses testified on behalf of the Meneses brothers. Among them were Regidor Juan de Mendoza, who was the first alcalde of Mérida at the time, and Regidor Luis Magaña Dorantes. They were members of the pro-governor faction on the city council.

Juan del Castillo was defended by Cristóbal de la Cámara, a descendant of a conquistador and a member of the encomendero class. He argued that Castillo should be absolved because there had been no abuses when he was in charge of the repartimiento of Alonso Meneses, and indeed he had remedied the abuses of his predecessor. As always, it was noted that the repartimiento was for the good of the native people because it gave them the means of paying their tribute and that it had always been done. Among the witnesses for his defense was Carlos Fernández de Texada, the city attorney who had helped bring forward the charges against Fernando Meneses.[31]

Francisco de Arostegui testified and also called witnesses in his defense. He pointed out that "although it is true that I whipped the Indian leaders of the village of Maní" and of other villages, he did that because he had received direct orders from the governor to "carry out the collection [of the wax that was owed] with all of the rigor of lashes."[32] This, of course, is the classic defense of the underling: he was just following orders.

The verdict and sentence passed down reveal the difficult balance that the crown tried to maintain in ruling over its territories in America. On the one hand, the royal government did not have the resources to pay its officials properly, which necessarily resulted in corruption. That same lack of resources meant that the crown would have limited means of coercion because it could not afford to keep a large number of troops in America.

At the same time, the government needed the active cooperation of the ruling elites in America. It was the provincial militia, not units of regular soldiers, that responded to threatened invasion or raids by the English or by pirates. The same people maintained order in the province and sometimes put down native rebellions, thereby assuring the payment of tribute by the indigenous people. Tribute, after all, was the major source of government revenue in Yucatán.

This meant that the government had to tolerate some infractions on the part of its officials for otherwise no one would be willing to serve. But at the same time, since medieval times the Spanish kings believed that one of their most important duties was to provide their subjects with justice. That meant that not all infractions could be ignored, especially if the actions of government officials resulted in unrest among either the Hispanic population or among the native people—or both.

Former Governor Vértiz tried to thread that needle, and thread it he did.[33] His rulings were as follows:

He found Alonso Meneses guilty of disobeying the order of the Audiencia and fined him 2,000 pesos (charge #1).

He found Fernando Meneses not guilty for arresting the regidores (Aldana and Ayora) (#2).

He found Alonso Meneses guilty of interfering in city elections by bringing in soldiers to intimidate the regidores and fined him 200 pesos (#3).

He found Alonso Meneses not guilty of carrying out an abusive repartimiento, but his brother was found guilty (#5).

Fernando Meneses was fined 1,488 pesos 6 reales for changing the weights and measures used, and another 6,065 pesos 5 reales for carrying out three repartimientos per year, when the custom had always been two. Another 5,000 pesos was added to the fine because the governor had ignored the effects that a bad harvest had been having on the Maya women's ability to produce cloth.

He found Alonso Meneses not guilty but his brother guilty of forcing the native people to pay to have their village leaders confirmed in office (#7); he fined Fernando Meneses 2,000 pesos, half to be returned to the Maya villagers, and the other half as punishment for doing it.

He found Fernando Meneses not guilty for lack of evidence on the charge of smuggling with the French (#8).

He found Fernando Meneses not guilty of reading other people's confidential correspondence (#9).

Finally, he refused to rule on the charge of paying a ransom to pirates (#10 against Fernando Meneses) and recommended that the matter be sent to the Council of the Indies because of the special circumstances of the case.

Alonso Meneses was thus fined a total of 2,200 pesos. His brother Fernando was fined 12,554 pesos 3 reales and was ordered to return the money to the native people in the districts most affected by his abusive practices. It is not known if the money was ever paid.

The judge also found Francisco de Arostegui guilty of whipping the native leaders to force them to pay the debts owed by their villages. He was fined 100 pesos, the money to be paid to the villagers of Maní and Tipikal.[34]

Then the presiding judge concluded the case against the Meneses brothers by praising them for their actions in defending the province and declaring them to be "good ministers whom His Majesty could continue to occupy in his service and grant favors and give thanks."[35] It was in fact routine to end a residencia with that statement. It was the royal government's admission that it had to put up with corruption and abuse carried out by its own officials.

Juan del Castillo was found not guilty.

IV. Soft Power

Perhaps lost in the details is a significant fact: throughout the whole political conflict, Juan del Castillo was always on the winning side. To explain this, it is important to look beyond simple personal self-interest and see how he got others to follow him.

Political actors are human beings who do not always judge situations by mere calculation of cost and benefit. They are sometimes affected by passion, affection, friendship, and even principle. It is clear from what we have already seen that some people despised other people. The record of social interaction, on the other hand, shows that friendship may also have played a role in political alliances in Mérida. Since many of the friendships that can be identified were more than just sentimental relationships but also served political interests, they might be classified as what are known as instrumental friendships.[36]

We shall start, of course, with Juan del Castillo. His supporters on the city council were Alonso de Aranda y Aguayo, Francisco de Solís, Juan de Mendoza, and Luis Magaña Dorantes. A documented relationship between Aranda y Aguayo and Castillo goes back to 1697, before either one of them was on the city council or had been elected to office. In that year Aranda y Aguayo got married, and Castillo was his matrimonial sponsor. Both men, of course, were the sons of important people (Aranda y Aguayo's father had been a regidor and Castillo's father was a former alcalde), and Aranda y Aguayo was marrying the sister of Castillo's (first) wife, whom he had married in 1691. Moreover, Castillo's grandfather, José de Arrúe, was a witness at the ceremony. The marriage therefore demonstrates the strengthening of a relationship between families.

Social interaction between the families continued. In 1716 Castillo served as the matrimonial sponsor of María Josepha Aranda y Aguayo, a foundling left at the door of Aranda y Aguayo's brother, a priest who was a member of the Cathedral Chapter. She had taken on the name of the Aranda y Aguayo family. The presence of two important men as witnesses (Regidor Antonio de la Helguera and Alcalde Pedro de Lira), in addition to Castillo, suggests that María Josepha was not just any foundling.

Alonso de Aranda y Aguayo was not as socially active as Castillo, and he did not serve as a matrimonial sponsor of anyone until the 1720s. Moreover, he did not serve as a witness at any wedding. Juan de Mendoza was similarly inactive, and his support for Castillo cannot be explained by the same ties as those of Aranda y Aguayo. Luis Magaña Dorantes was more active, but his ties were mostly with family members of his wife, who was not from a politically active family. An important exception was when he served as a witness in 1715 of the wedding of Juan del Castillo's son. This was a year of great political conflict, and Magaña Dorantes's presence in the wedding party was manifestation, if not a demonstration, of his political affiliation and perhaps instrumental friendship.

On the other hand, Castillo's ties with his fellow regidor Francisco de Solís were even stronger than those to Aranda y Aguayo. As early as 1708 both men, regidores by then, were witnesses at the wedding of a relative of Governor Martín Urzúa, who served as the matrimonial sponsor. Three years later they were witnesses again, this time at the wedding of Sevillian-born Andrés Vázquez Moscoso, who eventually became one of the four most-elected men in Mérida's politics. When Castillo remarried in 1711 after the death of his first wife, his second wife, María de Solís y Lara, was the niece of fellow regidor Francisco de Solís, who served as the matrimonial sponsor of the bride and groom. Then, in 1714, when Inés Solís Barbosa, the daughter of Regidor Francisco de Solís, married into the important Salazar family (members of which served as regidores and alcaldes in the late seventeenth century), Castillo served as the matrimonial sponsor. Finally, in 1723 the son of Francisco de Solís married Castillo's youngest daughter. She was thirteen at the time. Ties between the two regidores could hardly have been tighter.

Over the years, Juan del Castillo established or cultivated relationships with many politically important people, some of whom would be allies and others of whom would be opponents. As early as 1698 he served as the matrimonial sponsor of an immigrant from Seville (Juan José de Castro) who would be elected alcalde in the following year. In 1700, when alcalde himself for the first time, he was a witness at the wedding of a member of the Salazar family whose matrimonial sponsor was the (first) Count of Miraflores. The latter's brother-in-law, Lucas de Villamil y Vargas—who would be Castillo's opponent in 1712–1715—served in 1707 as the godfather of Castillo's older daughter. This demonstrates that the two factional leaders had not always been antagonistic. In 1701 Castillo, still a relatively unimportant person, was a witness at the wedding of two of the daughters of Antonio Ruiz de la Vega, the man who eventually was elected to office more than anyone else. In 1714 he was a witness at the wedding of the widowed Andrés Vázquez Moscoso, the former son-in-law of Antonio Ruiz de la Vega.

And, of course, people on their way up gravitated to Castillo's social circle. At his second wedding in 1711, one of the witnesses was the Cantabrian immigrant Antonio de la Helguera, who would become a regidor in 1715, right in the middle of the worst years of political conflict.

Meanwhile, Francisco de Solís established relationships in addition to those that he had with Juan del Castillo. Most importantly he became connected to the circle of the just mentioned, and often mentioned, Cantabrian Antonio Ruiz de la Vega. In 1708 Solís was a witness at the wedding of Ruiz de la Vega's daughter Ignacia. In the same year he was a witness at the wedding of a royal treasury officer who married the daughter of a royal treasury officer. In 1714 he joined with Juan del Castillo as a witness at the wedding of the just-mentioned Andrés Vázquez Moscoso. Finally, in 1718 he served as the matrimonial sponsor of Bernardo Bermejo Magaña, who would later be elected alcalde and whose brother Joseph would also be elected alcalde and eventually become a regidor. Two years later Joseph Bermejo Magaña would marry Josepha del Castillo, the above-mentioned thirteen-year-old daughter of Juan del Castillo, thus linking the Castillo, Solís, and Bermejo families. (The mother of Joseph and Bernardo Bermejo, Magdalena Magaña, was the woman who served for years as the treasurer of the Tribunal de Indios and collected a good salary for doing so.)

Juan del Castillo and two fellow regidores, Alonso de Aranda y Aguayo and Francisco de Solís, were thus a powerful political combination tied together over years of social interaction and probably friendship. After all, people do not usually invite people they dislike to be their matrimonial sponsors or witnesses or to serve as godparents of their children.

What about the people in the faction opposed to Juan del Castillo? They can be identified by their voting record or behavior during the political conflict between 1712 (when the second Count of Miraflores was thrown off the city council) and 1715. Obviously, the second Count of Miraflores was one of the leading figures in this group, and his supporters included his uncle, Lucas de Villamil y Vargas, as well as Nicolás Carrillo de Albornoz. Sometimes on their side were regidores Gregorio de Aldana and Felipe de Ayora y Porras (the two city councilmen who had been exiled by Governor Alonso Meneses). We shall leave out the regidores who joined the cabildo after the conflict of 1715.

We shall begin with the first Count of Miraflores, Pedro de Garrástegui. What is striking about the record of his social interaction with others at weddings is how little he participated in the twenty years before his death and before the expulsion of his son from the city council in 1712. He served only once as a matrimonial sponsor, and that was for his widowed brother-in-law Lucas de Villamil y Vargas, who married his second wife in 1697. Moreover, he was a witness only once. That was in 1706, when he attended the wedding of a Juan de Vergara, a Basque, and Eugenia de la Cerda, who was tied to the Basque community. (This was the couple that later in the year took in the illegitimate child of the count's son and of Josepha de la Cerda, the younger sister of Eugenia.) The first count therefore did not try, or else failed, to extend a web of friendship or influence that might have helped strengthen his son during the conflict.

The second count, Pedro de Garrástegui y Villamil, was only slightly more successful than his father in establishing a web of influence in the years before the crisis of 1712–15. He served as a matrimonial sponsor as early as 1704, at the wedding of an immigrant from Seville, but he did not have that role again until 1716, when he was the matrimonial sponsor of Juan de Vergara, the widower of one of his wife's sisters, the man who had taken in his illegitimate son a few years before.

Even at his own marriage to Josepha de la Cerda in 1707, relationships were truncated. No one served as the matrimonial sponsors, possibly because of the scandal resulting from the illicit sexual relationship that he had maintained with Josepha de la Cerda before they were married (as is demonstrated by the birth of their illegitimate son the year before). The witnesses were his wife's three brothers-in-law (the just-mentioned Basque Juan de Vergara, the *isleño* Juan Pardío Quiñones, and Agustín García, apparently a nonentity). There were no ties established to anyone outside of the family. On the other hand, in 1717, after the crisis, the weddings of his sisters Josepha and Nicolasa were attended by both of the city's alcaldes (Pedro de Lira and Andrés Vázquez Moscoso).

Clearly the Counts of Miraflores had a limited network of friendship or influence outside of their immediate family, and it was limited almost entirely to the Basque community. They did not succeed in establishing close relationships with anyone of importance—except for Lucas de Villamil y Vargas.

The latter, the first count's brother-in-law and the second count's uncle, was a much more successful leader. Over the years he reached out and established a web of influence that while not as extensive as that of Juan del Castillo was nonetheless significant. In 1701 he served as matrimonial sponsor of Felipe de Ayora y Porras, the son of Regidor Antonio de Ayora y Porras, a native of Seville. The son became a regidor himself that same year and supported the Miraflores–Villamil y Vargas faction in 1714–15. In 1708 Villamil y Vargas served as the matrimonial sponsor of the son of a royal treasury official who married the daughter of a royal treasury official. Those were important connections that favored his economic interests but only indirectly his political interests. Then, in the following year he was the matrimonial sponsor of Nicolás Carrillo de Albornoz, who had become a regidor in 1706. Both Ayora y Porras and Carrillo de Albornoz were firmly on the side of those who resisted Juan del Castillo and his people during the crisis of 1712–15. Thus, we see that Villamil y Vargas had already established important ties of influence and probably friendship years before he needed them during the conflict.

Then, in 1715, in the midst of the crisis, Villamil y Vargas served as the matrimonial sponsor of Juan del Campo, one of the dissidents on New Year's Eve, 1714. In 1716, del Campo was elected city attorney and, as we have seen, he moved to bring charges against Governors Fernando and Alonso Meneses. He became a regidor in 1720.

Villamil y Vargas of course maintained his ties with the Garrástegui family. In 1717 he served as the matrimonial sponsor of his niece Nicolasa Garrástegui y Villamil, the sister of the second count. And in 1719 he was the matrimonial sponsor of the granddaughter of the first count.

On the other hand, although Villamil y Vargas succeeded in establishing strong ties with two people who became regidores and allies, he never served as a witness. One suspects that he was just not as successful as Juan del Castillo when it came to establishing extensive networks of influence and support. Most of his ties were within the circle of the family of his brother-in-law, the first Count of Miraflores.

Nicolás Carrillo de Albornoz, a vociferous member of the Miraflores–Villamil y Vargas faction, did not tie important people to him by serving as a matrimonial sponsor. He served in that capacity but only for political nonentities. Similarly, he was not invited to be a witness of anyone of importance until 1715, when soon-to-be regidor Juan del Campo married. Carrillo de Albornoz served as a witness at the wedding, while, as we have seen, Villamil y Vargas was the matrimonial sponsor.

Gregorio de Aldana, one of the other regidores who supported the Miraflores–Villamil y Vargas side, was also relatively inactive in social events that helped consolidate political relationships. He was a matrimonial sponsor three times, but never for anyone of political importance. Interestingly, he was a witness at a wedding in 1715 that included Juan del Castillo as the matrimonial sponsor and the latter's father-in-law as a fellow witness. This may have been part of the desire on the part of someone to effect some kind of reconciliation between some members of the political elite in conflict.

Felipe de Ayora y Porras, the last of the regidores on the side of the Miraflores–Villamil y Vargas faction, was similarly less tied to important people through participation in social activities. As we have seen, he became attached early on to Villamil y Vargas, who served as matrimonial sponsor at his wedding in 1701. He himself served as the matrimonial sponsor in 1703 of a regidor who had been the *alférez real* of the city council before that post was acquired by Juan del Castillo. After that, however, he was not active in elite weddings until 1716, when he was a witness at a wedding of an important person from Valladolid who was marrying a relative of fellow dissident regidor Gregorio de Aldana. Attending as matrimonial sponsor was Juan de Castillo and his wife. This is another sign of the waning of political passions after the Meneses brothers were out of office.

What we see, therefore, is that when the political factions in Mérida prepared for action, their leaders received the support of many of the people with whom they had instrumental friendships. Juan del Castillo's success in politics can be attributed in part to his success in establishing those relationships, while the other side seems to have been less active in the recruitment of support by means of such friendships. Castillo seems to have been a very adept politician.

Weaving in and out of both factions were two politically important men who never became regidores. These were Antonio Ruiz de la Vega, who was the most frequently elected official (elected ten times) and Andrés Vázquez Moscoso (elected six times). The former was the father-in-law of the latter, and both immigrant men served as matrimonial sponsors and witnesses for people in both of the political factions. Their frequent election meant that they had considerable support among many regidores, for the latter were the electors. Presumably they were successful not just because they created few enemies but also because they had instrumental friendships and/or shared economic interests with everyone else who was important. They had few permanent enemies and were on good terms with practically everyone. Like Juan del Castillo, they were good at politics.

There is no evidence that rivalry between the American-born and the Spanish-born or Canary Island–born played any role in political conflict in

Mérida in the early eighteenth century. The two leaders and their followers were all born in Mérida. Both sides also had close ties to those born in Spain.

Political conflict in Mérida certainly concerned primarily economic interests. People were fighting for a share of the surplus produced by the conquered Maya population, for it was the indigenous people who produced the cotton cloth and wax that were Yucatán's most important exports. The fight was over who would get the lion's share and who would get the scraps left behind.

Conflict, however, is between human beings who are not motivated entirely or exclusively by economic interests. The pursuit of economic interest is made more successful through cooperation with others. Indeed, as we have already noted, trade depended to a great extent on trust. Therefore, people tried to find others to trust, and when family was unavailable, friendship could be useful.

The examples of relationships between people resulting from joint participation in the sacraments demonstrates one of the ways in which friendship could aid economic interests. Similarly, economic interests could foster friendships. It becomes impossible to untangle the two, but it is clear that these ties between people with similar interests cannot be accidental. Friendship, even if of the instrumental rather than affective type, was an important part of politics and of life itself. Indeed, it is likely that social life in Mérida to a great extent revolved around births and baptisms, marriages and weddings, and deaths and funerals. Sacraments in fact forged political alliances and instrumental friendships. They were the means of connecting families with other families in ways other than kinship. The result was the creation of the social network of class.

CONCLUSION
America, Yucatán, and Mérida

SEVERAL FACTORS SHAPED THE history of European colonization and settlement in America. First, geography determined what crops could and could not be grown. Plantation slavery thus emerged in some places but not in others, and wheat could not be grown everywhere. Geography also provided the framework for the development of a communications network, which resulted in either easy or difficult connections to the outside world. It also created a disease environment, which determined which diseases could become epidemic or endemic and which people would be devastated by some diseases and not by others.

The nature of indigenous society also determined certain outcomes. Where the indigenous people had economies of low productivity, Europeans found them to be almost useless, except as slaves, and as a result they usually enslaved them, drove them off, or exterminated them. Where there were surplus-producing economies, Europeans found that native people if left in possession of their land could be exploited. The colonists could live off the production and labor of the indigenous people. That was the essence of the encomienda system in Mesoamerica and the Andes. The result was the survival of Indians, and even now indigenous people are a majority in some places and native culture has survived.

Almost all European colonies in America were therefore unique because of the particular ways in which all of these factors interacted throughout history. Latin American cities, on the other hand, had a great deal of similarity. This is because people from Spain and Portugal brought with them to

America urban institutions derived from Roman models. They also arrived with an urban culture that defined what cities were and ought to be. As a result, the urban centers set up all over Latin America always had something in common with each other.[1] Therefore a study of one can tell us a lot about them all.[2]

Mérida, Yucatán was of course almost exactly the same in some ways as all colonial Latin American cities. However, at the same time it was distinct, different and—like all urban centers—unique because of the combination of several factors. First, whereas in many places the indigenous population dwindled and sometimes almost ceased to exist because of disease and the violence perpetrated by conquistadors and colonists, in the area around Mérida the Maya survived. They suffered catastrophic epidemics just like all indigenous people, but they recovered somewhat and throughout the entire colonial period greatly outnumbered the Hispanic and African people living in the province. In this respect Mérida was quite different from many other Hispanic communities in America. At the same time, of course, it was similar to others, especially in Mesoamerica and the central Andes.

Second, the indigenous people in the hinterland were surplus-producing and provided the maize and other foodstuffs needed in the city. This allowed the Spaniards to live off the Maya. Indeed, the conquered people of Yucatán usually produced more than enough food to feed themselves and everyone else. This was made possible by markets, grain purchases from indigenous producers by city councils, and the tribute of encomiendas. Spaniards did not need to establish their own structure of production (except for cattle). There were no wealthy hacendados (owners of haciendas) in Yucatán until later in history. Once again, there were few other places in Spanish America where the indigenous people provided almost all of the food for the city for two centuries.

Third, the hinterland around Mérida had soil and climate that would not permit the cultivation of any grain crop except maize. Sugarcane could be grown in parts of the Peninsula to the south and southeast of the city, but access to labor was scarce, thereby preventing cane production on a significant scale. Very few other settlements in Spanish America faced these material restrictions. In other parts of Latin America, the ability to produce wheat allowed Hispanic people to bring nearby land under cultivation and even settle outside the city. This happened in central Chile, where the existence of agricultural opportunities and the absence of a large indigenous population resulted in a process of ruralization, as Hispanic people moved out into the countryside.³ This could not have happened in Yucatán.

An important result of these factors was the great difficulty of getting rich. Compared to other regions of Spanish America, the Hispanic people of Mérida were quite poor. Only one person accumulated enough money to purchase a title of nobility, and the income of that noble family was derived from commerce in goods acquired from the Maya, not from any kind of production carried out on its own properties. The poverty of Yucatán thus imposed on Hispanic society a social structure that was not characterized by extremes of wealth and poverty. Some were a lot better off than others, of course, but no one was rich by the standards of central Mexico and Peru.

Next, Mérida was in close proximity to maritime trade routes (through Campeche and Sisal) and was the capital of a province with a long coastline. Few other regions with a substantial indigenous population were so situated because the tropical diseases endemic in lowland, coastal areas usually wiped out the native people (as in the Caribbean Islands). In this way Mérida's situation was quite different from that of most societies with large indigenous populations in Mesoamerica and the Andes.

Proximity to the sea had political results for it meant exposure to attacks by pirates and other foreigners. The crown therefore appointed a high-ranking military officer—a captain general—who also served as governor. Other places in America had governors but few had no such powerful local commander in residence with military forces under his command.

The external threat had social as well as political effects on the Hispanic community of Mérida. In Yucatán, the encomienda never lost its initial function as the basis for a regional militia to be called to serve at a moment's notice. Encomenderos in many parts of America had lost that function by the early seventeenth century, once the threat of indigenous rebellion had greatly diminished. Not in Mérida. Moreover, all able-bodied men, whether or not they were encomenderos, were organized into militia units, including at one point a company of heavy cavalry. Large numbers of citizens held military rank and everyone, including immigrant merchants, proudly identified themselves using their positions as ensign (*alférez*), captain (*capitán*), major (*sargento mayor*), or colonel (*maestre de campo*). Adding to their prestige was the real military service that they provided in an age when elite status and military function still had some connections.

Finally, the survival in Yucatán for two centuries of the encomienda meant that encomenderos and their descendants had more social prestige than in some other regions. Moreover, they were members and frequently commanders of militia units that actually fought against pirates and English invaders. This added to their prestige and social position. Indeed, as Mario Góngora pointed out some decades ago regarding social structure in Spanish America, "American stratification derived, as did that in ancient and medieval Europe, from military stratification. 'Social' institutions have sacred and military origins."[4]

Everywhere in Spanish America people who were descendants of the original conquerors proudly reminded others of their "noble" ancestors. In Yucatán, however, these people could still call themselves "Encomenderos of Indians for His Majesty" because they were indeed encomenderos and part-time warriors. The prestige of military titles and the social value of military service also continued to exist in other places in America, such as in Chile (and probably in many coastal cities), where the urban centers were in danger of attacks by pirates or the unconquered indigenous people beyond the frontier. In these places, as in Mérida, lived a society organized for war.[5]

Furthermore, as time went on more and more encomiendas were subdivided into smaller pieces in order to reward more and more supposedly deserving people.[6] This meant that both encomenderos and descendants of encomenderos continually increased in number. By the late seventeenth century they were numerous enough to form both an upper class and a middle class who could claim higher status than the majority of the people in the Hispanic community.[7]

The class structure of Hispanic society in Mérida a century and a half after the conquest was not like that of the sixteenth century. It was also not like that of the late colonial period. The nature of classes was changing as time went on. This study shows that in the late seventeenth and early eighteenth centuries, the upper class in Mérida was made up of people of high status who were categorized as *hidalgos*, members of the lower nobility. Many of these people were descendants of conquistadors and encomenderos. The majority of the upper-class people had inherited their status. Spanish-born government officials who settled in Mérida were always accepted as hidalgos, and so were their children. There was also a small but important group of immigrant merchants from northern Spain who acquired hidalgo status after acquiring wealth and serving as officers in the provincial militia. There was an even smaller number of locally born people who did the same after acquiring capital through commerce and/or cattle raising.

The members of Mérida's upper class were people in possession of or with access to political power. Some of the men were either city councilmen or served in elective offices. Men and women in the upper class frequently owned stores. They frequently owned estancias. The merchants among them had gained wealth through the import and export economies. This upper class was quite different from that of central Mexico. In Yucatán the only family with a noble title was not nearly as wealthy as the people in the titled nobility of central Mexico. Many upper-class people in Mérida had and maintained commercial enterprises as well as relatively small landed estates.

This, then, was a social class that was not defined merely by its economic position or property ownership. It therefore does not correspond to the definition of class used by Max Weber. Since only a small number of these people—all men of course—actually wielded political power through control of important offices, the Marxist term "ruling class" also seems to be too narrowly restricted.

All of this means, therefore, that while social classes exist virtually everywhere, their nature differs from place to place. The upper class in Yucatán was not merely an economic class or a political class. It was a social class characterized by high status and with varying connections to the economy and to political institutions. Many of the members of the class were part of the power elite. While the upper class was generally wealthier than most of the people within society, not everyone in it was wealthy, and people below them in the social structure sometimes had more wealth.

Below the upper class in Mérida was a middle class. Its members also were of the hidalgo class. Many, and possibly most, of them were descendants of conquistadors and encomenderos (which in many cases was why they qualified to be hidalgos). They sometimes participated in politics by holding elective offices, but they did not hold permanent offices on the city council. Moreover, they were not elected very often. Their access to political power therefore was more limited than that of the upper class. Many of these people owned stores but most were not involved in overseas trade like some of the members of the upper class. Many of them owned estancias, and just as their political participation in office can be counted, sometimes their share of the urban meat market can be measured. Their wealth was usually less than that of those in the class above them, but if they got wealthy they could aspire to membership in the upper class after family members began serving as officers in the militia.

Below the middle class was the majority, approximately three-quarters, of the Hispanic population. Some of them were in the position of a lower middle class. They were not hidalgos and therefore were called neither *don* nor *doña*. Some of them probably were descendants of conquistadors and encomenderos but because of the loss of wealth had experienced social mobility downward. Some probably had ancestors who were Maya or African, and if that were well known, their chances of social mobility upward were not good. They did not hold political office. Some of them were artisans or skilled workers like tailors, hatmakers, shoemakers, and jewelers. Some owned small shops catering to the urban poor and middle class as well as to the wealthy. Some of them owned small ranches and probably had hopes of improving their economic position. Indeed, a small number of non-hidalgo people managed to acquire some wealth and eventually pass themselves off as hidalgos, after suitable militia service. Their descendants then had the possibility of moving into the middle class if they had some wealth, married women of the hidalgo class, and served in the militia.

Below the lower middle class was a Hispanic working class, the size of which is impossible to measure. In Mérida most people in the working class were indigenous people or mulattoes, but some of them were classified as *españoles*. Some may have been former members of the lower middle class who had failed at petty business or small-scale ranching. Many of them were undoubtedly poor. Indeed, as has been shown, many people classified as Spaniards could not afford to pay for the last rites.

Because of the interaction of several historical factors, Mérida's Hispanic community was unique. Nevertheless, it also had much in common with communities in other cities, and it is useful to explore those commonalities. This book, it should be remembered, is a community study, and the purpose of a community study is to take from the particular and apply to the general. Such was the intent of the classics of anthropology by Robert Redfield and J. A. Pitt-Rivers. It is hoped, therefore, that the history of Hispanic people in Mérida can tell us something about many other, but of course not all, Hispanic societies in America in the late seventeenth and early eighteenth centuries.

First, the history of the Hispanic people of Mérida reveals the demographic importance of transatlantic immigration. One of eight marriages in the capital of Yucatán in the late Hapsburg and early Bourbon eras involved one or more immigrants. Thus every year people from Europe and the Canary Islands helped increase the number of people in the community. Of course, since the immigrants were overwhelmingly male, this meant that locally born women had a better chance of marrying someone who was socially desirable than would otherwise have been the case.

Locally born men, on the other hand, may have found themselves in a situation that offered a less than ideal choice of a wife. To marry at all, some undoubtedly had to forego matrimony with women who could bring a dowry into the marriage. The gender imbalance could also have permitted women and their parents greater say in choosing a partner, since there were more potential husbands to choose from. At the same time, the imbalance may have resulted in liaisons of men with women whom they did not choose to marry. Hispanic males of the hidalgo class almost never married women of lower social status. On the other hand, some non-hidalgo Hispanic men did marry women who were classified as Maya or mulatto. That meant marrying outside of the Hispanic community. In short, to find wives some men were forced to move down the social scale, perhaps in part because of the arrival of male immigrants. The result, nevertheless, would have been increased demographic growth. Hispanic communities with little immigration would have had few such consequences. These sometimes died out and disappeared.

The history of Mérida's Hispanic community also demonstrates the political importance of immigration. The city council always contained a significant number of people from either Europe or the Canary Islands. It also included a number of regidores and elected officials who were the sons of immigrants. In fact, first- and second-generation immigrants together outnumbered the city councilmen who were the sons of men born in Yucatán, that is, the traditional elite descendant from conquistadors and the original encomenderos. As a result, this outpost of colonialism must have seemed to be quite "Spanish" in nature.

This situation was by no means unique, for the prominence of the foreign-born was also evident in the case of the city councils of Popayán (Colombia) and Santiago de Guatemala.[8] However, it also contrasted significantly with the experience of much wealthier Mexico City, where foreign-born merchants or even Mexican-born merchants rarely, if ever, attained positions on the city council.[9] Despite the importance of foreigners, however, in Mérida there was as of yet apparently little hostility between the Spanish-born and the American-born. The city council of Mérida seems to have represented both groups reasonably well and its members always united whenever their interests were threatened. Only in the struggle between the Franciscans and the secular clergy over control of parishes is there any sign of conflict between the American-born and the Spanish-born.

That in turn means that the rulers of the Hispanic community in Mérida represented both mercantile and landowning interests. Once again, this was not unique, for merchants and landowners frequently served together on city councils in other regions of Spanish America. In Mérida, however, this was likely the result in part of the impossibility of getting rich from the production of landed estates. Many immigrants, especially those from the Basque Country and Cantabria, began their lives in Yucatán as merchants. Many went on from there to become landowners. At the same time, however, some regidores from the traditional encomendero class also had mercantile interests. Some owned stores and never became prominent landowners. In short, members of the ruling elite may have been proud of their conquistador ancestors and of being called an "Encomendero of Indians for His Majesty," but they frequently kept their hands in the non-aristocratic and supposedly degrading activities of merchants.

This was an upper class that did not disdain wealth gained through commerce. These were not "feudal" lords in the usual sense of the term. Had landowners been powerful and wealthy like those in northern Mexico, they would have dominated politics and perhaps have crowded commercial interests out of the ruling elite. Other Hispanic communities settled in regions of limited economic possibilities may have had a similar historical experience of a relatively weak landowning elite.

The rapid growth of the Hispanic community in Mérida meant that the large surrounding Maya society would not overwhelm Spanish society. The city would be "an island in a sea of Indians," but it would not sink beneath the indigenous waves, as almost happened in Ciudad Real (modern-day San Cristóbal de las Casas, Chiapas), where the Hispanic population eventually became too small to support a city council. Moreover, the growth of Hispanic society meant growing social stratification over time. A century and a half after the conquest, society was no longer made up overwhelmingly of conquistadores and their families. The population of 5,000 or so *españoles* was much too large to be considered the upper class of the city. Many people had to struggle to survive, and not all succeeded in staying prosperous. About 25 percent of society had the status of hidalgos, that is, ladies and gentlemen, but even they were too large in number to count as an upper class within Hispanic society, even if they were—and most probably were—descended from the original conquistadors or government officials who had arrived later.

This means that a middle class gradually emerged. These people participated in the political system and in the ranching economy even if they were not members of the ruling or ranching elite. The latter got the lion's share but there was quite a bit left for the others, and there was even significant participation in the urban meat market by Hispanic people who were not of the hidalgo class and by indigenous religious brotherhoods. The primary distinction between the upper and middle classes was wealth and political power. Evidence presented in previous chapters shows conclusively that a significant proportion of Hispanic society participated in the holding of elective office and in raising livestock for sale in the market. The upper class did not monopolize offices or ranching; rather, the middle class participated in office-holding to a lesser degree, which can be counted, and generally got a smaller share of the meat market, which can be measured. These were signs of the existence of class lines. What distinguished upper- and middle-class people from those below them in the social hierarchy was primarily their hidalgo status.

These developments may have been paralleled in other Hispanic American societies. In San Antonio de Béxar, for example, the Hispanic community was if anything even poorer than that in Mérida, and because it was equally impossible to get rich in Texas as in Yucatán, the society that developed was less socially stratified or more egalitarian than in regions with a rich upper class. People classified as *españoles* frequently worked with their hands and some even served as servants of the wealthier people.[10] Class differences could not have been sharply marked and what economic opportunity existed was to a great extent shared by all. Social mobility was possible. Other regions of relatively poor Spaniards probably also experienced the same conditions of less marked social classes and exclusivity, possibilities of social mobility, and economic opportunity. Much of colonial Spanish America, especially regions without the possibility of extreme enrichment, may not have been extremely hierarchical, as is so often assumed. There were rich and there were poor, but there were also a lot of people in between, and many of them may have experienced, or would later experience, social mobility upward.

On the other hand, where possibilities for enrichment existed, some people got rich and most people did not. Class lines therefore were more sharply drawn in northern Mexico and Peru and in other places with silver or gold deposits, like Popayán, where gold resulted in a different historical trajectory compared to that of Mérida. Once the indigenous people had declined drastically in number, merchants imported African slaves to do the hard labor in the mines. Wealth accumulated and men decayed (in the memorable words of Oliver Goldsmith).

However, since history is about change as well as continuity, we can be sure that the Hispanic community in Mérida in 1800 was by no means the same as it had been in 1700. Bourbon commercial reforms would have affected the merchant class in ways that need to be investigated, and perhaps the importance of immigrants and of immigrant merchants declined over time. On the other hand, haciendas—rural estates combining agriculture with stock-raising—became much more important as a source of income and as an economic base of upper- and middle-class people. Landowners became more important and probably transformed the city council into an institution that was dominated by hacendados rather than by merchants and merchant-landowners.[11] This new upper class may have felt itself to be more aristocratic than before. All of this may have made Mérida more typical of other Hispanic cities as Spanish America moved into the nineteenth century, when upper-class landownership combined with political power to become at times a defining feature of the age. That was the case in Yucatán until the Mexican Revolution.

Society in colonial Yucatán was never static. Over time a non-Indian society emerged in the large Maya villages. Although many of these people were mestizos or of part African origin, many others were *españoles* who were unconsciously creating new Hispanic communities outside of the original three cities. These residents were mostly small farmers, although some were small-scale merchants. After Independence, these people became the ruling elite in the villages.[12] The emergence of a class of small farmers who were not Maya shows that colonial society was quite different in 1800 compared to what it had been two and a half centuries before.

In a parallel fashion, historical change also affected the Hispanic people of Mérida. The population increased dramatically in size primarily as the result of demographic growth, although the arrival of immigrants would certainly have contributed to demographic expansion. Since these people show up in the documentation, we have been able to use the information in these sources to learn about their behavior.

It is important to note that the clergy, an important part of the elite, has appeared only sporadically in this study. They show up mostly as landowners, ranchers, moneylenders or borrowers, businessmen, chaplains of chantries, record keepers, fathers of illegitimate children, sons or brothers of important people, and curates of parishes outside of Mérida. Fortunately, recent scholarship has made it unnecessary to repeat what is already known about the clergy. The work by Adriana Rocher Salas in particular has added a great deal to our knowledge of the regular clergy in colonial Yucatán.[13] Similarly, Michael J. Fallon's study of the secular clergy contributes to our knowledge of the late-colonial period.[14] That means, however, that an analysis of the secular clergy—priests who were not Franciscans or Jesuits or members of the Order of Saint John of God (devoted to maintaining hospitals)—in the late seventeenth or early eighteenth century needs to be done.

At the same time, more research is needed regarding the three-quarters of the Hispanic population who were not in the hidalgo class. The sources to study these people are not abundant because the non-hidalgos frequently had no property and therefore do not appear in notarial or governmental records. Many of them would have been artisans or working class. Many undoubtedly served in the militia units as common soldiers commanded by hidalgos.

These non-elites do show up, however, in the sources receiving the sacraments, and it has been possible to learn something about their behavior as revealed in the records of marriage, baptism, and the last rites. They were more likely to live as couples who cohabitated and declined marriage until they were on their deathbeds. Many of them, especially the women, were certainly illiterate. Not even middle- or upper-class women were always literate. Men and women from the artisan class probably had little chance of rising in society, and so the barrier between the upper and middle classes and the rest of Hispanic society was strong. The Hispanic poor may have made up one-fourth of the total population.

Of course, it should not be forgotten that in a fundamental way Mérida was not like small cities in Spain and that its class structure therefore was different. The capital of Yucatán existed in the midst of an urban indigenous society. The Maya lived in urban villages organized as parishes. They comprised a great part of the social structure of the city even though they were not part of Hispanic society. To a great extent they occupied the ranks of the working class, leaving little space for others. Colonialism itself, therefore, insured that Mérida would not have the same social structure as small cities in Spain.

Regardless of social class, however, there is a great deal that is unknown or even secretive about Hispanic society in Mérida. Low rates of literacy contributed to this lack of information. No one in Yucatán kept a diary. No private letters have survived. Keeping diaries and writing letters seem to have been almost foreign to the culture. There was no printing press, and hence no newspapers or periodicals, until the early nineteenth century. That makes sense, given the low level of literacy. So much about life—such as what happened to the large number of foundlings left on doorsteps—was unrecorded and thus left unknown to us. Anthropologists can learn much more about a community because they can ask questions. Historians of the distant past cannot.

Nevertheless, the available sources, while telling us little about what people thought, tell us about human behavior. Records of baptisms, marriages, and extreme unction reveal more than just who was born, who got married, and who died. They permit us to study not just demography but also a community.

These and many other sources tell us a great deal about Hispanic society, Mérida, and Yucatán in the mid-colonial period, that is, the late seventeenth and early eighteenth centuries. They show that the economy and society had changed since the sixteenth century and that they were not as would be a century later. A process of change was always in existence and nothing remained static. Indigenous society changed and so did the Hispanic community. Both rural and urban society became more complex and more and more stratified.

However, at the same time in Mérida social structures assumed to be rigid and virtually unchanging in fact were flexible and always being transformed. The upper class was not a hereditary aristocracy, for many outsiders entered it. Society in Yucatán was not seigneurial, for upper-class wealth was only partly based on landownership and in any case the great majority of the people outside the cities were free farmers/peasants who lived in farming communities. Most of the Maya, therefore, were not under the domination of landowners, and those landowners in turn had no political control over the members of the free farming communities in the villages. Yucatán did not have a "natural" or a "feudal" economy, for it was highly commercialized and tied into the world economy through imports that were paid for by exports.

And in Hispanic society, too many people had the inherited prestige of encomenderos and conquistadors to be consigned to social oblivion by an exclusive upper class. This community in Mérida did not blend into the much larger Maya society. Nor did it maintain itself unchanging and completely "Spanish" to the core. It became, instead, Spanish American.

NOTES

Chapter One

1. For what follows, see AGI, E. C. 323ª, Residencia de Fernando and Alonso Meneses Bravo de Sarabia, Pesquisa en Mérida (ca. 1721).

2. This person was referred to as either Magaña Dorantes or Dorantes Magaña. This book will use the former. The use of surnames had not yet been standardized at this time, and most people used only the patronymic. Others used either the matronymic alone or the patronymic combined with the matronymic.

3. See José F. de la Peña, *Oligarquía y propiedad en Nueva España 1550–1624* (México: Fondo de Cultura Económica, 1983), 142–80; Thomas Calvo, *Guadalajara y su región en el siglo XVII. Población y economía* (Guadalajara: El Ayuntamiento de Guadalajara, 1992); Calvo, *Poder, religión y sociedad en al Guadalajara del siglo XVII* (México: Centres d'Études Mexicaines et Centramericaine, 1992).

4. Francisco Chacón Jiménez, "¿De nuevo la familia? No, es la sociedad. Reflexiones y nuevas orientaciones sobre las familias en perspectiva comparada," In *Familia y redes sociales: Cotidianida y realidad del mundo iberoamericano y mediterráneo*, ed. Sandra Olivero Guidobono, Juan Jesús Bravo Cato, and Rosalva Loreto López (Madrid: Editorial Iberoamericana, Vervuerte, 2021), 25–7.

5. For just a few examples of local studies useful for comparison with this one, see Luis González y González, *Pueblo en vilo: Microhistoria de San José de Gracia* (Mexico City: El Colegio de México, 1968) (about a town in northern Michoacán, Mexico); Peter Marzahl, *Town in the Empire. Government, Politics, and Society in Seventeenth-Century Popayán* (Austin: The University of Texas Press, 1978) (central Colombia); John K. Chance, *Race and Class in Colonial Oaxaca* (Stanford: Stanford University Press, 1978); and Jesús F. de la Teja, *San Antonio de Béxar: A Community on New Spain's Northern Frontier* (Albuquerque: The University of New Mexico Press, 1995) (Texas).

6. An important exception is the work by Calvo about seventeenth-century Guadalajara, *Guadalajara y su región* and *Poder, religion y sociedad*. For excellent studies of important components of Hispanic society in late-colonial Buenos Aires, see Susan

Migden Socolow, *The Merchants of Buenos Aires, 1778–1810: Family and Commerce* (Cambridge: Cambridge University Press, 1979); Socolow, *The Bureaucrats of Buenos Aires, 1769–1810: Amor al Real Servicio* (Durham: Duke University Press, 1988); Mariana Alicia Pérez, *En busca de mejor fortuna. Los inmigrantes españoles en Buenos Aires desde el Virreinato a la Revolución de Mayo* (Buenos Aires: Prometeo Libros, Universidad Nacional de General Sarmiento, 2010).

7. Robert Redfield, *Chan Kom, a Maya Village* (Washington, D.C.: Carnegie Institution of Washington, 1934); Redfield, *The Folk Culture of Yucatan* (Chicago: The University of Chicago Press, 1942); J. A. Pitt-Rivers, *The People of the Sierra* (New York: Criterion Books, 1954).

8. Classic works by U.S. scholars are Ralph L. Roys, *The Indian Background of Colonial Yucatan* (Washington: Carnegie Institution of Washington, 1943); Roys, *The Political Geography of the Yucatan Maya* (Washington: Carnegie Institution of Washington, 1957); Robert S. Chamberlain, *The Conquest and Colonization of Yucatan* (Washington: Carnegie Institution of Washington, 1948), which, unlike the books by Roys, has withstood the test of time. Somewhat more recent publications by non-Yucatecan scholars include Manuela Cristina García Bernal, *Yucatán: Población y encomienda bajo los Austrias* (Sevilla: Escuela de Estudios Hispano-Americanos de Sevilla, 1978); Nancy M. Farriss, *Maya Society Under Colonial Rule: The Collective Enterprise of Survival* (Princeton: Princeton University Press, 1984); Inga Clendinnen, *Ambivalent Conquests: Maya and Spaniard in Yucatan, 1517–1570* (Cambridge and New York: Cambridge University Press, 1987); Robert W. Patch, *Maya and Spaniard in Yucatán, 1648–1812* (Stanford: Stanford University Press, 1993); Matthew Restall, *The Maya World: Yucatec Culture and Society, 1550–1850* (Stanford: Stanford University Press, 1997); Philip C. Thompson, *Tekantó, A Maya Town in Colonial Yucatán* (New Orleans: Tulane University, Middle American Research Institute, 1999); John Chuchiak, "Towards a Regional Definition of Idolatry: Reexamining Idolatry Trials in the 'Relaciones de Méritos' and their Role in Defining the Concept of 'Idolotría' in Colonial Yucatán, 1570–1780," *Journal of Early Modern History* 6, no. 2 (2002): 140–67; Robert W. Patch, *Maya Revolt and Revolution in the Eighteenth Century* (Armonk, New York and London: M. E. Sharpe, 2002); Wolfgang Gabbert, *Becoming Maya: Ethnicity and Social Inequality in Yucatán Since 1500* (Tuscon: The University of Arizona Press, 2004); Matthew Restall, *The Black Middle: Africans, Mayas, and Spaniards in Colonial Yucatán* (Stanford: Stanford University Press, 2009).

9. Marta Espejo-Ponce Hunt, *Colonial Yucatan: Town and Region in the Seventeenth Century* (PhD diss., UCLA, 1974); Sergio Quezada, *Pueblos y caciques yucatecos, 1550–1580* (México: El Colegio de México, 1993); Pedro Bracamonte y Sosa and Gabriela Solís Robleda, *Espacios mayas de autonomía: El pacto colonial en Yucatán* (Mérida: Universidad Autónoma de Yucatán, 1996); Sergio Quezada, *Los pies de la república: Los indios peninsulares, 1550–1750* (México: CIESAS, 1997); Gabriela Solís Robleda, *Bajo el signo de la compulsión: El trabajo forzoso indígena en el sistema colonial yucateco, 1540–1730* (México: Editorial Porrúa, 2000); Pedro Bracamonte y Sosa, *La Conquista inconclusa de Yucatán: Los mayas de la montaña, 1560–1680* (México: CIESAS, 2001);

Bracamonte y Sosa, *Los mayas y la tierra: La propiedad indígena en el Yucatán colonial* (México: CIESAS, 2003); Bracamonte y Sosa, *La encarnación de la profecía: Canek en Cisteíl* (México: CIESAS, 2004); Gabriela Solís Robleda, *Entre la tierra y el cielo: Religión y sociedad en los pueblos mayas del Yucatán colonial* (México: CIESAS, 2005); Paola Peniche Moreno, *Ámbitos de parentezco: La Sociedad maya en tiempos de la colonia* (México: CIESAS, 2007); Gabriela Solís Robleda, *Las Primeras letras en Yucatán: La Instrucción básica entre la Conquista y el Segundo Imperio* (México: CIESAS, Editorial Porrúa, 2008); Paola Peniche Moreno, *Tiempos aciagos: Las calamidades y el cambio social del siglo XVIII entre los Mayas de Yucatán* (México: CIESAS, 2010); Adriana Rocher Salas, *La Disputa por las almas. Las Órdenes religiosas en Campeche, siglo XVIII* (México: CONACULTA, 2010); Laura Machuca Gallegos, *Los hacendados de Yucatán, 1785–1847* (México: CIESAS, Instituto de Cultura de Yucatán, 2011); Gabriela Solís Robleda, *Entre litigar justicia y procurar leyes: La Defensoría de indios en el Yucatán colonia* (México: CIESAS, 2013); Sergio Quezada, *Maya Lords and Lordship: The Formation of Colonial Society in Yucatán, 1350–1600* (Norman: University of Oklahoma Press, 2014); Sergio Eduardo Carrera Quezada, "La Política agraria en el Yucatán colonial: Las Composiciones de tierras en 1679 y 1710," *Historia Mexicana* LXV, no. 1 (2015): 65–109; Genny Negroe Sierra, *Impedimentos y dispensas matrimoniales en Yucatán colonial* (Mérida: Ediciones de la Universidad de Yucatán, 2018).

10. Victoria González Muñoz and Ana Isabel Martínez Ortega, *Cabildos y élites capitulares en Yucatán: Dos estudios* (Sevilla: Escuela de Estudios Hispano-Americanos de Sevilla, Consejo Superior de Investigaciones Científicas, 1989); Ana Isabel Martínez Ortega, *Estructura y configuración socioeconómica de los cabildos de Yucatán en el siglo XVIII* (Sevilla: Excma. Diputación Provincial de Sevilla, 1993); Hunt, "Colonial Yucatan."

11. Machuca Gallegos, *Los hacendados de Yucatán*; Machuca Gallegos, *Poder y gestión en el Ayuntamiento de Mérida, Yucatán (1785–1835)* (México: CIESAS, Publicaciones de la Casa Chata, 2016); Gabriela Solís Robleda, *Los Beneméritos y la Corona. Servicios y recompensas en la conformación de la sociedad colonial yucateca* (Mérida: CIESAS, M. A. Porrúa, 2019). See also Solís Robleda's earlier book, *Las Primeras letras*.

12. Pablo Emilio Pérez-Mallaina y Bueno, *Comercio y autonomía en la Intendencia de Yucatán, 1797–1814* (Sevilla: Escuela de Estudios Hispano-Americanos de Sevilla, 1978).

13. For summaries of the historiography of the era of Charles II and its significance, see Henry Kamen, *Spain in the Later Seventeenth Century, 1665–1700* (London and New York: Longman, 1980); Christopher Storrs, *The Resilience of the Spanish Monarchy 1665–1700* (Oxford: Oxford University Press, 2006); Herbert S. Klein and Sergio T. Serrano Hernández, "Was There a 17th-Century Crisis in Spanish America?" *Revista de Historia Económica, Journal of Iberian and Latin American Economic History* 37, no. 1 (2018): 43–80.

14. Guillermina del Valle Pavón, "En torno a los mercaderes de la Ciudad de México y el comercio de Nueva España. Aportaciones a la historiografía de la Monarquía Hispana del período 1670–1740," in *Los Virreinatos de Nueva España y del Perú*

(1680–1740). Un balance historiográfico, ed. Bernard Lavallé (Madrid: Collection de la Casa de Velázquez, 2019), 135–50; Del Valle Pavón, "Contrabando, negocios y discordias entre los mercaderes de México y los cargadores peninsulares," *Studia Historica, Historia Moderna,* Ediciones Universidad de Salamanca 42, no. 2 (2020): 115–43.

15. Calvo, *Guadalajara y su región,* 161–62.

16. Calvo, *Guadalajara y su región,* 159–62; D. A. Brading, *Miners and Merchants in Bourbon Mexico, 1763–1810* (Cambridge: Cambridge University Press, 1971); Pérez, *En busca de mejor fortuna.*

17. Peter Boyd-Bowman, "Patterns of Spanish Emigration to the Indies until 1600," *The Hispanic American Historical Review* 56, no. 4 (1976): 580–604; Carlos Martínez Shaw, *La Emigración española a América, 1492–1824* (Colombres, Asturias: Archivo de Indianos, 1994); Auke P. Jacobs, *Los movimientos migratorios entre Castilla e Hispanoamérica durante el reinado de Felipe III, 1598–1621* (Amsterdam: Rodopi, 1995); Isabelo Macías Domínguez, *La Llamada del Nuevo Mundo: la emigración española a América, 1701–1750* (Sevilla: Universidad de Sevilla, 1999).

18. For a detailed study of Spanish immigration after Independence, see the excellent book by José C. Moya, *Cousins and Strangers: Spanish Immigration in Buenos Aires, 1850–1930* (Berkeley: The University of California Press, 1998).

19. García Bernal, *La Sociedad de Yucatán,* 38–40, 49–50; García Bernal, *Yucatán: Población y encomienda,* 345–46, 354–55.

20. Ángel Hermilo Gutiérrez Romero, "Carrera eclesiástica, ascenso y movilidad de los miembros del cabildo eclesiástico de Yucatán, siglos XVI y XVII," in *Poder y privilegio: Cabildos eclesiásticos en Nueva España, siglos XVI-XIX,* ed. Leticia Pérez Puente y Gabino Castillo Flores (México: La Universidad Nacional Autónoma de México, La Universidad Real de México, 2016), 163.

21. Patch, *Maya and Spaniard,* 119, 143–4.

22. John Tutino, "Power, Class, and Family in the Mexican Elite, 1750–1810," *The Americas* 34 (Jan. 1983): 361.

23. Patch, *Maya and Spaniard,* 34, 148, 178, 197, 200.

24. Simon Kuznets, *Modern Economic Growth: Rate, Structure, and Spread* (New Haven: Yale University Press, 1967).

25. See Mario Góngora, "Urban Social Stratification in Colonial Chile," *Hispanic American Historical Review* 55, no. 4 (Aug. 1975): 421–48; Tutino, "Power, Class, and Family," 360–1.

26. See Colin MacLachlan and Jaime Rodríguez, *The Forging of the Cosmic Race: A Reinterpretation of Colonial Mexico* (Berkeley: University of California Press, 1980), 225–6, for a useful generalization about classes in colonial Mexico. Mérida in the late seventeenth and early eighteenth centuries does not fit neatly into those authors' class analysis, in part because they tended to generalize from studies of large cities.

27. Melchor Campos García has made a strong case for Gerónimo del Castillo, a Mexican military officer, as the author. See Melchor Campos García, ed., *Guerra de Castas en Yucatán: Su origen consecuencias y su estado actual 1866* (Mérida, Yucatán, México: Universidad Autónoma de Yucatán, 1997).

28. Tutino, "Power, Class, and Family," 378-9.

29. James Lockhart, *Spanish Peru, 1532-1560: A Colonial Society* (Madison: The University of Wisconsin Press, 1964).

30. James Lockhart, *The Men of Cajamarca; A Sociological and Biographical Study of the First Conquerors of Peru* (Austin: The University of Texas, 1972).

31. Hunt, "Colonial Yucatan"; Ida Altman and James Lockhart, eds., *Provinces of Early Mexico. Variants of Spanish American Regional Evolution* (Los Angeles: UCLA Latin American Center Publications, the University of California, Los Angeles, 1976).

32. Restall, *The Black Middle*; Restall, *The Maya World*; Thompson, *Tekantó*.

33. For British America, see the classic community study by John Demos, *A Little Commonwealth; Family Life in Plymouth Colony* (New York: Oxford University Press, 1970).

34. Murdo MacLeod, *Colonial Spanish Central America: A Socioeconomic History, 1520-1720* (Berkeley: University of California Press, 1973), 217-20; Marzahl, *Town in the Empire*, 7-8.

Chapter Two

Parts of chapter 2 are developed from Robert W. Patch, "Salazar's World: Colonial Mérida, Yucatán," in *Salazar: Portraits of Influence in Spanish New Orleans 1785-1808*, ed. Cybèle Gontar (New Orleans: Ogden Museum of Southern Art/University of New Orleans Press, 2018), 34-51.

1. For the importance of cities and regional development, see Ida Altman and James Lockhart, eds., *Provinces of Early Mexico. Variants of Spanish American Regional Evolution* (Los Angeles: UCLA Latin American Center Publications, the University of California, Los Angeles, 1976).

2. Hernán Cortés, *Letters from Mexico* (New Haven: Yale University Press, 1971), 24-8; Bernal Díaz, *The Conquest of New Spain* (London: Penguin Press, 1964), 114.

3. For urban government and local sovereignty after the conquest, see Jordana Dym, *From Sovereign Villages to Nation States: City, State, and Federation in Central America, 1759-1839* (Albuquerque: The University of New Mexico Press, 2006), 13-16.

4. For studies of international commerce in colonial Spanish America, see Antonio García-Baquero González, *Cádiz y el Atlántico (1717-1778)* (Seville: Escuela de Estudios Hispano Americanos de Sevilla, 1976); Geoffrey Walker, *Spanish Politics and Imperial Trade, 1700-1789* (Bloomington: Indiana University Press, 1979); Lutgardo Garcia Fuentes, *El comercio español con América, 1650-1700* (Seville: Escuela de Estudios Hispanos-Americanos de Sevilla, 1980); John Kicza, *Colonial Entrepreneurs: Families and Business in Bourbon Mexico City* (Albuquerque: University of New Mexico Press, 1983).

5. Diego López de Cogolludo, *Historia de Yucatán*, 2 vols. (Campeche: Comisión de Historia, 1954), 1:263-7; Juan Francisco Molina Solís, *Historia de Yucatán durante la dominación española*, 3 vols. (Mérida: Impresa de la Lotería del Estado, 1904-1913), vol. 1; Robert S. Chamberlain, *The Conquest and Colonization of Yucatan* (Washington, D.C.: The Carnegie Institution of Washington, 1948); Marta Espejo-Ponce Hunt, *Colonial Yucatan: Town and Region in the Seventeenth Century* (PhD diss., UCLA, 1974).

6. Silvio Zavala, *La Encomienda indiana* (Madrid: Centro de Estudios Históricos, 1935); Manuela Cristina García Bernal, *Yucatán: Población y encomienda bajo los Austrias* (Sevilla: Escuela de Estudios Hispano-Americanos de Sevilla, 1978).

7. Elena Laurie, "A Society Organized For War: Medieval Spain," *Past & Present* 35, no. 1 (1966): 54–76; James F. Powers, *A Society Organized For War: The Iberian Municipal Militias in the Central Middle Ages, 1000–1284* (Berkeley and Los Angeles: The University of California Press, 1988). See Solís Robleda, *Los beneméritos y la Corona* for numerous examples of the services performed by the militia officers in colonial Yucatán.

8. "Relación de la Ciudad de Mérida," *Colección de documentos inéditos relativos al descubrimiento, conquista y organización de las antiguas posesiones españolas de ultramar* (Madrid: Real Academia de la Historia, 1898), 11:38.

9. Robert W. Patch, *Maya and Spaniard in Yucatan, 1648–1812* (Stanford: Stanford University Press, 1993), 31–2; Archivo del Ayuntamiento de Mérida, Libros de Cabildo, 1840–1847.

10. Fray Antonio Ciudad Real, "El viaje de Fray Alonso Ponce por las provincias del Santo Evangelio," *Colección de documentos inéditos para la historia de España*, vols. LVII, LVIII (Madrid: Real Academia de la Historia, 1872); Francisco Cárdenas Valencia, *Relación historial eclesiástica de la provincia de Yucatán de la Nueva España: Escrita el año de 1639* (México: Antigua Librería Robredo, J. Porrúa e Hijos, 1937), 36–9; Cogolludo, *Historia de Yucatán*, 1:366–84. The classic study of the founding and early construction of Mérida is J. Ignacio Rubio Mañé, *La Casa de Montejo en Mérida, Yucatán* (México: Imprenta Universitaria, 1941).

11. The definitive study is Rubio Mañé, *La Casa de Montejo*.

12. Ciudad Real, "El viaje de Fray Alonso Ponce."

13. See Hunt, *Colonial Yucatan*, 163–7, for a discussion of the sources regarding the Spanish population of Mérida. I accept her assessment because it conforms to the size of a population that had over 200 births annually with 40 births per 1,000 people. For more, see below chapter four.

14. AGI, México 1020, Representación del procurador don Antonio Ruiz de la Vega, México, Sept. 3, 1722.

15. Ciudad Real, "El viaje de Fray Alonso Ponce"; Cogolludo, *Historia de Yucatán*, 1:366–84.

16. For the interesting history of convents in colonial Spanish America, see Kathryn Burns, *Colonial Habits: Convents and the Spiritual Economy of Cuzco, Peru* (Durham, North Carolina: Duke University Press, 1999); Asunción Lavrín, *Brides of Christ: Conventual Life in Colonial Mexico* (Stanford: Stanford University Press, 2008).

17. Patch, *Maya and Spaniard*, p. 121.

18. This process is explained in detail in Hunt, *Colonial Yucatan*, 152–237.

19. Biblioteca "Crescencio Carrillo y Ancona," Manuscritos, Año de 1753, Cuentas de propios del espresado año; Año de 1753, Licencias de tiendas dadas por los Señores regidores Don Juan José de Bergara y Don Diego de Aranda y Cano en dicho año de 53.

20. Archivo General del Arzobispado, Libros de Matrimonios, Mérida, 1690–1740; summarized also in Hunt, *Colonial Yucatan*, 26–138.
21. Patch, *Maya and Spaniard*, 36, 81–91.
22. Restall, *The Black Middle*.
23. BCCA, Special Collection, Libro 12, Synodo Diocesano . . . (1722); Gabriela Solís Robleda, *Contra viento y marea: Documentos sobre las reformas del obispo Juan Gómez de Parada al trabajo indígena* (México: Centro de Investigaciones y Estudios Superiores en Antropología Social, Instituto de Cultura de Yucatán, 2003).
24. Patch, *Maya and Spaniard*, 218–24.
25. Hunt, *Colonial Yucatan*, 147–51.
26. The sources for what follows are: Archivo del Ayuntamiento de Mérida, Libros de Cabildo, Acuerdos 1747–1760; AGI, Escribanía de Cámara, 321A, 321B, 321C, 322A, 322B, 323A, 323B, 323C, 324A.
27. Biblioteca "Crescencio Carrillo y Ancona," Manuscritos, Quentas dadas por el Capitan y Rexidor Decano Don Joseph de Marcos Vermejo como Sindico Procurador General, que fue en el año proximo pasado de 1756.

Chapter Three

Parts of chapter 3 are developed from Robert W. Patch, "Sacraments and Disease in Mérida, Yucatán, Mexico, 1648–1727," *The Historian* 58, no. 4 (1996): 731–43, https://doi.org/10.1111/j.1540-6563.1996.tb00971.x. Copyright © Phi Alpha Theta, reprinted by permission of Taylor & Francis Ltd, https://www.tandfonline.com on behalf of © Phi Alpha Theta.

For excellent discussions of the theory and practice of the estates system, see Karen Spalding, "Social Climbers: Changing Patterns of Mobility among the Indians of Colonial Peru," *Hispanic American Historical Review* 50, no. 4 (1970): 645–64; John K. Chance and William B. Taylor, "Estate and Class in a Colonial City: Oaxaca in 1792," *Comparative Studies in Society and History* 19, no. 4 (1977): 454–87; Robert McCaa, Stuart B. Schwartz, and Arturo Grubessich, "Race and Class in Colonial Latin America: A Critique," *Comparative Studies in Society and History* 21, no. 3 (1979): 421–42; Patricia Seed, "Social Dimensions of Race: Mexico City, 1753," *Hispanic American Historical Review* 62, no. 4 (1982): 569–606; Robert McCaa, "Calidad, Clase, and Marriage in Colonial Mexico: The Case of Parral, 1788–90," *Hispanic American Historical Review* 64, no. 3 (1984): 477–501.

1. For summaries of the large literature on the defining of *indios* and the use of racial categories, see María Elena Martínez, *Genealogical Fictions: Limpieza de Sangre, Religion, and Gender in Colonial Mexico* (Stanford: Stanford University Press, 2008); Rebecca Earl, *The Body of the Conquistador: Food, Race and the Colonial Experience in Spanish America, 1492–1700* (Cambridge: Cambridge University Press, 2012). For issues specifically related to the African or Afro-American population, see Ann Twinam, *Purchasing Whiteness: Pardos, Mulattos, and the Quest for Social Mobility in the Spanish Indies* (Stanford: Stanford University Press, 2015).

2. See Restall, *The Maya World*, for a discussion of the importance of Maya surnames to the Maya themselves. It is important to note that surnames did not exist among the Nahua and many other indigenous people in Mexico. During the colonial period they were therefore required to use such names, and to do so they usually took on Hispanic surnames, thereby making it impossible to distinguish between indigenous people and Hispanic people simply by surnames.

3. The terms used were *hijo/hija natural*, less frequently *de padres desconocidos* or *hijo* or *hija ilegítimo (a)*, and *expósito (a)*.

4. Calvo, *Guadalajara y su región*, 42–3; Calvo, *Poder, religión y sociedad*, 243; De la Teja, *San Antonio de Béxar*, 24–8.

5. For what follows, see Patch, *Maya and Spaniard*, 441–5; Robert W. Patch, "Sacraments and Disease in Mérida, Yucatán, Mexico, 1648–1727," *The Historian* 58, no. 4 (1996): 731–43.

6. AGA, Españoles, Libro 2 de Entierros, 1697–1714, fols. 16–19.

7. For a detailed study of the vector and its relationship with its environment, see Sir S. Rickard Christophers, *Aëdes Aegypti (L.) The Yellow Fever Mosquito: Its Life History, Bionomics and Structure* (Cambridge, 1960).

8. For 1648, see AGA, Españoles, Libro 1 de Entierros, 1639–1660, fol. 32 seqq. For nineteenth century comments on the disease, see Archivo General del Estado de Yucatán (Mérida), Poder Ejecutivo Oficio del Jefe Político de Ticul (Fernando de la Luz Patrón) al Secretario General de Gobierno, July 29, 1843; Oficio de la Comandancia Militar de Sisal (Eulogio Rosado) al Secretario General de Gobierno, Oct. 5, 1843.

9. Thomas Calvo, "Demographie historique d'une paroisse mexicaine: Acatzingo (1606–1810)," *Cahiers des Amériques Latines* 6 (1972): 33; Claude Morin, "Population et épidémies dans une paroisse mexicaine: Santa Inés Zacatelco (XVIIe-XIXe siècles)," *Cahiers des Amériques Latines* 6 (1972): 53, 58; América del Villar Molina, "Tributos y calamidades en el centro de la Nueva España, 1727–1762: Los límites del impuesto justo," *Historia Mexicana* LIV, no. 1, no. 213, (Julio–Septiembre, 2004): 34.

10. AGA, Españoles, Libros de Entierros, no. 3.

11. "An Occurrence at Owl Creek Bridge."

12. ANEY, J. A. Baeza, March 14, 1691, fol. 253.

13. Entierros, Jan. 24, 1700.

14. AGI, E. C. 322B, Residencia del Gobernador Alvaro Rivaguda, Pesquisa en Mérida (1709), fol. 188.

15. Gabriela Solís Robleda, ed., *Contra viento y marea. Documentos sobre las reformas del obispo Juan Gómez de Parada al trabajo indígena* (Mérida: Centro de Investigaciones y Estudios Superiores en Antropología Social, 2003), Aug. 22, 1722, 344–5.

16. ANEY, B. Magaña, Jan. 12, 1729, no foliation.

17. AGA, Españoles, Entierros, Nov. 24, 1716.

18. AGI, Mexico 892, Informe del gobernador interino Santiago Aguirre, Aug. 5, 1734; Carta del Gobernador Manuel Salcedo al Rey, Jan. 22, 1737.

19. Calvo, *Guadalajara y su región*, 64.

20. ANEY, J. A. Baeza, April 11, 1691.

21. ANEY, J. A. Baeza, June 8, 1691, fols. 283-6. Sosa was recorded as the surname of both the husband and the wife who were supposed to provide part of the dowry.
22. ANEY, J. A. Baeza, June 13, 1689, fols. 40-2.
23. ANEY, M. Montero, April 16, 1720, fols. 54-60.
24. ANEY, M. Montero, Oct. 9, 1720, fols. 201-4.
25. ANEY, B. Magaña, Nov. 18, 1729.
26. The word is of Nahuatl, not Maya, origin.
27. ANEY, M. Montero, June 18, 1718, fol. 87ff.
28. ANEY, J. A. Baeza, date unknown, sometime in October 1690, fols 165-71.
29. ANEY, M. Montero, July 22, 1722, fols. 462-3.
30. ANEY, J. A. Baeza, Dec. 2, 1691, fols. 356-7.
31. What follows is from ANEY, J. A. Baeza, August 13, 1692, fols. 541-3.The deteriorated nature of the document makes it impossible to read the full surname of Carvajal's wife. The first four letter are "Mont" and I am guessing the rest.
32. ANEY, J. A. Baeza, Nov. 24, 1692.
33. For a detailed analysis of chantries in the eighteenth century, see Gisela von Wobeser, *Vida eterna y preocupaciones terrenales: Las capellanías de misas en la Nueva España, 1700-1821* (Mexico City: La Universidad Nacional Autónoma de México, 1999).
34. ANEY, J. A. Baeza, July 24, 1689, fols. 49-52. For more references to cofradías in Mérida, see ANEY, J. A. Baeza, April 12, 1690, fols. 127-9; April 11, 1691, fols. 256-61; June 10, 1692, fols. 494-5. The cofradías of colonial Mérida have yet to be studied. For a Maya village cofradía, see Robert W. Patch, "Una cofradía y su estancia en el siglo XVIII: Notas de investigación," *Boletín de la Escuela de Ciencias Antropológicas de la Universidad de Yucatán* 8 (Jan.-April 1981): 56-66.
35. Beatriz Cáceres Menéndez and Robert W. Patch, "'Gente de mal vivir': Families and Incorrigible Sons in New Spain, 1721-1729," *Revista de Indias* LXVI, no. 237 (2006): 363-92.
36. The same was true everywhere else in Spanish America. See Charles Gibson, *The Aztecs under Spanish Rule: A History of the Indians of the Valley of Mexico, 1519-1821* (Stanford: Stanford University Press, 1964), 112-4.
37. Kathryn Burns, *Colonial Habits: Convents and the Spiritual Economy of Cuzco, Peru*. (Durham, North Carolina: Duke University Press, 1999), 3-6, 132-52.
38. Manuscript collection of the ex-Instituto Yucateco de Antropología e Historia, Book 12, Synodo Diocesano, 1722 (hereafter cited as Synodo Diocesano), Libro I, Tit. 4, fol. 21v. This is in a collection of manuscripts now in possession of the Archivo del Ayuntamiento de Mérida.
39. ASA, Asuntos Terminados, Expediente 1, March 24, 1751.
40. ANEY, A. Baeza, Jan. 23, 1692, fols. 421-2.
41. ANEY, A. Baeza, Feb. 8, 1692, fols. 429-31.
42. ANE, M. Montero, no date (August or September) 1720, fol. 151.
43. ANEY, J. A. Baeza, Sept. 18, 1690, fols. 160-2.
44. ANEY, F. A. Savido, Jan. 10, 1736, fols. 227-32.

45. ANEY, Indice de 1749 a 1803, Libro de Cappellanías de la Villa de San Francisco de Campeche mandado ayer por mando de su Sría., Ylustrísimo el Obispo mi Señor Dn Fray de San Buenaventura en la visita que hizo de estas capellanías, Año de 1749, fol. 97.

46. ANEY, Indice de 1749 a 1803, Libro de Cappellanías de la Villa de San Francisco de Campeche, fol. 73.

47. ANEY, J. A. Baeza, date unknown because of missing pages, but sometime in October 1690, fols. 165–71.

48. AGA, Matrimonios, May 2, 1709, fol. 112.

Chapter Four

1. AGA, Matrimonios, Mérida, Libro 6, fols. 71; Libro 5, Nov. 13, 1709, fol. 119.

2. See, for example, Robert W. Patch, "Decolonization, the Agrarian Problem, and the Origins of the Caste War," in *Land, Labor, and Capital in Modern Yucatán: Essays in Regional History and Political Economy*, ed. Jeffrey T. Brannon and Gilbert M. Joseph (Tuscaloosa: University of Alabama Press, 1991), 75–82.

3. ANEY, M. Montero, Oct. 29, 1720, fols. 228–30.

4. For a discussion of many of the issues regarding race, categories, and classification, see above, chapter 3, note 1.

5. For an analysis of the usage of *don* and *doña* in colonial Mérida, see the excellent treatment of the theme in Hunt, *Colonial Yucatán*, 61–3. Hunt shows that the usage expanded over time but never lost its significance as a status marker.

6. The status distinction between *don/doña* and everyone else was still being vigorously maintained in small-town Andalucía well into the middle of the twentieth century. See Pitt-Rivers, *The People of the Sierra*, 72–4, 81–3.

7. AGA, Libro 3 de Entierros (1714–1733).

8. AGA, Libro 6 de Bautismos, 1709–1716, Feb. 5, 1710, fol. 15.

9. AGA, Libro 6 de Bautismos, 1709–1716, Mar. 31, 1712, fol. 67v.

10. Susan M. Socolow, "Acceptable Partners: Marriage Choice in Colonial Argentina, 1778–1810," in *Sexuality and Marriage in Colonial Latin America*, ed. Asunción Lavrín (Lincoln and London: The University of Nebraska Press, 1989), 220.

11. Pérez, *En busca de mejor fortuna*, 166.

12. Góngora, "Urban Social Stratification," 434.

13. Xabier Lamikiz, "Basques in the Atlantic World, 1450–1824," *Oxford Research Encyclopedia of Latin American History* (Online: October 2017), 6.

14. For good examples, see AGI, México 957, Asuntos de encomiendas (various years); México 892, Carta del Gobernador (Salcedo) al Rey, Jan. 22, 1737; México 997, Asuntos de Encomiendas (1754); México 3083, Asuntos de Encomiendas (1765).

15. José María Valdés Acosta, *A través de las centurias*, 3 vols. (Mérida, Yucatán: Talleres "Pluma y Lápiz," 1926), I, 229–30, 385–6.

16. Manuela Cristina García Bernal, *La Sociedad de Yucatán* (Sevilla: Escuela de Estudios Hispano-Americanos de Sevilla, 1972), 55, 63; "Incorporación a La Real Corona

de las Encomiendas de Yucatán: Distrito de las Reales Cajas de Mérida y Campeche," *Boletín del Archivo General de la Nación* 9, no. 3 (1938): 469–567.

17. For a detailed study of the struggle against arranged marriages in Mexico, see Patricia Seed, *To Love, Honor, and Obey in Colonial Mexico: Conflicts over Marriage Choice, 1574–1821* (Stanford: Stanford University Press, 1992). See also Margarita Estrada Iguíniz and América del Villar Molina, *Matrimonio: Intereses, afectos conflictos: Una Aproximación desde la antropología, la historia y la demografía (siglos XVIII-XXI)* (Mexico City: Centro de Investigaciones y Estudios Superiores en la Antropología Social, 2015).

18. Kimberly Gauderman, *Women's Lives in Colonial Quito: Gender, Law, and Economy in Spanish America* (Austin: University of Texas Press, 2003), 22–7.

19. AGA, Matrimonios, Feb. 9, 1698, fol. 8.

20. AGA, Bautismos, Oct. 30, 1711; June 15, 1722; Mar. 23, 1726.

21. Ann Twinam, "Sexualidad, ilegitimidad y género en España y América, siglo XVIII: Una Comparación," in *Familia y redes sociales*, ed. Olivero Guidobono, Cato, and López, 37–8.

22. AGA, Bautismos, Sept. 17, 1727.

23. AGA, Bautismos, 1729, extra folios (between folios 32 and 33), dated Sept. 19, 1752, and Nov. 15, 1756.

24. Calvo, *Guadalajara y su región*, 93–5.

25. For the genealogy, see Valdés Acosta, *A través de las centurias*.

26. Robert McCaa, "Tratos nupciales: la constitución de uniones formales e informales en México y España, 1500–1900," in *Familia y vida privada en la historia de Iberoamérica*, ed. Pilar Gonzalbo Aizpuru and Cecilia Rabell Romero (México: El Colegio de México, 1996), 21–57.

27. ANEY, J. A. Baeza, March 10, 1692, fols. 451–2.

28. Silvia Arrom, *La Mujer mexicana ante el divorcio eclesiástico (1800–1857)* (México: Secretaría de Educación Pública, Dirección General de Divulgación, 1976).

29. AGA, Entierros, May 21, 1698, fol. 6.

30. AGA, Entierros, Mar. 7, 1720, fol. 50v.

31. AGA, Matrimonios, June 20, 1708, fol. 104.

32. AGA, Matrimonios, April 18, 1709, fols. 111–2.

33. AGA, Matrimonios, June 8, 1699, fol. 16.

34. AGA, Matrimonios, Feb. 14, 1702.

35. AGA, Matrimonios, July 9, 1703.

36. AGA, Matrimonios, Sept. 10, 1721, fols. 100–1.

37. AGA, Matrimonios, Dec. 29, 1724, fol. 129.

38. Robert McCaa, "Tratos nupciales," 21–57; Ann Twinam, *Public Lives, Private Secrets: Gender, Honor, Sexuality and Illegitimacy in Colonial Spanish America* (Stanford: Stanford University Press, 1999), 37–41.

39. AGA, Bautismos, Sept. 23, 1706, fol. 106.

40. Twinam, *Public Lives, Private Secrets*, 66–73.

41. AGA, Matrimonios, Aug. 11, 1700.

42. For the embellished story, see Valdés Acosta, *A través de las centurias*, II, 433–5.

43. Góngora, "Urban Social Stratification," 444; Calvo, *Guadalajara y su región*, 91–2; Twinam, *Public Lives, Private Secrets*, 7–13; Susan Migden Socolow, *The Women of Colonial Latin America* (Cambridge: Cambridge University Press, 2000), 74.

44. AGA, Bautismos, 1729–1736, Dec. 17, 1730, with additional document dated Oct. 15, 1781.

45. José M. Torres Pico, *Los expósitos en la sociedad colonial: La Casa Cuna de la Habana, 1710–1832* (La Habana: Instituto de la Historia de Cuba, Editora Historia, 2013), 29; Pilar Gonzalbo Aizpuru, "La Casa de Niños Expósitos de la Ciudad de México: Una fundación del siglo XVIII," *Historia Mexicana*, no. 123 (1992): 409–30. See also René Salinda Mesa, "Orphans and Family Disintegration in Chile: The Mortality of Abandoned Children, 1750–1930," *Journal of Family History* 16, no. 3 (1991): 316–29; Susan M. Socolow, *The Merchants of Buenos Aires, 1778–1810: Family and Commerce* (New York: Cambridge University Press, 1978), 220.

46. Ondina E. González, "Consuming Interests: The Response to Abandoned Children in Colonial Havana," in *Raising an Empire: Children in Early Modern Iberia and Colonial Latin America*, ed. Ondina E. González and Bianca Premo (Albuquerque: University of New Mexico Press, 2007), 137–62; Ann Twinam, "The Church, the State, and the Abandoned: *Expósitos* in Late Colonial Havana," in *Raising an Empire*, 163–86.

47. ANEY, M. Montero, Aug. 21, 1738, no foliation.

48. ANEY, B. Magaña, Sept. 26, 1729, no foliation.

49. AGA, Matrimonios, Jan. 7, 1706; Matrimonios, May 21, 1731.

50. AGA, Matrimonios, May 12, 1737.

51. ANEY, J. A. Baeza, no date, sometime in October 1690, fols. 165–7.

52. ANEY, B. Magaña, Mar. 24, 1728; May 26, 1728; July 8, 1729; Aug. 6, 1729.

53. AGA, Bautismos, May 17, 1717; Bautismos, Jan. 27, 1724; April 25, 1724.

54. AGA, Bautismos, Oct. 8, 1711; AGA, Matrimonios, Jan. 10, 1729, f. 164.

55. ANEY, B. Magaña, Jan. 3, 1728, no foliation.

56. AGI, E. C. 322A, Residencia del Gobernador Martín Urzúa, el Conde de Lizarraga, Cuaderno de la Demanda del Cap. Don Juan Manuel Carrillo de Albornoz contra el Conde de Lizarraga (1707), fols. 48–52.

57. ANEY, J. A. Baeza, December 14, 1692, fols. 602–4.

58. For a discussion of the signifiers of class differences, see the next chapter.

59. Calvo, *Guadalajara y su región*, 103–7.

60. Archivo de la Secretaría del Arzobispado, Representaciones y Ynformes del Yllmo. Y Rmo. Señor Don Fray Luis de Piña y Mazo Dignmo. Obispo de estas Provincias de Yucatán al Rey Ntro. Señor en su Real y Superior Consejo de las Yndias, y En la Real Audiencia de México. Desde el año de 1780, Informe de July 18, 1782.

61. Twinam, *Public Lives, Private Secrets*, 91–6.

62. Quoted in Earl, *The Body of the Conquistador*, 89.

63. Asunción Lavrín and Edith Couturier, "Dowries and Wills: A View of Women's Socioeconomic Role in Colonial Guadalajara and Puebla, 1640–1790," *Hispanic*

American Historical Review 59, no. 2 (May 1979): 280-304; Calvo, *Guadalajara y su region*, 316-18; Pilar Gonzalbo Aizpuru, "Las cargas del matrimonio. Dotes y vida familiar en la Nueva España," in *Familia y vida privada*, Gonzalbo Aizpuru and Rabell Romero, 216.

64. Pilar Gonzalbo Aizpuru, "Las cargas del matrimonio. Dotes y vida familiar en la Nueva España," in *Familia y vida privada*, Gonzalbo Aizpuru and Rabell Romero, 225.

65. Gonzalbo Aizpuru, "Las Cargas del matrimonio," 25.

66. ANEY, J. A. Baeza, May 24, 1692, fols. 471-2.

67. ANEY, M. Montero, Oct. 13, 1720, fols. 208-9.

68. ANEY, J. A. Baeza, Sept. 18, 1690, fols. 160-2.

69. ANEY, J. A. Baeza, Oct. 8, 1692, fols. 575-7.

70. ANEY, J. A. Baeza, June 11, 1692, fols. 496-9.

71. ANEY, J. A. Baeza, Dec. 15, 1692, fols. 611-3.

72. ANEY, B. Magaña, Aug. 6, 1729, no foliation.

73. García Fuentes, *El comercio español con América*, 302-6; García-Baquero González, *Cádiz y el Atlántico (1717-1778)*, vol. 1, 309-36; Walker, *Spanish Politics and Imperial Trade*; Stanley J. Stein and Barbara H. Stein, *Silver, Trade, and War: Spain and America in the Making of Early Modern Europe* (Baltimore and London: Johns Hopkins University Press, 2000), 58-86, 142-4.

74. Góngora, "Urban Social Stratification," 433.

75. Synodo Diocesano, 1722, Libro 5, Título X, fol. 186v. The bishop called attention to "el uso pernicioso de vestirse las mujeres españolas el traje disoluto y lascivo de Meztizas, en que estando casi desnudas es preciso el que provoquen y hagan atrollar la mayor honestidad, y justos respectos del parentesco aunque sea solo dentro de sus casas, y delante de los parientes solos." By that point in time in Yucatán it is possible that the word *mestiza* had come to be used as a synonym for Maya woman.

76. Information found in the will of Juan del Castillo's mother, Doña Antonia de Arrúe, drawn up in Maní, in ANEY, J. A. Baeza, 8 June 1691, fols. 283-5.

77. AGI, Escribanía de Cámara 323A, Residencias de Fernando Meneses Bravo de Sarabia and Alonso Meneses Bravo de Sarabia, 1715, Pesquisa en Mérida, fol. 221-2.

78. Earl, *The Body of the Conquistador*, 50-2.

79. Sínodo Diocesano, 1722, Libro 1, Tit. 1, Sección 2, fol. 14.

80. AGI, México 1020, Representación del procurador de Mérida, Campeche y Valladolid al gobernador, Sept. 3, 1722; Carta del Cabildo de Mérida al Rey, Sept. 18, 1722. The documents regarding Gómez de Parada's attempted reform and the resistance to it are published in *Contra viento y marea: Documentos sobre las reformas del obispo Juan Gómez de Parada al trabajo indígena*, ed. Gabriela Solís Robleda (Mérida: Instituto de Investigaciones y Estudios Superiores en Antropología Social, Instituto de Cultura de Yucatán, 2003).

81. This is one of the main themes of Earl, *The Body of the Conquistador*.

Chapter Five

1. Richard E. Boyer, *Lives of the Bigamists: Marriage, Family, and Community in Colonial Mexico* (Albuquerque: University of New Mexico Press, 1995).
2. AGA, Matrimonios de Españoles, Libro 6, Nov. 6, 1718, March 5, 1726.
3. In the documents, the home villages of two of the 129 people were illegible.
4. Patch, *Maya and Spaniard*, 232–43.
5. AGI, E. E. 321A, Residencia del governador Juan de Arechaga, Proceedings in Campeche (1684), fol. 5ff. One of the witnesses called to testify was Captain Juan Antonio Calvo y Moreno, who was identified as the "factor del Consulado de Negros."
6. AAM, 1747–1751, fols. 15–17; AGA, Matrimonios, Oct. 1, 1724, fol. 127.
7. AGI, México, 997, Encomiendas, fol. 581 ff.
8. For the study of emigration from Spain and immigration in America, see José C. Moya, "Migration and the Historical Formation of Latin America in a Global Perspective," *Sociologias*, Porto Alegre (2018), 20, 49, 24–68; Carlos Martínez Shaw, *La Emigración española a América, 1492–1824* (Columbres, Asturias: Archivo de Indianos, 1994). Most of the literature on Spanish emigration and immigration is cited in Hillel Eyal, "Beyond Networks: Transatlantic Immigration and Wealth in Late Colonial Mexico City," *Journal of Latin American Studies* 47, no. 2 (2015): 317–48.
9. Calvo, *Guadalajara y su región*, 155–60.
10. In Mexico City in the eighteenth century, 40 percent of immigrant merchants did not get married. See Paloma Fernández Pérez and Juan Carlos Sola-Corbacho, "Regional Identity, Family and Trade in Cádiz and Mexico City in the Eighteenth Century," *Journal of Early Modern History* 8, no. 4 (2004): 370–1.
11. ANEY, J. A. Baeza, Feb. 19, 1692, fols. 438–9.
12. Eyal, "Beyond Networks," 320–1.
13. Peter Boyd-Bowman, "Patterns of Spanish Emigration to the Indies until 1600," *Hispanic American Historical Review* 56, no. 4 (November 1976): 580–604.
14. J. Ignacio Rubio Mañé, *Gente de España en la Ciudad de México. Año de 1689* (México, 1939), 349–51.
15. There were 164 immigrants from Spain, but one of these was said to be from "Castile." Since his regional origin is unknown, he is excluded from the sample.
16. Kris E. Lane, *Pillaging the Empire: Piracy in the Americas 1500–1750* (Armonk, New York: M. E. Sharpe, 1998).
17. There are numerous references to these military matters in AGI, México 888, no foliation, military positions.
18. Francisco Morales Padrón, "Colonos canarios en Indias," *Anuario de Estudios Americanos* VIII (1951): 399–441.
19. Sergio Solbes Ferri, "La navegación directa de Canarias a América y su papel en el sistema comercial atlántico, 1718–1778," *América Latina en la Historia Económica*" (Jan.–April 2018): 36–97.
20. AGI, México 3080, Carta del Gobernador (Crespo) al Ministro de la Marina (Arriaga), July 1, 1762.

21. ANEY, M. Montero, Dec. 8, 1720, fols. 246-8.
22. Ancestry.com information shared with the author by Víctor Manuel Cáceres Menéndez of Mérida, Yucatán. I thank him for the information.
23. Morales Padrón, "Colonos canarios," 13, 16.
24. ANEY, M. Montero, April 16, 1720, fols. 54-60.
25. ANEY, M. Montero, July 7, 1720, fols. 116-9; Dec. 7, 1721, fols. 372-5; Dec. 8, 1720, fols. 246-8.
26. ANEY, M. Montero, Dec. 7, 1721, fols. 372-5.
27. Boyd-Bowman, "Patterns of Spanish Emigration."
28. Jacobs, *Los movimientos migratorios*, 127-50.
29. Juan Carlos Jurado Jurado, "Forasteros y transeúntes en América, Siglo XVIII: El caso de Francisco Fernández de la Fuente," *Revista de Indias* LX, no. 220 (Sept.-Dec. 2000): 655-6.
30. Calvo, *Guadalajara y su región*; Pérez, *En busca de mejor fortuna*.
31. The gender imbalance was even more extreme in Antequera (Oaxaca City) in the 1690s. Only two of sixty Spanish-born immigrants who married between 1693 and 1700 were female. See John K. Chance, *Race and Class in Colonial Oaxaca* (Stanford: Stanford University Press, 1978), 132-7.
32. Rubio Mañé, *Gente de* España, 349.
33. Rubio Mañé, *Gente de España*, 351.
34. Brading, *Miners and Merchants*, 104-9.
35. Brading refers to these people as *montañeses*. That term does not appear in the documents regarding Yucatán, and so in this study I am employing the somewhat anachronistic term Cantabrian instead.
36. Cited in Fernando Barreda y Ferrer de la Vega, *Prosperidad de Santander y desarrollo industrial de esta provincia desde el siglo XVIII* (Santander: Editorial Cantabria, 1957), 2.
37. For the Basque presence in Mexico, see Amaya Garritz, ed., *Los vascos en las regiones de México Siglos XVI-XX*, 3 vols. (México: Universidad Nacional Autónoma de México, Ministerio de Cultura del Gobierno Vasco, Instituto Vasco-Mexicano de Desarrollo, 1996). The studies in these books concentrate on individuals and religious brotherhoods but not on Basque immigration as a whole.
38. Patch, *Maya and Spaniard*, 82-3.
39. Álvaro Aragón Ruano and Alberto Angulo Morales, "The Spanish Basque Country in World Trade Networks in the Eighteenth Century," *International Journal of Maritime History* 25, no. 149 (2013): 149-72; Xabier Lamikiz, "Basques in the Atlantic World, 1450-1824," *Oxford Research Encyclopedia of Latin American History* (Online: October 2017): 1-22.
40. Aragón Ruano and Angulo Morales, "The Spanish Basque Country," 149.
41. ANEY, J. A. Baeza, Dec. 13, 1691, fols. 372-3; no date (late October or early November 1691), fols. 332-4.
42. José Moya, *Cousins and Strangers: Spanish Immigrants in Buenos Aires, 1850-1930* (Berkeley, Los Angeles, London: The University of California Press, 1998).

236   Notes to Chapters Five and Six

43. The Spanish Basque Country consists of the Lordship (*Señorío*) of Vizcaya (Biscay), the Province of Guipúzcoa (Gipuzcoa), the Province of Álava, and the Kingdom of Navarre. The latter two are inland, while the first two are in a basin leading to the sea and are considered to be the maritime Basque provinces.

44. Moya, *Cousins and Strangers*, 96.

45. AGI, México 891, Carta del Gobernador Cortayre al Rey, Aug. 16, 1721.

46. Libro 5 de Baptismos, Jan. 3, 1703.

47. AGI, Mexico 892, Carta del Gobernador Capitan General al Rey, Aug. 14, 1739.

48. Informe del Fiscal y del Consejo de Indias, attached to AGI, Mexico 892, Carta del Gobernador Capitan General al Rey, Aug. 14, 1739.

49. There is a plaque commemorating Figueroa's accomplishment on the façade of the church of Santa Ana in Mérida.

50. Charles F. Nunn, *Foreign Immigrants in Early Bourbon Mexico 1700–1760* (London, New York, Melbourne: Cambridge University Press, 1979), 11–29.

51. Nunn, *Foreign Immigrants*, 2.

52. Libro 5 de Matrimonios, 1697–1712, fol. 116.

53. Libro 6 de Matrimonios, 1712–1729, fol. 39.

Chapter Six

1. *Instrucciones que los vierreyes de Nueva España dejaron a sus sucesores*, 2 vols. (México, 1873), I, 258 (quoted in Brading, *Miners and Merchants*, 105).

2. Francisco de Ajofrín, *Diario del viaje que hizo a América en le siglo XVIII*, 2 vols. (México, 1964), I, 63 (quoted in Brading, *Miners and Merchants*, 109).

3. See José Ramón Díaz de Durana Ortiz de Urbina, *La Otra nobleza. Escuderos e hidalgos sin nombre y sin historia. Hidalgos e hidalguía universal en el País Vasco al final de la Edad Media (1259–1525)* (Bilbao: Servicio Editorial de la Universidad del País Vasco, 2004) for a detailed study of the claim to *hidalguía* in the various regions of the Basque Country.

4. AGI, México 895, Carta del Gobernador Salcedo al Rey, Jan. 22, 1737.

5. Góngora, "Urban Social Stratification," 439.

6. Díaz de Durana, *La Otra nobleza*, 19.

7. ANEY, J. A. Baeza, undated, Aug. 1691, fol. 319.

8. Eyal, "Beyond Networks," 335–48.

9. Lamikiz, "Basques in the Atlantic World, 1450–1824," 6.

10. AGI, 321B, Residencia del Gobernador y Capitán Juan Bruno Tello de Guzmán, Cargos y Descargos (1687), fol. 272ff.

11. AGI, México 888, Petitions for encomiendas, Relación de Méritos de Antonio de la Helguera, no foliation.

12. ANEY, M. Montero, no date (1729), fols. 192–5.

13. De la Teja, *San Antonio de Béxar*, 24–5.

14. Fernández Pérez and Sola-Corbacho, "Regional Identity," 373–5.

15. Eyal, "Beyond Networks," 327–35.

16. Xabier Lamikiz, *Trade and Trust in the Eighteenth Century Atlantic World: Spanish Merchants and Their Networks* (London: Royal Historical Society, 2010).

17. Eyal, "Beyond Networks," 326–35.

18. John E. Kicza, *Colonial Entrepreneurs: Families and Business in Bourbon Mexico City* (Albuquerque: University of New Mexico Press, 1983), 150–1.

19. Aragón Ruano and Angulo Morales, "The Spanish Basque Country in World Trade Networks," 149.

20. Del Valle Pavón, "Contrabando, negocios y discordias," 119.

21. María Conde's second surname does not appear in the records of her marriage or in those of her daughters. It is found in a notarial document drawn up in 1738. The document refers to a capellanía founded for her in around 1714 by Antonio Ruiz de la Vega. See ANEY, F. A. Savido, June 14, 1738, fols. 127–31.

22. As just noted, María Conde Pinacho may have been the daughter of an Italian merchant.

23. Unless otherwise stated, all of the following information about marriages is from the AGA, Matrimonios de Españoles, Libros 4–7.

24. For an interpretation emphasizing Garrástegui's marriage into the elite rather than the marriage of his daughters to Spaniards, see María Isabel Campos Goenaga, "Arraigar en Yucatán: De Garrástegui y Oleada a Calderón y Marcos Bermejo. Una Mirada a la sociedad Novohispana del siglo XVIII," in *Identidad y estructura de la emigración vasca y Navarra hacia Iberoamérica Siglos (XVI-XXI)*, ed. José Manuel Azcona (Thomas Reuters Aranzadi: Madrid, 2015), 125–40.

25. Patch, *Maya and Spaniard*, 82.

26. Archivo Notarial del Estado de Yucatán (Mérida), J. A. Baeza, Jan. 25, 1689, fol. 2.

27. Upon the death of his first wife, he remarried in 1700. His second wife, María del Puerto, was from the local encomendero elite.

28. AGA, Libros de entierros, July 20, 1698; Oct. 13, 1712; Oct. 2, 1726.

29. William B. Taylor, *Landlord and Peasant in Colonial Oaxaca* (Stanford: Stanford University Press, 1972), 164; Chance, *Race and Class in Colonial Oaxaca*, 141.

30. García Bernal, *Yucatán: Población y encomienda*, 261.

31. ANEY, J. A. Baeza, April 15, 1689, fols. 18–22.

32. ANEY, M. Montero, Feb. 23, 1720, fols. 20–4.

33. AGI, México 1020, Quaderno 2°. Aug. 19, 1722.

34. Solís Robleda, *Bajo el signo de la compulsión*, 218–9.

Chapter Seven

1. This is not the same approach used by Max Weber in his famous essay, "Class, Status, and Party," in *From Max Weber*, ed. H. H. Gerth and C. Wright Mills (New York: Oxford University Press, 1946), 180–95. By "class" Weber means people of the same economic condition, while party as a category is inadequate for the study of the colonial period. His use of status, however, is very useful. In this study, therefore, I will use the concept of social class, made up of people who are similar in terms of capital, status, and/or power.

2. Calvo, *Poder, religión y sociedad*, 45–73.

3. The basic study is Constantino Bayle, *Los cabildos seculares in América Española* (Madrid: Sapienta S. A. de Ediciones, 1952). The historiography of city councils in colonial Spanish America is extensive. For a good summary see Laura Machuca Gallegos, *Poder y gestión en el Ayuntamiento de Mérida, Yucatán (1785–1835)* (México: Centro de Investigaciones y Estudios Superiores en Antropología Social, 2016), 18–19, and the cited bibliography, 214–39.

4. González Muñoz and Ana Martínez Ortega, *Cabildos y élites capitulares en Yucatán*; Martínez Ortega, *Estructura y configuración*; Machuca Gallegos, *Poder y gestión*.

5. Martínez Ortega, *Estructura y configuración*, 29–48, 58–60.

6. Martínez Ortega, *Estructura y configuración*, 58–9.

7. Most people at the time used only paternal surnames. In this chapter maternal surnames are also added for clarification of identity. This is, of course, unavoidably anachronistic.

8. In a few cases a single office was filled by two people because the first person either resigned or died and was replaced.

9. The Hispanic population was approximately 5,000. Leaving out women and children (who were ineligible to hold office), the adult male population probably numbered around 1,250. Between 20 and 25 percent of these men were likely to be hidalgos (see chapter 4), so the total adult male population of hidalgo status would have been approximately 250–300. This, of course, is a very rough estimate.

10. Góngora, "Urban Social Stratification," 433.

11. Three other people—Bartolomé de la Garma, Antonio Casanova, and Íñigo de Mendoza—were also elected to office three times in all if we count elections before 1694. But they are not counted here among the elite in order to emphasize the period after 1696.

12. Góngora, "Urban Social Stratification," 433.

13. In the case of the regidores, the period examined begins in 1694.

14. Both Hunt (*Colonial Yucatán*, 423) and Martínez Ortega (*Estructura y configuración*, 104, 258) assert that Francisco Méndez Pacheco was of an old encomendero family. However, Hunt provides no evidence to prove that. Martínez Ortega follows Hunt and in addition cites genealogical information in Valdés Acosta about the Pacheco family. In fact, however, Valdés Acosta does not show that Francisco Méndez Pacheco belonged to the prominent Pacheco family founded by conquistadores. Hunt seems to have based her conclusion on the maternal surname, but Pacheco is a common surname and by itself does not prove that Méndez Pacheco was a member of that family.

15. AAM, 1747–1751, fols. 19–21.

16. Martínez Ortega, *Estructura y configuración*, 67–89.

17. Martínez Ortega, *Estructura y configuración*, 96–9.

18. Martínez Ortega could not identify the origins of Regidores Martín de Echanagucia, Juan del Campo, José González de la Madriz, and Antonio de Ayora y Porras.

Marriage records in Mérida show that the first three were born in Spain, and a petition for an encomienda shows that Ayora y Porras too was from Spain. (AGI, México 1020, Cuaderno sobre encomiendas, 1757, fol. 23ff.) She also mistakenly states that Antonio Ruiz de la Vega was a regidor. Francisco de Zea Moscoso could not be identified as either foreign-born or America-born. However, he was the son of a regidor in Valladolid (Yucatán), and so it is highly likely that he was born in Yucatán. His father's origins could not be identified.

19. Martínez Ortega, *Estructura y configuración*, 99–104. Regidor Felipe de Ayora y Porras y Argaiz was the son of Regidor Antonio de Ayora y Porras, an immigrant from Andalucía. Felipe was born in Mérida and therefore was part of the community of second-generation immigrants.

20. Gaspar de Salazar y Córdoba was the son of a high-status official from Tabasco. Diego Rodríguez de Villamil, the father of Lucas de Villamil y Vargas, was from somewhere in New Spain, although it is not clear from where. Valdés Acosta says that Diego Rodríguez de Villamil "undoubtedly" was from the family of that name in New Spain but did not provide any evidence of a direct relationship to prove it. Valdés Acosta, *A través de las centurias*, I, 423. It remains possible that he was a first-generation immigrant from Spain who married well in Yucatán.

21. AGI, E. C. 323A, Residencia de Fernando and Alonso Meneses Bravo de Sarabia, Primera Pieza (1721), fols. 427–32.

22. AGI, E. C. 323B, Demanda hecha por el Conde de Miraflores en contra de Fernando y Alonso Bravo de Sarabia, fol. 322.

23. Here, Weber is useful. See Weber, "Class, Status, and Party," 180–95.

24. Stephen Webre, "El Cabildo de Santiago de Guatemala en el siglo XVII: ¿Una Oligarquía Criolla Cerrada y Hereditaria?" *Mesoamérica*, Año 1, Cuaderno 2 (June 1981): 1–19; José F. de la Peña y María Teresa López Díaz, "Comercio y poder: Los mercaderes y el cabildo de Guatemala, 1592–1693," *Historia Mexicana* XXX, no. 4 (April–June 1981): 469–505.

25. Chacón Jiménez, "¿De nuevo la familia?," in *Familia y redes sociales*, ed. Olivero Guidobono, Cato, and López, 25–7.

26. Antonio de Ayora y Porras, Francisco Solís Casanova, Domingo Rodríguez Vigario, Diego de Aranda y Aguayo, and the Count of Miraflores.

27. Pedro de Ancona.

28. Such as Nicolás Carrillo de Albornoz.

29. Such as Juan del Castillo y Arrúe.

30. This is based on the assumption that the parents of immigrants from Spain were born in Spain, the parents of immigrants from the Canary Islands were born in the Canary Islands, the parents of the immigrants from Portugal were born in Portugal, and the parents of the immigrant from Italy were born in Italy.

31. Apparently the first historian, but not the last, to argue that in colonial Yucatán the upper class was an endogamous caste was García Bernal, *La Sociedad de Yucatán*, 89–92. See also García Bernal, "La aristocracia de Yucatán (siglo XVII)," in *América: Encuentro y asimilación* (Granada: Diputación de Provincial de Granada, 1988), 317–31,

wherein she modifies the interpretation by pointing out that Spanish-born government officials sometimes intermarried with local elite women.

32. Webre, "El Cabildo de Santiago de Guatemala," 1–19.
33. Pitt-Rivers, *The People of the Sierra*, 100–3. The Andalusian saying is:
Tu hijo se casa
Y pierdes a tu hijo.
Tu hija se casa
Y ganas a otro.
34. ANEY, B. Magaña, July 8, 1728, no foliation.
35. AGA, Matrimonios, Libro 7, June 23, 1730, fol. 3.
36. Pitt-Rivers, *People of the Sierra*, 106–9.
37. García Bernal, *La Sociedad de Yucatán*, 79–80; García Bernal, *Población y encomienda*, 425–74; Martínez Ortega, *Estructura y configuración*, 124–30.

Chapter Eight

1. The records are found in AGN, Tierras, 483, Exp. 2 (1728), fols. 1–39.
2. For excellent studies of the functioning of the ranching economy and its relationship with markets, see Ramón Serrera Contreras, *Guadalajara ganadera: Estudio Regional novohispano, 1760–1805* (Sevilla: Escuela de Estudios Hispano-Americanos de Sevilla, 1977); Eric Van Young, *Hacienda and Market in Eighteenth-Century Mexico: The Rural Economy of the Guadalajara Region, 1675–1820* (Berkeley: The University of California, 1981).
3. De la Teja, *San Antonio de Béxar*, 97–117.
4. AGN, Tierras, 483, Expediente 2 (1728), fols. 60–73.
5. AGI, E. C. 322B, Residencia del Gobernador Roque de Soberanis, Pesquisa en Mérida (1709), fol. 237.
6. Patch, *Maya and Spaniard*, 213–7.
7. ANEY, M. Montero, Oct. 4, 1737, no foliation.
8. Peter Marzahl, "Creoles and Government: The Cabildo of Popayán," HAHR 54, no. 4 (November 1974): 650–2. See also Calvo, *Poder, religion y Sociedad*, 45–73.
9. AGI, E. C. 327, Causa criminal fulminada (1716), fol. 319; ANEY, J. A. Baeza, April 11, 1690, fols. 123–5.
10. ANEY, M. Montero, April 3, 1719, fols. 276–7; ANEY, B. Magaña, July 20, 1728, no foliation.
11. AGI, E. C. 322B, Residencia del Maestre de Campo Don Alvaro de Ribaguda Enciso y Luyando, Pesquisa en Mérida (1709), fol. 151.
12. Solís Robleda, *Contra viento y marea*, 213.
13. ANEY, B. Cetina Yzarraga, Jan. 3, 1721, fols. 255–6.
14. ANEY, M. Montero, Mar. 22, 1721, fols. 275–6.
15. ANEY, B. Magaña, Mar. 7, 1728, no foliation.
16. ANEY, B. Magaña, Jan. 1, 1729, no foliation.
17. ANEY, B. Magaña, April 12, 1728, no foliation; ANEY, B. Magaña, July 18, 1728, no foliation.

18. ANEY, B. Magaña, Dec. 31, 1728, no foliation.
19. ANEY, B. Magaña, July 20, 1728, no foliation; July 19, 1728, no foliation; Nov. 11, 1729, no foliation.
20. Solís Robleda, *Contra viento y marea*, 213.
21. Góngora, "Urban Social Stratification," 436–8; Kicza, *Colonial Entrepreneurs*, 19–28.

Chapter Nine
1. For a good summary of the research on conflicts within cathedral chapters, see Alexandre Coello de la Rosa, "Conflictividad capitular y poderes locales en el Cabildo de Manila (1690–1697)," *Colonial Latin American Review* 25, no. 3 (2016): 325–50.
2. Robert W. Patch, "Imperial Politics and Local Economy in Colonial Central America, 1670–1770," *Past & Present*, no. 143 (May 1994): 79–107. This is a main theme of Robert W. Patch, *Indians and the Political Economy of Colonial Central America, 1670–1810* (Norman: University of Oklahoma Press, 2013).
3. Horst Pietschman, "*Alcaldes Mayores, Corregidores und Subdelegados*: Zum Problem des Distriksbeamtenschaft in vizekönigreich Neuspanien," *Jahrbuch für Geschichte von Staat, Wirtschaft und Gesellschaft Lateinamerikas* 10 (1973): Anhang I, 254.
4. AGI, E. C. 323A, Residencia de Fernando and Alonso Meneses Bravo de Sarabia, Pesquisa en Mérida (1721), fol. 244ff.
5. AGI, E. C. 323B, Demanda hecha por el Conde de Miraflores contra Fernando y Alonso Meneses Bravo de Sarabia (no date), fols. 218–21, 59, 125.
6. AGI, E. C. 323A, Residencia de Fernando and Alonso Meneses, Proceedings in Mérida (1721), fols. 13, 235.
7. AGI, E. C. 323B, Pieza (untitled), Demanda hecha por el Conde de Miraflores contra Fernando y Alonso Meneses Bravo de Sarabia (1721 copy), fol. 213.
8. AGI, E. C. 323B, Residencia de Fernando and Alonso Meneses Bravo de Sarabia, Pesquisa en Mérida (1721), fol. 385; Autos en Mérida (1721), fol. 10.
9. AGI, E. C. 323B, Demanda hecha por el Conde de Miraflores contra Fernando y Alonso Meneses Bravo de Saravia (no date), fol. 278.
10. AGI, E. C. 322A, Pleito entre Juan Manuel Carrillo de Albornoz y el Conde de Lizarraga (1708), fol. 251; E. C. 323A, Residencia de Fernando y Alonso Meneses de Bravo Sarabia, Pesquisa en Mérida (1721), fol. 23.
11. E. C. 323B, Demanda hecha por el Conde de Miraflores contra Fernando y Alonso Meneses Bravo de Saravia (no date), fols. 15–23, 280.
12. AGI, E. C. 323B, Demanda hecha por el Conde de Miraflores en contra de Fernando y Alonso Meneses Bravo de Sarabia (no date), no foliation.
13. AGI, E. C. 323B, Demanda hecha por el Conde de Miraflores (1721), fols. 328–9, 414–5.
14. AGI, E. C. 323C, Residencia de Fernando Meneses Bravo de Sarabia, Pieza 1A, de los autos en Mérida (Medina Cachón's proceedings) (1715), fols. 5–7.
15. AGI, E. C. 323A, Residencia de Fernando y Alonso Meneses Bravo de Sarabia, carried out by Governor-Captain General Don Juan Joseph Vertiz (1715).

242 Notes to Chapter Nine

16. AGA, Bautismos de Españoles, Aug. 20, 1714.

17. AGI, E. C. 323B, Demanda hecha por Don Carlos de Texada, procurador de Mérida, en contra de Fernando y Alonso Meneses Bravo de Saravia (1721), fol. 10.

18. AGI, E. C. 323C, Instrumentos de Composición y Aberío que hicieron los regidores los Regidores Don Felipe de Ayora y Don Gregorio de Aldana de no pedir en la residencia contra el Señor Don Alonso de Meneses por haver sido desterrados a Campeche, y recibos de las cantidades que expresan (1715).

19. AGA, Matrimonios, Nov. 17, 1717, fol. 58.

20. AGI, E. C. 323B, Demanda hecha por el Conde de Miraflores (1721), fol. 515.

21. AGI, E. C. 323B, Demanda hecha por el Conde de Miraflores en contra de Fernando y Alonso Meneses Bravo de Sarabia (no date), fol. 50.

22. AGA, Matrimonios, May 13, 1721.

23. AGI, E. C. 327, Causa criminal fulminada en virtud de comisión de S. M. Por el Sr. Don Juan Joseph de Vertiz Hortañón Governador y Capitán General . . . (1716).

24. What follows is from AGI, E. C. 323A, Residencia de Fernando and Alonso Meneses Bravo de Sarabia, Pesquisa en Mérida (1721).

25. AGI, E. C. 323A, Residencia de Fernando and Alonso Meneses Bravo de Sarabia, Pesquisa en Mérida (1721), fol. 13.

26. AGI, E. C. 323A, Residencia de Fernando and Alonso Meneses Bravo de Sarabia, Pesquisa en Mérida (1721), fol. 56.

27. AGI, E. C. 323A, Residencia de Fernando and Alonso Meneses Bravo de Sarabia, Pesquisa en Mérida (1721), fol. 221.

28. AGI, E. C. 323A, Residencia de Fernando and Alonso Meneses Bravo de Sarabia, Pesquisa en Mérida (1721), fol. 241.

29. AGI, E. C. 323A, Residencia de Fernando and Alonso Meneses Bravo de Sarabia, Pesquisa en Mérida (1721), fols. 446–52.

30. AGI, E. C. 323A, Residencia de Fernando and Alonso Meneses Bravo de Sarabia, Pesquisa en Mérida (1721), fols. 451–2.

31. AGI, E. C. 323A, Residencia de Fernando and Alonso Meneses Bravo de Sarabia, Pesquisa en Mérida (1721), fols. 550–62.

32. AGI, E. C. 323A, Residencia de Fernando and Alonso Meneses Bravo de Sarabia, Pesquisa en Mérida (1721), fol. 562.

33. AGI, E. C. 323A, Residencia de Fernando y Alonso Meneses Bravo de Safabia, Pesquisa en Mérida (1721), fols. 861–85.

34. AGI, E. C. 323A, Residencia de Fernando y Alonso Meneses Bravo de Safabia, Pesquisa en Mérida (1721), fols. 883–5.

35. AGI, E. C. 323A, Residencia de Fernando y Alonso Meneses Bravo de Safabia, Pesquisa en Mérida (1721), fol. 885–6.

36. For an exposition of the concept of instrumental friendship, see Neera Kapur Badhwar, *Friendship: A Philosophical Reader* (Ithaca, New York: Cornell University Press, 1993). For its application in a historical context, see Dale Kent, *Friendship, Love, and Trust in Renaissance Florence* (Cambridge, Massachusetts: Harvard University Press, 2009).

Conclusion

1. For a good scholarly anthology on urban history, see Louisa Schell Hoberman and Susan Migden Socolow, eds., *Cities & Society in Colonial Latin America* (Albuquerque: University of New Mexico Press, 1986).
2. For an analysis of how local conditions determined historical outcomes in cities in colonial Chile, see Góngora, "Urban Social Stratification," 421–48.
3. Góngora, "Urban Social Stratification," 425–7.
4. Góngora, "Urban Social Stratification," 427.
5. Góngora, "Urban Social Stratification," 427–9.
6. García Bernal, *Población y encomienda*, 333–45; *La Sociedad de Yucatán*, 45–50.
7. For an analysis of the relationship between the encomienda and the history of different regions of Chile, see Góngora, "Urban Social Stratification," 427–36.
8. Webre, "El cabildo de Santiago de Guatemala en el siglo XVII."
9. Kicza, *Colonial Entrepreneurs*, 178–9.
10. De la Teja, *San Antonio de Béxar*, 119–22.
11. Machuca Gallegos, *Poder y gestión*, 90–1.
12. Patch, *Maya and Spaniard*, 138–54.
13. Rocher Salas, *La Disputa por las almas*; Adriana Rocher Salas, "Clero y élites en Yucatán durante el período colonial," in *Grupos privilegiados en la Península de Yucatán. Siglos XVIII y XIX*, ed. Laura Machuca Gallegos (Mexico City: Publicaciones de la Casa Chata, 2014), 21–53.
14. Michael J. Fallon, "The Secular Clergy in the Diocese of Yucatán, 1750–1800" (unpublished PhD diss., Catholic University of America, 1979).

BIBLIOGRAPHY

Primary Sources

AAM—Archivo del Ayuntamiento de Mérida, Libros del Cabildo.
AGA—Archivo General del Arzobispado, Mérida
ASRA—Archivo de la Secretaría del Arzobispado, Mérida
AGI—Archivo General de Indias, Seville
AGEY—Archivo General del Estado de Yucatán, Mérida
ANEY—Archivo Notarial del Estado de Yucatán
BCCA—Biblioteca "Crescencio Carrillo y Ancona," Manuscritas.
    Quentas dadas por el Capitan y Rexidor Decano Don Joseph de Marcos Vermejo como Sindico Procurador General, que fue en el año proximo pasado de 1756.
    Año de 1753, Cuentas de propios del espresado año.
    Año de 1753, Licencias de tiendas dadas por los Señores regidores Don Juan José de Bergara y Don Diego de Aranda y Cano en dicho año de 53.
    Libro 12, Synodo Diocesano . . . (1722).

Ajofrín, Francisco de. *Diario del viaje que hizo a América en el siglo XVIII*. 2 vols. México: 1964.

Cárdenas Valencia, Francisco. *Relación historial eclesiástica de la provincia de Yucatán de la Nueva España: escrita el año de 1639*. México: Antigua Librería Robredo, J. Porrúa e Hijos, 1937.

Ciudad Real, Fray Antonio. *El viaje de Fray Alonso Ponce por las provincias del Santo Evangelio*. Vols. LVII and LVIII, *Colección de documentos inéditos para la historia de España*. Madrid: Real Academia de la Historia, 1872.

Cortés, Hernán. *Letters from Mexico*. New Haven: Yale University Press, 1971.
Díaz del Castillo, Bernal. *The Conquest of New Spain*. London: Penguin Press, 1964.
Instrucciones que los virreyes de Nueva España dejaron a sus sucesores. 2 vols. México: 1873.
López de Cogolludo, Diego. *Historia de Yucatán*. 2 vols. Campeche: Comisión de Historia, 1954.
O'Gorman, Edmundo. "Incorporación a La Real Corona de las Encomiendas de Yucatán. Distrito de las Reales Cajas de Mérida y Campeche." *Boletín del Archivo General de la Nación* 9, no. 3 (1938): 469–567.
Relación de la Ciudad de Mérida. Vol. 11, *Colección de documentos inéditos relativos al descubrimiento, conquista y organización de las antiguas posesiones españolas de ultramar*. Madrid: Real Academia de la Historia, 1898.

Books & Articles

Altman, Ida, and James Lockhart, eds. *Provinces of Early Mexico. Variants of Spanish American Regional Evolution*. Los Angeles: UCLA Latin American Center Publications, 1976.
Aragón Ruano, Álvaro, and Alberto Angulo Morales. "The Spanish Basque Country in World Trade Networks in the Eighteenth Century." *International Journal of Maritime History* 25, no. 149 (2013): 149–72.
Arrom, Silvia. *La Mujer mexicana ante el divorcio eclesiástico (1800–1857)*. México: Secretaría de Educación Pública, Dirección General de Divulgación, 1976.
Badhwar, Neera Kapur. *Friendship: A Philosophical Reader*. Ithaca, New York: Cornell University Press, 1993.
Barreda y Ferrer de la Vega, Fernando. *Prosperidad de Santander y desarrollo industrial de esta provincia desde el siglo XVIII*. Santander: Editorial Cantabria, 1957.
Bayle, Constantino. *El protector de indios*. Seville: Escuela de Estudios Hispano-Americanos, Serie 1a, Anuario Núm. 5, 1945.
—. *Los cabildos seculares in América Española*. Madrid: Sapienta S. A. de Ediciones, 1952.
Borah, Woodrow. *Justice By Insurance: The General Indian Court of Colonial Mexico and the Legal Aides of the Half-real*. Berkeley: The University of California Press, 1983.

Boyd-Bowman, Peter. "Patterns of Spanish Emigration to the Indies until 1600." *The Hispanic American Historical Review* 56, no. 4 (1976): 580–604.

Boyer, Richard E. *Lives of the Bigamists: Marriage, Family, and Community in Colonial Mexico.* Albuquerque: University of New Mexico Press, 1995.

Bracamonte y Sosa, Pedro, and Gabriela Solís Robleda. *Espacios mayas de autonomía: El pacto colonial en Yucatán.* Mérida: Universidad Autónoma de Yucatán, 1996.

Bracamonte y Sosa, Pedro. *La Conquista inconclusa de Yucatán: Los mayas de la montaña, 1560–1680.* México: CIESAS, 2001.

—. *Los mayas y la tierra: La propiedad indígena en el Yucatán colonial.* México: CIESAS, 2003.

—. *La encarnación de la profecía: Canek en Cisteíl.* México: CIESAS, 2004.

Brading, D. A. *Miners and Merchants in Bourbon Mexico 1763–1810.* Cambridge: Cambridge University Press, 1971.

Burns, Kathryn. *Colonial Habits: Convents and the Spiritual Economy of Cuzco, Peru.* Durham, North Carolina: Duke University Press, 1999.

Cáceres Menéndez, Beatriz, and Robert W. Patch, "'Gente de mal vivir': Families and Incorrigible Sons in New Spain, 1721–1729." *Revista de Indias* LXVI, no. 237 (2006): 363–92.

Calvo, Thomas. "Demographie historique d'une paroisse mexicaine: Acatzingo (1606–1810)." *Cahiers des Amériques Latines* 6 (1972): 7–31.

Campos García, Melchor, ed. *Guerra de Castas en Yucatán: Su origen consecuencias y su estado actual 1866.* Mérida, Yucatán, México: Universidad Autónoma de Yucatán, 1997.

Campos Goenaga, María Isabel. "Arraigar en Yucatán: De Garrástegui y Oleada a Calderón y Marcos Bermejo. Una Mirada a la sociedad Novohispana del siglo XVIII." In *Identidad y estructura de la emigración vasca y Navarra hacia Iberoamérica Siglos (XVI-XXI)*, edited by José Manuel Azcona, 125–40. Thomas Reuters Aranzadi: Madrid, 2015.

Carrera Quezada, Sergio Eduardo. "La Política agraria en el Yucatán colonial: Las Composiciones de tierras en 1679 y 1710." *Historia Mexicana* LXV, no. 1 (2015): 65–109.

Chacón Jiménez, Francisco. "¿De nuevo la familia? No, es la sociedad. Reflexiones y nuevas orientaciones sobre las familias en perspectiva comparada." In *Familia y redes sociales: Cotidianida y realidad del mundo iberoamericano y mediterráneo*, edited by Sandra Olivero Guidobono,

Juan Jesús Bravo Cato, and Rosalva Loreto López, 25–7. Madrid: Editorial Iberoamericana, Vervuerte, 2021.

Chamberlain, Robert S. *The Conquest and Colonization of Yucatan*. Washington, DC: Carnegie Institution of Washington, 1948.

Chance, John K. *Race and Class in Colonial Oaxaca*. Stanford: Stanford University Press, 1978.

Chance, John K., and William B. Taylor. "Estate and Class in a Colonial City: Oaxaca in 1792." *Comparative Studies in Society and History* 19, no. 4 (1977): 454–87.

Christophers, Sir S. Rickard. *Aëdes Aegypti (L.) The Yellow Fever Mosquito: Its Life History, Bionomics and Structure*. Cambridge: Cambridge University Press, 1960.

Chuchiak, John. "Towards a Regional Definition of Idolatry: Reexamining Idolatry Trials in the 'Relaciones de Méritos' and their Role in Defining the Concept of 'Idolotría' in Colonial Yucatán, 1570–1780." *Journal of Early Modern History* 6, no. 2 (2002): 140–67.

Clendinnen, Inga. *Ambivalent Conquests: Maya and Spaniard in Yucatan, 1517–1570*. Cambridge and New York: Cambridge University Press, 1987.

Coello de la Rosa, Alexandre. "Conflictividad capitular y poderes locales en el Cabildo de Manila (1690–1697)." *Colonial Latin American Review* 25, no. 3 (2016): 325–50.

Demos, John. *A Little Commonwealth; Family Life in Plymouth Colony*. New York: Oxford University Press, 1970.

Díaz de Durana Ortiz de Urbina, José Ramón. *La Otra nobleza. Escuderos e hidalgos sin nombre y sin historia. Hidalgos e hidalguía universal en el País Vasco al final de la Edad Media (1259–1525)*. Bilbao: Servicio Editorial de la Universidad del País Vasco, 2004.

Domínguez, Isabelo. *La Llamada del Nuevo Mundo: La emigración española a América, 1701–1750*. Sevilla: Universidad de Sevilla, 1999.

Dym, Jordana. *From Sovereign Villages to Nation States: City, State, and Federation in Central America, 1759–1839*. Albuquerque: The University of New Mexico Press, 2006.

Earl, Rebecca. *The Body of the Conquistador: Food, Race and the Colonial Experience in Spanish America, 1492–1700*. Cambridge: Cambridge University Press, 2012.

Estrada Iguíniz, Margarita, and América Molina del Villar. *Matrimonio: Intereses, afectos conflictos: Una Aproximación desde la antropología, la*

historia y la demografía (siglos XVIII-XXI). Mexico City: Centro de Investigaciones y Estudios Superiores en la Antropología Social, 2015.
Eyal, Hillel. "Beyond Networks: Transatlantic Immigration and Wealth in Late Colonial Mexico City." *Journal of Latin American Studies* 47, no. 2 (2015): 317–48.
Farriss, Nancy M. *Maya Society Under Colonial Rule: The Collective Enterprise of Survival*. Princeton: Princeton University Press, 1984.
Fernández Pérez, Paloma, and Juan Carlos Sola-Corbacho. "Regional Identity, Family and Trade in Cádiz and Mexico City in the Eighteenth Century." *Journal of Early Modern History* 8, no. 4 (2004): 358–85.
Florescano, Enrique. *Precios del maíz y crisis agrícolas en México (1708–1810)*. México: El Colegio de México, 1969.
Gabbert, Wolfgang. *Becoming Maya: Ethnicity and Social Inequality in Yucatán Since 1500*. Tuscon: The University of Arizona Press, 2004.
García Bernal, Manuela Cristina. *La Sociedad de Yucatán*. Sevilla: Escuela de Estudios Hispano-Americanos de Sevilla, 1972.
—. *Yucatán: Población y encomienda bajo los Austrias*. Sevilla: Escuela de Estudios Hispano-Americanos de Sevilla, 1978.
García Fuentes, Lutgardo. *El comercio español con América, 1650–1700*. Seville: Escuela de Estudios Hispanos-Americanos de Sevilla, 1980
García-Baquero González, Antonio. *Cádiz y el Atlántico (1717–1778)*. Seville: Escuela de Estudios Hispano Americanos de Sevilla, 1976.
Garritz, Amaya, ed. *Los vascos en las regiones de México Siglos XVI-XX*. 3 vols. México: Universidad Nacional Autónoma de México, Ministerio de Cultura del Gobierno Vasco, Instituto Vasco-Mexicano de Desarrollo, 1996.
Gauderman, Kimberly. *Women's Lives in Colonial Quito: Gender, Law, and Economy in Spanish America*. Austin: University of Texas Press, 2003.
Gerth, H. H., and C. Wright Mills, eds. *From Max Weber*. New York: Oxford University Press, 1946.
Gibson, Charles. *The Aztecs under Spanish Rule: A History of the Indians of the Valley of Mexico, 1519–1821*. Stanford: Stanford University Press, 1964.
Góngora, Mario. "Urban Social Stratification in Colonial Chile." *Hispanic American Historical Review* 55, no. 4 (Aug. 1975): 421–48.
Gonzalbo Aizpuru, Pilar, and Cecilia Rabell Romero, eds. *Familia y vida privada en la historia de Iberoamérica*. México: El Colegio de México, 1996.

Gonzalbo Aizpuru, Pilar. "La Casa de Niños Expósitos de la Ciudad de México. Una fundación del siglo XVIII." *Historia Mexicana*, no. 123 (1992): 409–30.

—. "Las cargas del matrimonio. Dotes y vida familiar en la Nueva España." In *Familia y vida privada en la historia de Iberoamérica*, edited by Pilar Gonzalbo Aizpuru and Cecilia Rabell Romero, 207–26. México: El Colegio de México, 1996.

González y González, Luis. *Pueblo en vilo: Microhistoria de San José de Gracia*. México: El Colegio de México, 1968.

González, Ondina E., and Bianca Premo, eds. *Raising an Empire: Children in Early Modern Iberia and Colonial Latin America*. Albuquerque: University of New Mexico Press, 2007.

González, Ondina E. "Consuming Interests: The Response to Abandoned Children in Colonial Havana." In *Raising an Empire: Children in Early Modern Iberia and Colonial Latin America*, edited by Ondina E. González and Bianca Premo, 137–62. Albuquerque: University of New Mexico Press, 2007.

González Muñoz, Victoria, and Ana Isabel Martínez Ortega. *Cabildos y élites capitulares en Yucatán. Dos estudios*. Sevilla: Escuela de Estudios Hispano-Americanos de Sevilla, Consejo Superior de Investigaciones Científicas, 1989.

Gutiérrez Romero, Ángel Hermilo. "Carrera eclesiástica, ascenso y movilidad de los miembros del cabildo eclesiástico de Yucatán, siglos XVI y XVII." In *Poder y privilegio: Cabildos eclesiásticos en Nueva España, siglos XVI-XIX*, edited by Leticia Pérez Puente and Gabino Castillo Flores, 161–73. México: La Universidad Nacional Autónoma de México, La Universidad Real de México, 2016.

Hunt, Marta Espejo-Ponce. *Colonial Yucatan: Town and Region in the Seventeenth Century*. Unpublished PhD diss., UCLA, 1974.

Jurado Jurado, Juan Carlos. "Forasteros y transeúntes en América, Siglo XVIII. El caso de Francisco Fernández de la Fuente." *Revista de Indias* LX, no. 220 (Sept.–Dec., 2000): 651–62.

Kamen, Henry. *Spain in the Later Seventeenth Century, 1665–1700*. London and New York: Longman, 1980.

Kent, Dale. *Friendship, Love, and Trust in Renaissance Florence*. Cambridge, Massachusetts: Harvard University Press, 2009.

Kicza, John E. *Colonial Entrepreneurs: Families and Business in Bourbon Mexico City.* Albuquerque: University of New Mexico Press, 1983.
Klein, Herbert S., and Sergio T. Serrano Hernández. "Was There a 17th-Century Crisis in Spanish America?" *Revista de Historia Económica, Journal of Iberian and Latin American Economic History* 37, no. 1 (2018): 43–80.
Kuznets, Simon. *Modern Economic Growth: Rate, Structure, and Spread.* New Haven: Yale University Press, 1967.
Lamikiz, Xabier. *Trade and Trust in the Eighteenth Century Atlantic World: Spanish Merchants and Their Networks.* London: Royal Historical Society, 2010.
—. "Basques in the Atlantic World, 1450–1824." In *Oxford Research Encyclopedia of Latin American History*, 1–22. Online: October, 2017.
Lane, Kris E. *Pillaging the Empire: Piracy in the Americas 1500–1750.* Armonk, New York: M. E. Sharpe, 1998.
Laurie, Elena. "A Society Organized for War: Medieval Spain." *Past & Present* 35, no. 1 (1966): 54–76.
Lavallé, Bernard, ed. *Los Virreinatos de Nueva España y del Perú (1680–1740). Un balance historiográfico.* Madrid: Collection de la Casa de Velázquez, N. 172, 2019.
Lavrín, Asunción. *Brides of Christ: Conventual Life in Colonial Mexico.* Stanford: Stanford University Press, 2008.
Lavrín, Asunción, ed. *Sexuality and Marriage in Colonial Latin America.* Lincoln, Nebraska: The University of Nebraska Press, 1992.
Lavrín, Asunción, and Edith Couturier. "Dowries and Wills: A View of Women's Socioeconomic Role in Colonial Guadalajara and Puebla, 1640–1790." *Hispanic American Historical Review* 59, no. 2 (May 1979): 280–304.
Lockhart, James. *Spanish Peru, 1532–1560: A Colonial Society.* Madison: The University of Wisconsin Press, 1968.
—. *The Men of Cajamarca; A Sociological and Biographical Study of the First Conquerors of Peru.* Austin: The University of Texas Press, 1972.
MacLeod, Murdo J. *Colonial Spanish Central America: A Socioeconomic History, 1520–1720.* Berkeley: The University of California Press, 1973.
Machuca Gallegos, Laura. *Los hacendados de Yucatán, 1785–1847.* México: CIESAS, Instituto de Cultura de Yucatán, 2011.

—. *Poder y gestión en el Ayuntamiento de Mérida, Yucatán (1785–1835)*. México: CIESAS, Publicaciones de la Casa Chata, 2016.

Martínez Ortega, Ana Isabel. *Estructura y configuración socioeconómica de los cabildos de Yucatán en el siglo XVIII*. Sevilla: Excma. Diputación Provincial de Sevilla, 1993.

Martínez, María Elena. *Genealogical Fictions: Limpieza de Sangre, Religion, and Gender in Colonial Mexico*. Stanford: Stanford University Press, 2008.

Martínez Shaw, Carlos. *La Emigración española a América, 1492–1824*. Colombres, Asturias: Archivo de Indianos, 1994.

Marzahl, Peter. "Creoles and Government: The Cabildo of Popayán." *Hispanic American Historical Review* 54, no. 4 (Nov. 1974): 636–56.

—. *Town in the Empire. Government, Politics, and Society in Seventeenth-Century Popayán*. Austin: The University of Texas Press, 1978.

McCaa, Robert. "Calidad, Clase, and Marriage in Colonial Mexico: The Case of Parral, 1788–90." *Hispanic American Historical Review* 64, no. 3 (1984): 477–501.

—. "Tratos nupciales: la constitución de uniones formales e informales en México y España, 1500–1900." In *Familia y vida privada en la historia de Iberoamérica*, edited by Pilar Gonzalbo Aizpuru and Cecilia Rabell Romero, 21–57. México: El Colegio de México, 1996.

McCaa, Robert, Stuart B. Schwartz, and Arturo Grubessich. "Race and Class in Colonial Latin America: A Critique." *Comparative Studies in Society and History* 21, no. 3 (1979): 421–42.

Mesa, René Salinda. "Orphans and Family Disintegration in Chile: The Mortality of Abandoned Children, 1750–1930." *Journal of Family History* 16, no. 3 (1991): 316–29.

Mills, C. Wright. *The Power Elite*. New York: Cambridge University Press, 1959.

Molina del Villar, América. "Tributos y calamidades en el centro de la Nueva España, 1727–1762. Los límites del impuesto justo." *Historia Mexicana* LIV, nos. 1 and 213 (July–Sept. 2004): 34, 15–57.

Molina Solís, Juan Francisco. *Historia de Yucatán durante la dominación española*. 3 vols. Mérida: Impresa de la Lotería del Estado, 1904–1913.

Morales Padrón, Francisco. "Colonos canarios en Indias." *Anuario de Estudios Americanos* VIII (1951): 399–441.

Morin, Claude. "Population et épidémies dans une paroisse mexicaine: Santa Inés Zacatelco (XVIIe–XIXe siècles)." *Cahiers des Amériques Latines*, 6 (1972): 43–73.

Moya, José C. *Cousins and Strangers: Spanish Immigration in Buenos Aires, 1850–1930*. Berkeley: The University of California Press, 1998.

—. "Migration and the Historical Formation of Latin America in a Global Perspective." *Sociologias*, Porto Alegre 20, no. 49 (2018): 24–68.

Nunn, Charles F. *Foreign Immigrants in Early Bourbon Mexico 1700–1760*. London, New York, Melbourne: Cambridge University Press, 1979.

Olivero Guidobono, Sandra, Juan Jesús Bravo Cato, and Rosalva Loreto López, eds. *Familia y redes sociales: Cotidianida y realidad del mundo iberoamericano y mediterráneo*. Madrid: Editorial Iberoamericana, Vervuerte, 2021.

Patch, Robert W. "Decolonization, the Agrarian Problem, and the Origins of the Caste War." In *Land, Labor, and Capital in Modern Yucatán: Essays in Regional History and Political Economy*, edited by Jeffrey T. Brannon and Gilbert M. Joseph, 75–82. Tuscaloosa: University of Alabama Press, 1991.

—. "Imperial Politics and Local Economy in Colonial Central America, 1670–1770." *Past & Present*, no. 143 (May 1994): 79–107.

—. *Indians and the Political Economy of Colonial Central America, 1670–1810*. Norman: University of Oklahoma Press, 2013.

—. *Maya and Spaniard in Yucatán, 1648–1812*. Stanford: Stanford University Press, 1993.

—. *Maya Revolt and Revolution in the Eighteenth Century*. Armonk, New York and London: M. E. Sharpe, 2002.

—. "Sacraments and Disease in Mérida, Yucatán, Mexico, 1648–1727." *The Historian* 58, no. 4 (Summer 1996): 731–43.

—. "Una cofradía y su estancia en el siglo XVIII. Notas de investigación." *Boletín de la Escuela de Ciencias Antropológicas de la Universidad de Yucatán*, no. 8 (Jan.–April 1981): 56–66.

Peniche Moreno, Paola. *Ámbitos de parentezco: La Sociedad maya en tiempos de la colonia*. México: CIESAS, 2007.

—. *Tiempos aciagos: Las calamidades y el cambio social del siglo XVIII entre los Mayas de Yucatán*. México: CIESAS, 2010.

Peña, José F. de la. *Oligarquía y propiedad en Nueva España 1550–1624*. México: Fondo de Cultura Económica, 1983.

Peña, José F. de la, and María Teresa López Díaz. "Comercio y poder: Los mercaderes y el cabildo de Guatemala, 1592–1693." *Historia Mexicana* XXX, no. 4 (April–June 1981): 469–505.

Pérez, Mariana Alicia. *En busca de mejor fortuna. Los inmigrantes españoles en Buenos Aires desde el Virreinato a la Revolución de Mayo.* Buenos Aires: Prometeo Libros, Universidad Nacional de General Sarmiento, 2010.

Pérez-Mallaina y Bueno, Pablo Emilio. *Comercio y autonomía en la Intendencia de Yucatán, 1797–1814.* Sevilla: Escuela de Estudios Hispano-Americanos de Sevilla, 1978.

Pietschman, Horst. "Alcaldes Mayores, Corregidores und Subdelegados: Zum Problem des Distriksbeamtenschaft in vizekönigreich Neuspanien." *Jahrbuch für Geschichte von Staat, Wirtschaft und Gesellschaft Lateinamerikas"* 10, no. 1 (1973): 254.

Pitt-Rivers, J. A. *The People of the Sierra.* New York: Criterion Books, 1954.

Powers, James F. *A Society Organized for War: The Iberian Municipal Militias in the Central Middle Ages, 1000–1284.* Berkeley and Los Angeles: The University of California Press, 1988.

Quezada, Sergio. *Los pies de la república: Los indios peninsulares, 1550–1750.* México: CIESAS, 1997.

—. *Maya Lords and Lordship: The Formation of Colonial Society in Yucatán, 1350–1600.* Norman: University of Oklahoma Press, 2014.

—. *Pueblos y caciques yucatecos, 1550–1580.* México: El Colegio de México, 1993.

Redfield, Robert. *Chan Kom, a Maya Village.* Washington, DC: Carnegie Institution of Washington, 1934.

—. *The Folk Culture of Yucatan.* Chicago: The University of Chicago Press, 1942.

Restall, Matthew. *The Maya World: Yucatec Culture and Society, 1550–1850.* Stanford: Stanford University Press, 1997.

—. *The Black Middle: Africans, Mayas, and Spaniards in Colonial Yucatán.* Stanford: Stanford University Press, 2009.

Rocher Salas, Adriana. *La Disputa por las almas. Las Órdenes religiosas en Campeche, siglo XVIII.* México: CONACULTA, 2010.

Roys, Ralph L. *The Indian Background of Colonial Yucatan.* Washington, DC: Carnegie Institution of Washington, 1943.

—. *The Political Geography of the Yucatan Maya.* Washington, DC: Carnegie Institution of Washington, 1957.

Rubio Mañé, J. Ignacio. *Gente de España en la Ciudad de México. Año de 1689.* México: Boletín del Archivo General de la Nación, 2ª. Serie, T. VII, 1939.

—. *La Casa de Montejo en Mérida, Yucatán.* México: Imprenta Universitaria, 1941.

Seed, Patricia. *To Love, Honor, and Obey in Colonial Mexico: Conflicts over Marriage Choice, 1574–1821*. Stanford: Stanford University Press, 1992.

—. "Social Dimensions of Race: Mexico City, 1753." *Hispanic American Historical Review* 62, no. 4 (1982): 569–606.

Serrera Contreras, Ramón. *Guadalajara ganadera: Estudio Regional novohispano, 1760–1805*. Sevilla: Escuela de Estudios Hispano-Americanos de Sevilla, 1977

Socolow, Susan M. "Acceptable Partners: Marriage Choice in Colonial Argentina, 1778–1810." In *Sexuality and Marriage in Colonial Latin America*, edited by Asunción Lavrín. Lincoln and London: The University of Nebraska Press, 1989.

—. *The Bureaucrats of Buenos Aires, 1769–1810: Amor al Real Servicio*. Durham: Duke University Press, 1988.

—. *The Merchants of Buenos Aires, 1778–1810: Family and Commerce*. New York: Cambridge University Press, 1978.

—. *The Women of Colonial Latin America*. Cambridge: Cambridge University Press, 2000.

Solís Robleda, Gabriela. *Bajo el signo de la compulsión: El trabajo forzoso indígena en el sistema colonial yucateco, 1540–1730*. México: Editorial Porrúa, 2000.

—. *Entre la tierra y el cielo: Religión y sociedad en los pueblos mayas del Yucatán colonial*. México: CIESAS, 2005.

—. *Entre litigar justicia y procurar leyes: La Defensoría de indios en el Yucatán colonia*. México: CIESAS, 2013.

—. *Las Primeras letras en Yucatán: La Instrucción básica de entre la Conquista y el Segundo Imperio*. México: CIESAS, Editorial Porrúa, 2008.

—. *Los Beneméritos y la Corona. Servicios y recompensas en la conformación de la sociedad colonial yucateca*. Mérida: CIESAS, M. A. Porrúa, 2019.

Solbes Ferri, Sergio. "La navegación directa de Canarias a América y su papel en el sistema comercial atlántico, 1718–1778." *América Latina en la Historia Económica* (Jan–April 2018): 36–97.

Spalding, Karen. "Social Climbers: Changing Patterns of Mobility among the Indians of Colonial Peru." *Hispanic American Historical Review* 50, no. 4 (1970): 645–64.

Stein, Stanley J., and Barbara H. Stein. *Silver, Trade, and War: Spain and America in the Making of Early Modern Europe*. Baltimore and London: Johns Hopkins University Press, 2000.

Storrs, Christopher. *The Resilience of the Spanish Monarchy 1665–1700*. Oxford: Oxford University Press, 2006.
Taylor, William B. *Landlord and Peasant in Colonial Oaxaca*. Stanford: Stanford University Press, 1972.
Teja, Jesús F. de la. *San Antonio de Béxar: A Community on New Spain's Northern Frontier*. Albuquerque: The University of New Mexico Press, 1995.
Thompson, Philip C. *Tekantó, A Maya Town in Colonial Yucatán*. New Orleans: Tulane University, Middle American Research Institute, 1999.
Torres Pico, José M. *Los expósitos en la sociedad colonial: La Casa Cuna de la Habana, 1710–1832*. La Habana: Instituto de la Historia de Cuba, Editora Historia, 2013.
Tutino, John. "Power, Class, and Family in the Mexican Elite, 1750–1810." *The Americas* 34 (Jan. 1983): 359–81.
Twinam, Ann. *Public Lives, Private Secrets: Gender, Honor, Sexuality and Illegitimacy in Colonial Spanish America*. Stanford: Stanford University Press, 1999.
—. *Purchasing Whiteness: Pardos, Mulattos, and the Quest for Social Mobility in the Spanish Indies*. Stanford: Stanford University Press, 2015.
—. "Sexualidad, ilegitimidad y género en España y América, siglo XVIII: Una Comparación." In *Familia y redes sociales: Cotidianida y realidad del mundo iberoamericano y mediterráneo*, edited by Sandra Olivero Guidobono, Juan Jesús Bravo Cato, and Rosalva Loreto López, 29–44. Madrid: Editorial Iberoamericana, Vervuerte, 2021.
—. "The Church, the State, and the Abandoned: *Expósitos* in Late Colonial Havana." In *Raising an Empire: Children in Early Modern Iberia and Colonial Latin America*, edited by Ondina E. González and Bianca Premo, 163–86. Albuquerque: University of New Mexico Press, 2007.
Valdés Acosta, José María. *A través de las centurias*. 3 vols. Mérida, Yucatán: Talleres "Pluma y Lapiz," 1926.
Van Young, Eric. *Hacienda and Market in Eighteenth-Century Mexico: The Rural Economy of the Guadalajara Region, 1675–1820*. Berkeley, California: The University of California, 1981.
Valle Pavón, Guillermina del. "Contrabando, negocios y discordias entre los mercaderes de México y los cargadores peninsulares." *Studia Historica, Historia Moderna, Ediciones Universidad de Salamanca* 42, no. 2 (2020): 115–43.

—. "En torno a los mercaderes de la Ciudad de México y el comercio de Nueva España. Aportaciones a la historiografía de la Monarquía Hispana del período 1670-1740." In *Los Virreinatos de Nueva España y del Perú (1680-1740). Un balance historiográfico,* edited by Bernard Lavallé, 135-50. Madrid: Collection de la Casa de Velázquez, 2019.

Walker, Geoffrey. *Spanish Politics and Imperial Trade, 1700-1789.* Bloomington: Indiana University Press, 1979.

Webre, Stephen. "El Cabildo de Santiago de Guatemala en el siglo XVII: ¿Una Oligarquía Criolla Cerrada y Hereditaria?" *Mesoamérica* 1, no. 2 (June 1981): 1-19.

Wobeser, Gisela von. *Vida eterna y preocupaciones terrenales: Las capellanías de misas en la Nueva España, 1700-1821.* Mexico City: La Universidad Nacional Autónoma de México, 1999.

Zavala, Silvio. *La Encomienda indiana.* Madrid: Centro de Estudios Históricos, 1935.

INDEX

Abasto de carne (meat supply), 17, 169, 179
Adoption, 77–79
Adultery, 81–82
Africans/African Americans, 17, 19, 27, 29, 58, 63, 88
Alarcón, Manuel, 191, 193, 196
Alcaldes (magistrates-mayors), 1, 138, 139, 140–44, 151, 156
Aldana Malpica, Gregorio de, 141, 146, 147, 150, 151, 157, 162; and politics, 189, 192, 194, 195, 203, 205, 206; and ranching, 177–78
Ancona, Francisco Antonio, 156, 161, 156, 161
Ancona Hinostrosa, Pedro, 141, 147, 150, 239n27
Andalucía, 6, 28, 43, 47, 91, 109, 113, 115, 146, 147, 159, 160, 230n6; and immigration, 96, 97, 100, 102
Andalusians, 132, 149, 151, 152, 196; community, 128–31; immigration of, 104, 115, 118, 119, 122, 123, 127
Andes, 20, 208, 209, 210
Antwerp, 96, 127
Aragon, 28, 97, 100, 110

Aranda y Aguayo, Alonso, 141, 146, 147, 150, 152, 157, 162; and politics, 3–4, 187, 192, 195, 201–202; and ranching, 174, 175, 180
Aranda y Aguayo, Diego, 49, 147, 150, 156, 161, 163, 239n26
Aranda y Aguayo, José, 174, 176, 180, 201
Arostegui, Francisco, 197, 198, 199, 200
Arrúe, Antonia de, 47
Arrúe, José de, 47, 201
Ávila y Carranza, Isabel María de, 48
Ávila y Carranza, Lorenzo de, 142, 176, 180
Ayora y Porras, Antonio de, 135, 142, 150, 204–205, 239n19, 239n26
Ayora y Porras, Felipe de, 43, 238–39n18; friends of, 203, 204, 206; and politics, 143, 147, 150, 152, 156, 161, 162, 189, 192, 194; and ranching, 174, 177

Bacalar, Salamanca de, 22, 23
Banns (wedding), 56, 71–72, 73
Barbosa, María, 173, 176, 177
Basque (language), 122, 148
Basque Country (País Vasco/Vizcaya), 28, 61, 62, 97, 146, 147, 215, 236n43;

259

Basque Country (*continued*)
  immigration from, 100, 101, 104, 105, 106, 110, 113, 121, 126
Basques, 113, 127, 135, 204; and city council, 152, 153, 159; community, 123–26; immigration of, 102, 104–106, 115, 130, 131, 149, 181; marriage patterns, 118–122, 132
Belgium, 10, 28, 108
Belize, 98, 109
Beltrán de Mayorga, Matías, 49, 147, 150, 161, 162
Bermejo Magaña, Bernardo, 177, 203
Bermejo, Clemente de Marcos, 142, 149, 156, 177
Bermejo, José, 142, 162, 163, 177, 203
Bermejo Magaña, Nicolás, 19
Bilbao, 7, 105
Bolio Solís, Juan, 46
Borreli de la Mota, Ana, 127–28
Bourbon Reforms, 121, 217
Boyd-Bowman, 102, 104
Brading, David, 10, 104, 235n25
Buenos Aires, 10, 61, 76
Burns, Kathryn 5

Cabrera, Pedro, 144, 159
Cabildo. *See* city council
Cacao, 12, 24, 84, 118
Cádiz, 28, 105, 106, 107, 121, 123, 126, 12
Calderón y Garrástegui, Pedro, 142, 162
Calderón y Robles, Pedro, 142, 156, 161
Calvo, Thomas, 10, 101
Cámara Osorio, Juan de la, 147, 150, 161
Campeche, 22, 25, 29, 49, 108, 168, 188, 190, 194, 198; and capellanías, 53–55; and migration, 92–93: and trade, 28, 93, 107, 134, 178, 183, 189, 210

Campo, Juan del, 45, 238–39n18; and city council, 141, 146, 147, 150, 152, 157, 161, 141, 146, 147; and politics, 176, 182, 194, 205
Campos García, Melchor, 224n27
Canary Islanders (*isleños*), 151, 152, 159, 194, 204, 206; community of, 127–28; and immigration, 102, 104, 113, 119, 122, 127–28, 129, 130, 133
Canary Islands, 5, 10, 19, 28, 48, 61, 70, 85, 134, 147, 148, 149, 158, 214; immigration from, 96, 102, 107, 108, 109, 113, 114, 115, 118, 126, 131, 134
Cantabria, 28, 104, 107, 109, 110, 113, 121, 124, 146, 147, 148, 215
Cantabrians, 135, 136, 149, 152, 153, 159, 181, 182, 203; community of, 126–27; immigration of, 102, 104, 115, 117, 118, 119, 120, 122, 123, 125, 128, 131, 132
Cántabro (language), 123, 148
Capellanías (chantries), 17, 49, 50, 51–55, 158, 184
Capellán (chaplain), 51, 52, 53
Carbajal, Rosa, 43, 50
Cárdenas, Mateo Carlos de, 43, 141, 161
Caribbean Sea, 102, 210
Carrillo, Juan Manuel, 43, 190, 198
Carrillo de Albornoz, Nicolás, 143, 147, 150, 152, 156, 157, 161, 162 169, 239n28; friends of, 203, 205; and politics, 2–3, 192, 194, 195; and ranching, 172, 177, 178
Casa de Montejo, 25
Castas, 27, 59
Caste, 63, 144, 156, 158, 181
Castile, 28, 48, 83, 113, 115
Castillo y Arrúe, Juan del, 2, 47, 126–27, 239n29; and city council, 141, 145, 146, 147, 148, 150, 152, 156, 157, 160, 162, 163;

friends of, 201–203, 204, 205, 206; and politics, 187, 190, 191, 192, 193, 194, 195, 197, 198, 200; and ranching, 174, 175, 178, 179, 182
Castillo y Cano, Juan del, 145, 146
Castro, Juan José de, 129, 130, 142, 161, 162, 175, 202
Catalonia, 29, 124
Cathedral Chapter, 12, 18
Catholic culture, 51, 53, 170
Cepeda y Lira, Pedro, 135, 141, 146, 152, 157, 161, 163, 201, 204
Cerda, Eugenia de la, 204
Cerda, Josepha de la, 204
Chacón, Juan Antonio, 160, 162
Chacón, Rodrigo, 143
Chacón y Ascorra, Alonso, 142, 156
Chacón y Ascorra, Ignacio, 141, 161, 193
Child mortality, 16, 41–43
Chile, 11, 62, 113, 183, 209, 211
City council, 5, 15, 30–32, 137–38, 169–70, 172, 187, 188, 189, 191, 195
Ciudadela (citadel), 27, 43
Class. *See* social class
Clothing, 84, 86–87
cofradías (religious brotherhoods), 51, 168, 171–172
Colombia, 11, 19
Commerce, 28, 29, 86, 98, 104–105, 106, 120–121, 122, 154, 181, 184
Conde Pinacho, María, 121, 237n21, 237n22
Convent, (of Immaculate Conception), 26, 76
Córdoba (Spain), 109, 129
Corpus Christi, 31
Cortayre, Antonio (governor), 107–108
cotton/textiles/thread, 2, 55, 80, 87–88, 186, 187, 197; exports of, 12, 29, 104, 134, 182, 188–89; tribute in, 2, 11, 24
creoles, 9, 116, 132, 148

doctor, 26, 31, 45, 108
Domínguez, Juan, 43, 50
doweries, 16, 26, 47–50, 55, 77, 83–87, 178

Echanagucia, Alonso de, 144, 176, 181
Echanagucia, Martín de, 147, 150, 156, 238–39n18
Encomienda, 11, 13, 22, 49, 62, 133, 135, 146, 149, 164–66; and exports, 12; income, 63–64; individuals, 49, 113; and politics, 23, 187
encomenderos, 7, 11, 63, 131, 135, 144, 151, 154, 158, 164–66, 182; class, 64, 119, 124, 132, 133, 198; as militia – 98, 133, 165
endogamy, 63, 101, 118, 119, 158
England, 10, 28, 43, 49, 55, 58, 78, 105, 107, 115
epidemic, 15, 35–41, 46, 48, 76, 132, 171
Escribanía de Gobernación y Guerra, 80, 190
estancias/estancieros, 13, 15, 54, 69, 134, 146, 167–169, 171
Estrella, Joseph de. *See* Fernández de Estrella, Joseph de
exports, 3, 11–13, 21. *See also* cotton, wax
expósitos. See foundlings
Extremadura, 23, 73, 102, 124, 126
Extreme Unction, 35, 36, 38, 40
Eyal, Hillel, 120

family, 70, 77, 123; and social network, 5, 123–32, 155
famine, 39, 41, 76, 168, 170–73
fathers-in-law (*suegros*), 159, 160–63

Fernández Palomino, José, 49, 55
fiel executor (market inspector), 138, 140–44
Figueroa y Silva, Antonio de (governor), 48, 109, 236n49
Flanders, 103, 115, 118
foundlings (*expósitos*), 34, 46, 57, 58, 72, 73, 74–82, 87
France, 10, 16, 28, 58, 102, 124, 126
Franciscans, 10, 26
friendship, 4

Galicia, 106, 107, 109, 110, 113, 114, 115, 131
Gallegos, 102, 119, 122, 127, 130
García Bernal, Manuela Cristina, 6, 239–240n31
Garrástegui y Oleaga, Pedro (First Count of Miraflores), 3, 104, 239n26; and Basque community, 123–26, 130, 131, 133; and city council, 139, 147, 150, 156, 161, 163; friends of 202, 203–204; and politics, 187, 189
Garrástegui y Villamil, Pedro (Second Count of Miraflores), 139, 143, 147, 150, 152, 155, 157, 162; friends of, 203–204, 205; and politics, 2, 4, 187, 190–91, 193, 194, 195, 196
Garrástegui y Villamil, Francisca, 124; Josefa, 124, 204; María, 124–126; Nicolasa, 124, 204, 205
Genoa, 103, 107, 108, 118, 126, 128
gente de color, 58
Gibraltar, 106, 128, 129
Gómez de Parada, Bishop Juan, 53, 57, 135, 149
Góngora, Mario, 144
González, Ignacio, 143, 162, 172

González de la Madriz, José, 147, 150, 152, 157, 161, 163, 178, 238–39n18
Granada, 109, 126
granary, 25, 31
Guadalajara (New Galicia), 10, 34, 46, 81, 84, 104, 138
Guanche (language), 122, 148 Guatemala, 20

Haciendas, 12, 13, 41, 64
Hapsburg monarchy/period, 8–9, 86, 109, 121, 213
Havana, 28, 45, 76
Helguera, Antonio de la, 117, 135; and city council, 141, 147, 150, 152, 157, 162; friends of, 201, 203; and ranching, 175, 181, 182;
Herrera, Cristóbal, 61, 142, 143
Herrera y Córdoba, Cristóbal, 114, 147, 150, 152, 157, 161, 194
Hidalgo/hidalgos, 64, 79, 132, 137, 145, 164; class, 16, 59, 60, 67, 81, 112, 114, 115, 121, 128, 140, 144, 151, 153, 166; and social mobility, 178–79
Honduras, 12, 24
Hunt, Marta Espejo-Ponce, 6, 17, 148, 226n13; 230n5; 238n14

illegitimacy/illegitimate, 16, 34, 57, 67, 72, 73–82, 87, 155
immigrants/immigration, 9, 10, 14, 15, 18–19, 25, 28, 59, 65, 66, 69, 74, 85. *See also* Andalusians; Basques; Belgium; Cantabrians; Canary Islanders; *Gallegos*; England; France; Ireland; Italy
imports, 12, 21
indigo, 12–13

indulgences, 2, 63, 124
infant mortality, 41–42
Inquisition, Holy Office of, 90, 196
Ireland, 10, 28, 58, 103, 107, 108, 115
Italy, 10, 16, 28, 58, 103, 115, 117, 130, 158
Izamal, 25, 44, 173, 179

Jacobs, Auke Peter, 101

Kicza, John, 121
Kuznets, Simon, 13

labor services, 24, 89, 135, 166
Laguna de Términos, 109, 198
landed estates, 9, 12, 52, 53, 54, 134, 137, 167. *See also* estancias.
Lara, Francisca de, 49, 55
La Mancha, 110, 130
last rites (Extreme Unction), 36, 132, 151
Lazagavaster, Juan Ascencio, 141, 146, 152, 157, 193, 197
Latin America, 14, 16, 19, 20
Lebrija, 109, 129
literacy, 21, 47, 115, 154, 218–219
Livorno, 107, 117
Lizarraga, Pedro de, 142, 163
Lockhart, James, 17
Low Countries, 58, 105

Maldonado Jurado, Cristóbal, 129, 150, 161
Magaña, Magdalena, 149, 176, 177, 195, 203
Magaña Dorantes, Luis, 1–3, 114; and city council, 141, 146, 147, 150, 152, 155, 157, 163; friends of, 201, 202; and politics, 187, 192, 193, 195, 197, 198; and ranching, 174, 177, 182
Maní (village), 47, 187, 199, 200

marriage 59–60, 65–67, 68–69, 70–71, 77, 78, 81, 82, 83, 90–100, 123, 158–59, 164; arranged, 118, 119–120, 121, 122, 124–25, 132, 158–59, 164; among Andalusians, 128–31; among Basques, 123–26; among Canary Islanders, 127–28; among Cantabrians, 126–27
Martínez Ortega, Ana Isabel, 15, 139, 146, 148, 14n238
Maya (people), 2, 11, 22–23, 29, 34, 89
Mayan language, 5, 88, 92
Mayordomo del pósito (granary custodian), 138, 140–44
measles, 39–40, 48
Medina Cachón, Francisco, 186–87, 190, 192, 196
Medina Cachón, Juan Francisco, 192, 193
Méndez Pacheco, Francisco, 141, 145, 146, 148, 150, 152, 153, 157, 162, and politics, 190, 198; and social mobility, 153, 238n14
Mendicuti, Francisco de, 143, 173, 176
Mendoza, Juan de, 141, 146, 147, 150, 152, 157, 175; and politics, 187, 192, 195, 198, 201
Meneses Bravo de Sarabia, Alonso (governor), 2–4, 189, 190, 191; residencia of, 192, 194, 195, 197–200, 203, 205
Meneses Bravo de Sarabia, Fernando (governor), 10, 186–87, 188, 189; residencia of, 192, 193, 195, 197–200, 205
merchants, 86, 99, 100, 104, 105, 106, 113, 121, 127, 133–34, 153, 154. *See also* commerce
Mesoamerica, 208, 209, 210
Mexico City, 7, 17, 28, 65, 76, 106, 136, 149, 191, 214; Council of, 57; and immigration, 96, 103, 112, 118, 121

264 *Index*

Mexico (New Spain), 9, 12, 14, 16, 19, 20, 21, 29, 35, 112, 116, 124, 210, 212, 216, 228n2; Audiencia de, 74, 82, 84, 135, 136, 190, 191, 198, 199; and immigration, 147, 149, 158
militia/militia officers, 98, 113, 117, 122, 153, 165, 179
Mimenza, Gerónimo, 143, 162
Miraflores, Count of. *See* Garrástegui, Pedro and Garrástegui y Villamil, Pedro
Moya, José, 107

Navarre, 47, 109
New Castile, 109, 110
New Spain. *See* Mexico
Noguera, Martín Antonio de, 48, 175, 178
Nunn, Charles, 109

Oaxaca, 107, 133–34, 235n31
Ortiz del Barrio, Francisco, 48, 143, 162, 190
Osorio Cervantes, Manuela, 48–49

Padrino de Boda (matrimonial sponsor) 3, 16, 126, 160–63, 179. *See also* marriage
Pardío Ordóñez, Juan, 148, 150, 152, 157, 172, 178, 204
Pardo, 58, 59
Pérez, Francisco, 175, 178–79, 180, 182
Pérez, Juan, 176, 179
Pérez, Mariana Alicia, 10, 61, 101
Peru, 17, 210, 216
pirates, 22, 50, 54, 97, 98, 186, 211
Pitt-Rivers, J. A., 6
political participation, 144, 153–54
Popayán (Colombia), 214, 217
Portugal, 16, 19, 108, 147, 148, 158, 208
poverty, 16, 46, 47, 61, 75, 81, 132, 138

power (political), 5, 137, 144, 154, 164–66, 170, 177
power/ruling elite, 144, 145, 149, 151, 153, 155, 156, 163, 165–66
priests, 51–54, 68, 79, 112, 156, 174
procurador/procurator (city attorney), 135–36, 138, 140–44, 156
Puebla, 48, 84
Puerto, Gerónimo del, 143, 162
Puerto, María del, 133, 237n27
Puerto, Nicolás del, 142, 147, 150
Purgatory, 36, 51, 53

Race, 15, 58–59, 61
Ranchers (*estancieros*), 17, 18
Ranches/cattle ranches. *See* estancias
Ranching elite, 170–71, 174; and city council, 174–176, 179
Real estate, 52, 54, 154, 167
Real Hacienda, 126, 130. *See also* Royal Treasury
Redfield, Robert, 6
regidores (city councilmen), 1, 5, 18, 30, 38. *See also* city council
religious festivals, 31
repartimiento, 2, 11–12, 13, 44, 49, 88
República de Españoles (Commonwealth of Spaniards), 21
República de Indios (Commonwealth of Indians), 21
Residencia, 15, 116, 169
Restall, Mathew, 17
Ríos Reyes, Pedro de los (bishop), 57
Rivas Talavera, Diego de, 127–28, 131, 133, 176
Rivaguda, Álvaro (governor), 44
Rivero, Pedro, 53, 141
Rocher Salas, Adriana, 218

Rodríguez Moreno, Manuel, 141, 146, 152, 157, 163
Rodríguez Vigario, José, 49
Rodríguez Vigario Bohórquez, Domingo, 147, 150, 152, 157, 161, 239n26
Rodríguez Vigario Ortega, Juan, 143, 147, 150, 152, 156, 157
Rodríguez de Villamil, Diego, 239n20
Romero de Salazar, Juan, 54–55
Royal Treasury (Real Hacienda), 122, 126, 127, 130, 149. See also Real Hacienda
Rubio Mañé, 103
Ruela, Miguel de, 142, 176
Ruiz de la Vega, Antonio, 53, 121–22, 126–127, 129, 131, 133, 21n237; and city council, 141, 146, 152, 157, 163, 18n239; and politics, 195, 196, 202, 203, 206, 18n239; and ranching 172, 175, 180
Ruiz de la Vega, Ignacia, 203; María Olaya, 127; Petrona, 127, 133; Tomasa, 126–27
Ruiz Pérez, Juan, 144, 163

Salazar y Córdoba, Francisco, 192, 193
Salazar y Córdoba, Gaspar de, 135, 142, 147, 150, 156, 161, 176, 20n239
Salazar y Villamil, Simón de, 141, 175
Salcedo, Manuel (governor), 108, 113
Sánchez de Aguilar, Josefa, 173, 176, 177, 180, 194
San Antonio de Béxar (Texas), 34, 118, 168, 216
San Cristóbal (barrio), 25, 29, 46, 117
Sanlúcar de Barrameda, 106, 126, 129, 132, 182
Santander, 104, 121, 126, 130
Santiago de Guatemala, 107, 154, 158, 214
Santiago (barrio), 58, 8
Santa Ana (church and barrio), 28, 31, 44, 77, 236n49

Santa Cruzada, 2, 11, 124, 139, 149
Secobio Ceballos, Manuel, 173, 17
Seville, 15, 28, 45, 49, 102, 204; and immigration, 102, 106, 107, 109, 123, 124, 126, 129, 130, 135
Sisal, 210
Slavery/slaves, 29, 49, 50, 59, 84, 88
Smuggling, 186, 196, 198, 200
Social capital, 65–66, 132, 154, 159
Social class, 4–5, 8, 10, 13–14, 16, 18, 60, 61, 62, 63, 64, 83, 116, 122, 132, 137, 153, 155, 164; lower, 4; middle, 4, 64, 137, 144, 164, 166; upper, 4, 5, 54, 62, 64, 119, 135, 137, 149, 156, 158, 166, 177, 180. See also poverty
Social mobility, 8, 14, 54, 60, 63, 95, 114–115, 153, 158
Social networks, 4–5, 16, 123, 126, 127, 129, 131, 155, 159, 160, 164,
Social reproduction, 5, 8, 155, 158, 164
Social stratification, 7, 13–14, 132, 167
Solís, Ignacio, 142, 177
Solís Barbosa, Antonio, 143, 147, 150, 152, 157, 162, 178
Solís Casanova, Francisco, 147, 150, 152, 156, 157, 160, 162, 175; and politics, 187, 192, 195, 201
Solís Robleda, Gabriela, 7
Sosa, Juan Francisco de, 142, 161, 172
Spain, 8–9, 10, 16, 19, 21, 45, 74, 136, 149, 189, 208; different from America, 60, 62, 75, 82; and emigration, 49, 70, 104, 106, 111, 115, 118, 121, 122, 132, 134, 135, 145, 147–48
Spanish America, 4, 5, 6, 13, 14, 18, 217; compared with Mérida, 63, 75, 82, 183, 209, 210, 229n36

Status, 79, 83, 125, 132, 134, 151, 153; markers of, 21, 60–62, 64–67, 87, 92, 108, 112–114, 116, 137
Sugar cane, 12–13, 29

Tabasco, 12, 24
Tenerife, 48, 114, 128, 132
Tenorio, Fernando Martín, 182
Texada, Carlos de, 143, 194
Thompson, Phillip, 1
Tipikal (village), 197, 200
Tithes, 12, 127
Toledo, 110, 124, 130, 135
Tribunal de Indios, 149, 177, 195, 203
Tribute, 2, 11, 24, 168, 199
Trujeque, Nicolás, 47–48
Tutino, John, 16

Urgoitia y Carrillo, Domingo, 156, 157, 192; and cabildo, 141, 146–47, 150, 152; and ranching, 178
Urquizo y Tovar, Fernando, 44
Urzúa Arizmendi, Martín (governor), 44, 126, 190, 20

Valdés Acosta, J. M., 238n14, 239n20
Valladolid (Yucatán), 22, 25, 44, 53, 80, 108, 197, 239n18
Vázquez Moscoso, Andrés, 122, 127, 129–130, 131, 133; and city council, 141, 146, 152, 157, 163; friends of, 202, 204, 206; and ranching, 175
Veracruz, 7, 28, 29, 50, 182, 188, 189
Vértiz y Ortañón, Juan José de (governor), 43, 161, 193, 194, 195–96, 199–200
Villamil y Vargas, Lucas de, 48, 116, 239n20; and city council, 142, 147, 150, 152, 157, 161, 162, 163; and ranching, 173, 175, 180, 182; and politics, 2–4, 192, 194; and friends, 202, 203, 204–205
Villamil y Vargas, Micaela de, 2, 48, 124, 125, 149, 194, 196
Violante de Salcedo Enríquez y Navarra, María de, 43

Wax, 2, 133, 186, 187, 199; export, 134, 182, 189, 207; tribute in, 11, 24, 29, 80
Wealth/capital, 155, 158, 166; and cattle, 167, 178, 181, 183–84; and class, 137, 151, 153, 154; and status, 131, 132–34
Weber, Max, 212, 1n237
Widows/widowers, 68–69, 70, 72, 73, 74, 79, 83
Witnesses (weddings), 201–207. *See also* Basques; Cantabrians; Andalusians; Canary Islanders
Women/females, 74, 89, 96, 100, 101, 117; and cattle market, 174, 177; indigenous, 189, 198; and marriage, 118–119, 121–22, 124–125, 127, 154, 158, 164; and power, 16, 83, 149, 151; and remarriage, 69–70, and status, 65–67, 76

Yellow fever, 35–41. *See also* epidemics

Zara y Urquizu, Juan Antonio de, 147, 150, 152, 157, 161, 162
Zavalegui y Urzúa, Miguel de, 143, 162, 176, 180–81, 182
Zea Moscoso, Francisco de, 148, 150, 152, 157, 239n18
Zuazúa y Múxica, Juan de, 135, 143, 147, 150, 152, 157, 175
Zuazúa y Urquizu, Juan Antonio de, 142

The authorized representative in the EU for product safety and compliance is:
Mare Nostrum Group B.V.
Mauritskade 21D
1091 GC Amsterdam
The Netherlands
Email address: gpsr@mare-nostrum.co.uk

KVK chamber of commerce number: 96249943